HERE IN
NEW ENGLAND

ABOUT *HERE IN NEW ENGLAND*

"For 45 years at *Yankee* magazine, Mel Allen wrote about New England and New Englanders and what makes this place special. The stories take us to the last horse-and-buggy egg man; to a sardine packer in Maine; to a search for a lost boy; and to the people who tried to save a young man's life. This book is a love song to and a celebration of the unique people who call New England home."
— Ann Hood, *New York Times* bestselling author of *The Knitting Circle* and *The Stolen Child*

"Mel Allen writes love stories – but not the expected type. In his stories couples and families are united in their love for their work, their neighbors, their place in the world. Devotion is Mel's subject. If there's a secret to the magic that Mel conjures, it's this: he listens. That's devotion."
— Howard Mansfield, author of *I Will Tell No War Stories*

"These stories are about all of us, our hopes, fears, passions; our need for connection; our capability for resilience."
— Todd Balf, author of *Three Kings: Race, Class, and the Barrier-Breaking Rivals Who Launched the Modern Olympic Age*

"*Here in New England* is a beating heart here in your hands. Hold it close and hear the region speak."
— Suzanne Strempek Shea, author of *Selling the Lite of Heaven*

"I can open this book to any page and find a person I feel like I know in a place that feels familiar and so damn real. Mel Allen's gift for storytelling, honed over decades at *Yankee* magazine, is nothing short of a wonder."
— Brian Kevin, features editor, *National Geographic*

"Allen shows an uncanny ability to illuminate New England's hidden depths, revealing the profound through intimate portraiture, one story at a time."
— Wayne Curtis, author of *And a Bottle of Rum: A History of the New World in 10 Cocktails*

"The people in this collection could be characters straight from fiction. These stories run the scale of emotions: humorous, wise, and even heart-breaking. Millworkers, musicians, fishermen, factory workers, they all come alive on the page."
— Cathie Pelletier, author of *Northeaster, A Story of Courage and Survival in the Blizzard of 1952*

HERE IN NEW ENGLAND

Unforgettable stories of people, places,
and memories that connect us all

BY MEL ALLEN

EARTH SKY + WATER, LLC
PUBLISHING

All of the stories in this book, with the exception of the introduction, prefaces, and epilogues have appeared previously in *Yankee* magazine. In a few instances the stories are slightly abridged, and word usage has been updated to current standards.

For more information, visit: melallennewengland.com

ISBN-978-162126536-8

Published in the United States by Earth Sky + Water, LLC
PO Box 60, Wilton, New Hampshire 03086, www.earthskywater.net

Third Printing
Printed in the United States

Cover photograph, Sea Smoke, *by Peter Ralston*
Cover and book design by Ellen Klempner-Béguin

For the readers of *Yankee,* whose loyal support has made these stories possible; for the writers I have worked with over the decades who have made my days so worthwhile; for the men and women of New England who trusted me with their stories; and for the colleagues over the years whose ideas and feedback have made all the difference—this book is for all of you.

Contents

Introduction

Every book comes with an origin story: this is mine. One sweltering summer night in 1969 on the Colombian coast, where the heat and humidity are so intense that at times it seems even breathing takes effort, I am in a movie theater to see *Camelot.* In one of the first scenes, Richard Harris, as King Arthur, is perched in a tree with snow falling, singing, "I wonder what the king is doing tonight?" I recall nothing else from this evening, except that seeing the snow—even if Hollywood fake—jolted me. I knew then that I wanted to live where there was snow and changing seasons. Soon after, I was in a library where they had books from the United States, and I picked up a photography book, and there it was—a Maine winter landscape.

I knew nobody in Maine, but a few months later, back in the U.S., my wife and I were driving north. When we crossed into Maine, it began to snow; I had found my home. I taught fourth grade, then wrote stories for the Portland newspaper, then came to *Yankee* in Dublin, New Hampshire, and never left. *Yankee* is celebrating its 90th year as I write this in the early summer of 2025, and I have been part of it for half its life.

I landed at *Yankee* at a time when Jud Hale, the editor and nephew of *Yankee*'s founder, Robb Sagendorph, said to me, "Find stories. Go wherever you need to go. See the people who interest you, who touch you, whose stories deserve to be known." And I found more than stories: I heard the voices of New England, and I saw a New England that so few of us get to see.

In Mystic Seaport there is an exquisite scale model of the Connecticut sea town in the mid 19th century. One man, Arthur Payne, worked on that model for more than 50 years. If you lean down and see it at eye level, it seems as if the whole town he has created comes to life—people working, playing, ships loading or unloading.

I see the stories in these pages a little like that—miniature pictures of New England that reveal a larger life around them. To tell these stories, I have entered into the lives of people for hours or days—and when they open their own lives and their hearts, the words they speak become intimate albums. They tell me details of their lives that they may not tell anyone else. And it is up to me to treat those words with deep respect.

What *Yankee* means to people came home to me when I reached out to Alan Shepard, Jr., on the 30th anniversary of when he became the first American in space. He said he had been approached by every network and every major national magazine. He had declined them all. But he said yes to me because, he said, "*Yankee* is home."

The most important words in this book's title, for me, are "that connect us all." We live now in a time where division has become the backdrop to our lives. But when I look at the stories here about people overcoming seemingly impossible obstacles, of others reaching out to help their neighbors, of entire communities pulling together when all seems lost, or of thousands of people searching a wilderness for a lost child, I see a common humanity that has always been part of the New England landscape.

I will continue to find stories that matter. You can reach me at melallen716@gmail.com, and melallennewengland.com. I will write back.

ONE

ALWAYS BELIEVING

In February 2025 I flew to Vancouver, B.C., to meet my two sons—one arriving from Hawaii, another from Colorado, where they live. They had long wanted to ski at Whistler/Blackcomb; I simply wanted to be where they were, even if my days would be spent in a different way. I had a stack of index cards, pens, a laptop, and a briefcase filled with printed stories, dozens and dozens of stories. Each morning after we walked to the first ski lift together, they ascended, and I headed to the village library. At a quiet corner desk I spread the cards with the titles of my stories. Then I began to sort them into rough themes.

Many stories told about people who refused to accept failure, refused to give up a dream, refused to allow obstacles that might defeat many of us. There was something inside them, a will that cannot be taught or found in a book, that allowed them to persevere, to keep going, even when they had every reason to step away. Their stories, more than I could possibly fit into a single chapter, spoke to the tenacity that has always been part of the New England character. And I put them together, one after another, with a theme I called "Always Believing."

One summer evening in 2017 when I stood on a stage at the Alamo Theater in Bucksport, Maine, to talk about the meaning of community, I learned that the people in the audience had much to tell me about how a town pulls together when a mill town loses its mill. They refused to accept the script that says a town slowly falls apart, despair settles like a cloud, people leave, schools close. I did not know then that for the next many months I would come to know this town, its people, its spirit, with an intimacy that continues to call me back to "The Town That Refused to Die."

And here, in "Fire on the Farm," you will meet the Bachelder family in Epsom, New Hampshire. As small-herd dairy farmers, they already faced long odds of enduring; it is why so many hundreds of dairy farmers have sold out, the land of their toil now housing developments. A devastating fire should have sealed their fate. I wish you had all been there in Ruth's country kitchen as she talked about the joy of working from dawn to dusk, fighting to keep their little farm going.

A hard life, she said over and over, but one she would never trade. "I can't tell you how rewarding the farm life is," Ruth told me. "Every kid had chores. Then they'd go off and play, and when dinner was ready, I'd get out in the middle of the road and yell, and they'd come running." It was never a question for Ruth and her family to find a way to stay on the land.

Just as it was never a question when a 94-year-old hill farmer in the north country of New Hampshire asked his young friends, two transplants from New York, to keep his subsistence homestead alive as a museum, and they said yes. They had no idea how to make it happen. But they had made a promise, and they had to find a way to keep it.

Or when we think of Stephen King now, and see one of the most successful writers in the world, yet there was a time when rejection letters came one after another. He still believed that one day there would come a yes.

Of all the qualities we want to instill in our children, I cannot think of one more meaningful than this: to believe that no matter how distant a goal might be to reach, if you dig in, if you persist, you can find a way. A yes awaits.

A Promise Kept

Imagine a house that held everything that you'd ever touched. The books you read; diaries and journals; your toys; your clothes; your shoes; the board games you played and the jigsaw puzzles you pieced together on winter nights by the glow of lantern light. Baseballs plucked from the weeds after Fourth of July games, when the town men challenged the country boys; the quilts that warmed you as a child and that still warmed you when you were old.

The school papers you wrote; the maps that showed a world that seemed too big to ever grasp; the letters and cards that friends and family sent you telling of births and deaths and news from afar. The clothes you wore as a child, and those you wore as a grownup; the newspapers that recounted the comings and goings in your town from the day you were born to the day you died; magazines with cover stories on President Teddy Roosevelt. Every button that ever fell off; every fragment of cloth and string; pots that boiled beans and pans that fried bacon. Tools that helped you make a living; carts and buggies and harnesses and horseshoes and yokes for oxen; receipts for anything you ever bought, telling a story of hard times deeper than the numbers.

Then imagine the same house holding the life of your grandfather and of your father, too, who was born in 1835. And your mother, a sister, a brother. All the things needed to live a hardscrabble farm life in a five-bedroom house that had never known indoor plumbing, electricity, or running water; where the food was cooled in a room that stood above a clear, cold spring. And all the things that entered your life never ever left. Because if you paid for something, you needed it, and if you needed it, there would always be a way to use it. Always. The leather sole of a boot worn to the nub would resurface as a door hinge; a piece of wire mesh nailed to a stick killed flies. Layers and layers of stuff, a stratified human geology waiting to be unearthed. What would that look like?

On this summer day in Stewartstown, New Hampshire, seven miles north of Colebrook on Route 145, in Coos County in the far north of the Granite State, I am about to find out.

The sign for the Poore Family Foundation for North Country Conservancy, which everyone calls simply the Poore Family Farm, comes up abruptly. It's a clean summer morning, puffy clouds, bees buzzing, the smell of newly mown grass leading to walking trails through land that stretches for 100 acres on both sides of the road. I see a few cars parked in a shaded area, and a truck with Pennsylvania plates, bicycles tied to its roof. On a small rise is a pretty flower garden and a farmhouse and barn.

Richard (Rick) Johnsen and Mark Winer wait by the information booth, the size of a lemonade stand. A sign requests a donation to tour the grounds and the homestead/farm museum, but nobody is ever turned away. They're six-footers, in their early sixties: Rick with the ponytail he's worn since his youth, Mark in a white ball cap and a Poore Family Farm T-shirt. Their New York accents haven't been dulled much by their nearly 40 years in the north.

Rick hands me a map—a walking tour of all the outbuildings, with highlighted details. "A lot of people just want to wander," he says. "Others like to be guided.

"I want to tell you about Kenneth Poore," he begins. "We're here because of him. John Calvin Kenneth Poore was born in 1885 and died in 1983. He lived here his entire life. Mark knew him first, but I'll give the spiel." But before he says another word, a man bounds up to us.

"Can I interrupt you guys?" he says. His voice fairly trembles with excitement. "I don't know who you are. I'm from Pittsburgh, Pennsylvania, and I'm on my honeymoon, and I've just spent the last hour here. And it's unbelievable, fascinating. Without a doubt, this should be preserved with every ounce of effort. You have to sell the rights to HBO and they'll make a series. All the stories here!"

His name is Chris Lisowski. He tells us he's 35, a high-school art teacher and artist in the Pittsburgh area with hopes of one day teaching kids how to renovate old houses. He and his wife have been biking in Vermont and are now taking the North Country route to Maine. They saw the sign and pulled in. I ask what has him so excited. "You'll see it," he says. "It's a step back in time. It's a hoarder's dream. Everything in there is history." He's quiet for a moment, trying, it seems, to contain himself. "The letters—I just sat there reading the letters. You can't stop looking at stuff!"

Hours later, as I drove away, after I'd walked through the house, the barns, the sheds; walked through the fields and woods down to the stream; read the letters and heard the story of Kenneth Poore and the young people he embraced and who embraced him, and the promise they made, I thought that there may not be any other place like this anywhere. This is history peeled back, stripped of ceremony, as if the spirits of those who lived here still hover. If only the teacher from Pittsburgh had known how all this had come to be, all that he'd seen and touched. How excited would he have been then?

In one sense, the story begins with Moses Heath, "a Paul Bunyan-like character," Mark says. Heath cleared the land and built the first structures in the early 1820s, until he sold the farm to Job Poore in 1832, who left it to his son, John Calvin Poore, Kenneth's father, who, when he died in 1918, left it to Kenneth. "They were not rich people," Mark says as we walk to the farmhouse. "The rich people had the bottomland, the river land. These are the hill people. This was the far north. They came because they could homestead."

I could continue with who begat whom and how the branches spread, but those stories could once be told about any of hundreds of old farms where people were born and died under the same roof. Most of those farms are gone now, the stories all but lost, while this one still stands, so that's why this story begins on a spring day in 1974.

"I'm renting a house around the corner [from the Poore Farm]," Mark says. "I was a back-to-the-lander, escaping my upbringing. Like a lot of people, I didn't know what I was looking for. I had an old station wagon. I was driving by, and I see this old man shuffling up the road, tattered overalls, old hat. He was walking up from the cemetery with clippers in his hand. I soon learned that he was paid 50 cents each time he cleared around the headstones. I'm thinking I could give this old guy a ride. So I pull over. And I look out at this old, wizened face, and I look up to these blue sparkling eyes. He's nearly 90, and he has the eyes of a five-year-old. And before I can say anything, he says, 'I guess you're looking for me.' I said, 'Do you want a ride?' 'No, I live right there,' he says. I said, 'I live around the corner.' He goes, 'Oh, I heard there was a hippie in the neighborhood.'

"There were 64 years between us. But he was totally different from my grandfathers. They were from Russia, the old country. One was a very religious Hasidic Jew. The other never spoke to me. So I started going over [to Kenneth's]. I'd go into the house, and he was living now in one room. His housekeeper, Alfa, really the love of his life, had died 10 years before. You ever been with somebody you don't know that well and the silence is okay? It was fine with us. I'd come down and pitch hay or give him a ride to town. We got friendly. He was a true American Victorian. If he was working in the garden and a woman stopped by, he'd take off his old battered hat. Always polite. No teeth. Hard to understand him sometimes."

Rick Johnsen moved north from the city too, not long after, along with all the other young people who came looking for a sense of belonging in the '70s, who found one another and found in Kenneth Poore a touchstone. A man whose life was as straight as the blade of his axe: He woke early, worked hard for little money. He sold butter, cut wood, set traps in the freezing streams, traded with neighbors, dabbled in taxidermy: a little of everything, enough to keep going, enough to pay the taxes. There was food from the gardens and animals and the woods and waters. He read anything he could get from the town's tiny library. He wore frugality like a skin. He told stories of his father's Civil War and the day his father came back from Colebrook in his horse and buggy, carrying the news that Sitting Bull was dead.

"He loved people," Mark says. "He never married, never had children, and he loved this renaissance of people who came up from the cities. People were interested in the old skills, and Kenneth had lived those skills. He became a kind of celebrity to us. We took him to parties and came to the farm for parties. We took him to movie nights. We celebrated his birthday with him on July 5 every year."

"We wanted to get back to the land," Rick adds, "but Kenneth was already there. He'd never left it." Once Kenneth told them, "I don't know about this country, but with you young people maybe there's hope."

We enter the house gingerly. With the help of volunteers, young and old, they've strengthened it, bolstered it, put in electricity so that visitors can see better, but its hard life shows. We go to the bedroom where Kenneth slept on a straw-mattress rope bed; into another bedroom with women's clothes hanging from a line, all pressed as if waiting for someone to slip into them; into a parlor; and slide our way into the kitchen, which looks as if Kenneth has just left on an errand. In a corner hangs a calendar from 1953.

"He had the same breakfast every day," Mark says. "He had overalls on, he had his long johns on. I don't care if it was July or January, he wore the same clothes. He'd start a fire in the woodstove. He'd boil potatoes in the pot. He'd put coffee on. He'd fry some bacon. He'd take the bacon out, then fry the potatoes in the bacon grease. And he'd put the bacon back in and crack an egg in there. He'd eat all that for breakfast. Then he'd eat a doughnut with a piece of cheese and a second cup of coffee. He'd do that 365 days a year."

They warn me to watch my head as they lead me upstairs to a room that looks out to the garden. In 1975, when Kenneth Poore took a fall and could no longer care for himself on the isolated farm, Mark moved into this room. He tapped maple trees, pumped water, shaved Kenneth, shared his table. "I was a mystery to my father," Mark admits. "He couldn't understand what I was doing here."

In 1979, when Kenneth was 94, he told his friends of his vision and his hope. His vision was that somehow the homestead could be preserved after he died. With a lawyer's help, he formed the Poore Family Foundation for North Country Conservancy. When he died, the land and the buildings and all the things they held would go to the foundation. But a foundation is merely a name on paper. His hope was that his young friends would be the ones to keep it alive. Mark said he would. Rick said he would. Others said they would. On a summer day in 1983, Kenneth

Poore suffered a heart attack, lingered a few months, and then died in October.

He was buried in a plain wooden box in the cemetery whose stones he had kept clipped, beside his father and mother. Mark and Rick and their friends dug the grave by hand. They were now responsible for a farmstead that had stayed untouched since long before the Civil War. A house and barns, all falling down. No money. They had made a promise, but they had no idea how to keep it.

They call the next decade "the dark years." They had a foundation but no training: raw material, but no clear plan for how to make it a living museum. Rick crawled into attic eaves, looked beneath beds, searched outbuildings, finding boxes and trunks filled with papers and clothing, diaries and journals. So many things; unpacking them was like sweeping sand from a beach.

Every foray into a dark corner, every climb into a barn rafter unearthed something more. Mark moved back to the city for a while, and the homestead proved impossible to keep secure. Even today, 30 years later, Rick will receive a call or a letter saying that someone has found a Poore family keepsake in an attic where it didn't belong, and it makes its way home.

In 1994, with little meaningful progress toward opening a museum, and with even the local newspaper urging Rick and the others to give up the dream, the state attorney general took the foundation to court, seeking to dissolve it, wanting to sell the land and the buildings, with the proceeds going to other nonprofits that seemed to know what they were doing. "It was do or die," Rick says.

"That got us going," Mark adds. "[They] put our backs to the wall and we realized we'd gotten into perfection paralysis. We needed the public to see this." They reorganized the board, and Rick Johnsen became the chairman. "We fought, and we came out on top," Rick says. In 1995 they announced that on Kenneth Poore's birthday, July 5, they would open with cake and lemonade. They spruced up the grounds and repaired the split-rail fence. The house was too shaky for visitors to come inside, but they filled the upper floor of the large barn with displays. Rick's wife, Michele, made signs that announced *Museum Open* by the side of the road.

But would anyone show up?

The first day, maybe 100 curious locals came; word spread, and the next day it was double that. For many it was like seeing the lives of their grandparents come to life. Eugene Reid, who teaches building trades to high-schoolers in nearby Canaan, Vermont, came on board with his students, and for the past 15 years they've poured their sweat into making crumbling roofs and walls solid and whole. Volunteers cleared decades of manure from barns, cut trails; Rick learned the nuances of applying for grants. Volunteers built a sawmill and milled the lumber from the woods; they built a nature-center cabin and a stage so that performers could play to people sitting in the meadow. Exhibits grew, and still more stuff came out of boxes.

And then one day in 2004, a woman came for a tour and found her life's work. "We took on all these projects," Rick says, "but Linda Tillotson took on the house."

When Rick Johnsen first showed Linda around, she was stunned. Raised in Montreal, she had married Rick Tillotson, whose father was the most influential man in New Hampshire's North Country. "They were all doing the best they could," she says. "The rooms were packed with artifacts. I'm the type of person who likes to dig into dirty drawers and make them neat. I jumped in and I didn't stop."

She stripped the closets and drawers and boxes of their clothing, boiled and ironed every piece from long johns to dresses, and then displayed them in the house and barn. "I don't love ironing," she says, "but I loved every second of ironing those clothes—bringing these dirt-filled clothes into new life."

She carted home thousands of pages of diaries, journals, and letters; hour by hour she transcribed each one. "They gave an insight into a whole other world," she says. Now visitors can spend hours with the light slanting through the barn and relive the ordinary and extraordinary moments of lives long past.

"I grew to love the farm," Linda says. "I'd sit outside on the balcony, drink a cup of coffee, and feel Kenneth's father. I relived his life. Relived the Civil War." And one night she typed these words from John Calvin

Poore's diary: *"1885. A baby boy born 4 this morning."*

"I still have all of Kenneth's papers to do," Linda says. "It's part of my world, and I won't stop until it's done. This is the most wonderful thing that has ever happened in my life."

At the end of the day, I asked Rick and Mark about what lay ahead. They said that each year they run out of money; then they scrap and fight for a way to keep going. They want to put together a book of the Poore family's Civil War-era letters as a fund-raiser. They've hosted weddings here and want more. Each August they hold a big country concert, and they want other events. "I believe this area needs this," Rick said.

"We're just the stewards," Mark added. "We don't own this. This is part of Coos County. This is living history."

I drove away thinking of Kenneth Poore, thinking that I felt I already knew him, and thinking that if a place has the power to change lives, then sometimes people, too, can change a place. I'd found here on a country road people who cared about an old farmer and what his way of life meant, who found a way to keep it from vanishing, from the land and from memory. And I kept hearing Rick's voice as I said good-bye: "There's still so much stuff to unpack. So much stuff!"

Published March/April 2008

Since the Yankee *story, the Poore Family Homestead Historic Farm Museum has grown to include an amphitheater and covered bandshell for events and music. Mark Winer, Richard Johnsen, and Linda Tillotson continue to be fully involved.*

The Town That Refused to Die

THE LAST SHIFT

You learn what you're made of not when life is good, but when the ground beneath your feet gives way, and you are left afraid and uncertain of what to do. In the past year, I have found the same may be said about a town.

The one I am talking about is Bucksport, Maine. About 4,900 people live here, in modest, well-kept homes set back from the east bank of the Penobscot River where it spills into the deepwater bay. Important things have always been made here. Before the turn of the 20th century, shipbuilders lived along the river, and when Robert E. Peary set out for the North Pole, he sailed on the *Roosevelt*, built on neighboring Verona Island, with a Bucksport mariner as chief engineer.

At the northern edge of town, on a spit of land known as Salmon Point, a paper mill was built in 1930 where a tannery once stood. The site earned its name from the spawning runs that once churned the river thick with fish. Even with the Depression settling upon the country, Bucksport had resources needed to make paper: water, forests, and the newly constructed Wyman hydro dam 84 miles north to power the immense machinery that transformed pulp into paper. There was a port for ships to bring supplies in and take tons of paper out. And there were people hungry for work.

The men and women who lived in Bucksport and the rural hamlets that rimmed the town came from rugged stock: They were loggers, farmers, fishermen. Their families were large and self-sufficient, and they put meat on the table by knowing how to shoot game and how to fish on the lakes and ponds that rippled through the countryside. They would work themselves to exhaustion if asked—and they were.

Over the decades Bucksport became known for producing the finest lightweight coated paper in the world, paper that was used in such magazines as *Time* and *Sports Illustrated* and *Good Housekeeping* and *Newsweek,* and catalogs like L.L. Bean and Sears and Victoria's Secret and Avon. The boast was that any American who read magazines touched paper that came from the skill of Bucksport papermakers.

Hundreds of thousands of people pass by Bucksport every summer, on their way to Bar Harbor or Acadia National Park or the Blue Hill Peninsula. They view the town from two tourist sites across the river: 19th-century Fort Knox, the largest fort in New England, and the Penobscot Narrows Bridge, which has the tallest bridge observatory tower in the world. They ride the tower's elevator up 42 stories, and from that height Bucksport appears as a miniature village against the dark water, the smokestacks of the mill stabbing the sky. Crossing the river, they reach the town's lone stoplight. A right turn leads to Down East tourist towns; left, to Bucksport. Few turn left. It was a point of pride for many residents that they did not scrub sidewalks for summer visitors. In Bucksport there is neither high season nor low season. There is football and hunting season, snowmobiling season, fishing season, summer-camp-by-a-pond season. It was always papermaking season.

I learned much of this in the summer of last year [2017], just before the 225th anniversary of the town's founding by Jonathan Buck, which would be celebrated at the annual Bay Festival. It had been two and a half years since the paper mill was shuttered by its most recent owner—an out-of-state company called Verso—a decision that came with no warning and left the town reeling. Some 570 workers, half as many as had once worked at the mill, lost their jobs.

I had been invited to give a talk on the spirit of community at a weekly summer event called Wednesdays on Main, held at the historic redbrick Alamo Theatre. Community was not an abstract topic in Bucksport that evening. When a mill town loses its mill, it loses not only the core of its tax base, it loses its security, its future, its sense of who it is. "This was traumatic," says Tom Gaffney, a psychologist who has tended to local families since the early 1980s. "There was numbness. Fear. They all asked, 'What are we going to do now?' "

Everyone had seen what happened just 80 miles north when Great Northern Paper left town, wounding Millinocket and East Millinocket seemingly beyond recovery. Laid-off workers pulled up stakes, their houses on the market for $25,000 or less. Families were uprooted. Schools lost their students. Across the country, that's how the story usually goes when a company town loses its company.

When my talk ended, a tidy procession of people from the audience followed me up the street to a reception at MacLeod's, a restaurant that on Thanksgivings past had delivered more than 1,000 turkey dinners to mill workers round the clock, as papermaking did not stop for a holiday. They said the mill closing *should* have crushed the town—but didn't. Now something remarkable seemed to be bubbling up, even as the ground remained unsteady. The mill and its 274 acres had been bought by a Canadian metal recycling company, and the town had little control over what might happen next. What people could control was how they reacted. They told me that listening to each other had become an urgent task. A local poet was collecting memories of the mill where her father had spent his life and was putting them into a book. Organized committees and teams of volunteers were listening to neighbors to find out what they hoped Bucksport might become. Past, present, and future were swirling around one another in a web of voices; sometimes they all got tangled. People said they were still learning how to seed hope where despair could easily take hold. They were still learning how to move ahead while the carcass of the mill was visible to everyone.

When the night ended, I said I would return. I'd listen, too. It is the story I tell now. It begins with an ending, December 17, 2014, one week before Christmas Eve.

Everyone in Bucksport knew the mill would close one day—they could see what was happening in a world where people read magazines on their phones—but they thought it was still years away. For Danny Wentworth, whose family's papermaking roots go back more than 80 years, here is what that meant. He was driving home from the Fryeburg Fair on

October 1, 2014, when his cell phone rang. His supervisor said the mill was closing. Forever. Wentworth threw the phone against the dash and yelled, "We're done!" Panicked calls and texts flew back and forth across the towns that were home not only to mill workers but also to many who depended on the mill: loggers, truck drivers, shopkeepers, town officials who managed the local tax rate. Pretty much everybody.

Danny remembers the final weeks this way: coworkers struggling with anxiety; the bitter reality that the mill had been sold for scrap; shutting machines down one by one, like the lights of a city going out. He knows it's impossible for outsiders to understand the depth of feeling you can have for a machine that you're with as much as you are with your family. "When I shut down No. 1 paper machine, I got real emotional," he says. "It was the first one to start up when they opened the mill. That was my baby."

He tried to stay hopeful. But even as rumors spread that other paper companies wanted to buy and reopen the mill, "we all knew a scrapper was coming. We'd see them come in with their dark suits, and they seemed to be drooling over the brass in the machines. And we were all thinking, *This is what we've done our whole life.*" On the final shift of the last day of papermaking in Bucksport, Danny walked past the main gate just before 7 a.m. On this day, it was quiet. The scents of ground spruce and fir pulp swirled with chemicals had all but disappeared. He had eight hours to linger, with little to do except brood about the legacy he was leaving behind.

His maternal grandfather, Arthur Wight, Sr., was a New Brunswick native who came to Bucksport with his wife and children from Berlin, New Hampshire, and found work when the Maine Seaboard Paper Company opened the mill here in 1930. Danny's father, Charles Wentworth, Sr., started at the mill after graduating from Bucksport High School in 1942, then went to war in the Pacific. When he came home in 1946, he went back into the mill, now owned by St. Regis, where he would spend the next 40 years. He helped build No. 4 paper machine, then supervised the flow of paper stock. When Danny and his siblings were young, he would sometimes sneak them past the gate on nights when he had to come in to deal with a problem. To the children, with the rumbling noise and clouds of steam, it was a strange and exciting world.

Danny graduated from Bucksport High School, tried college for a year, and then in 1981, at age 20, he came home and "went into the mill." That was how you said it—"went into the mill"—as if it was a world unto itself. And it was. You spoke paper mill language: beater rolls, wet end breaks, drum barking, groundwood, swipers, riggers. Even with ear protection, the noise was so loud and piercing that you and your coworkers communicated with hand signals that would be a foreign code to much of the outside world. You shared the certainty that accidents happen and that machinery moving at high speed is unforgiving—"a lot of thin ice in a mill" is how they said it. You earned some of the highest wages in a poor state, and the heat, noise, bone-wearying hours, and lifetime of disrupted sleep cycles were the price you paid. In return, you escaped to the woods and camps in trucks, snowmobiles, and four-wheelers that took you to fresh air.

The mill was humming when Danny first came and would soon swell to 1,300 workers. In time, Danny rose to become tender on No. 1 paper machine. He was there when Champion International bought out St. Regis, and when International Paper forced Champion out, and when Verso took over in 2006. Every day he drove four miles across the bridge from Verona Island feeling the calm certainty of being where he belonged. *Love* is not a word used loosely about this work, but he'll say to anyone who asks, "I loved it there."

On December 17, in the final hours, Danny felt "like a family is breaking up. We are connected. And the connection is about to break." Later he would search for words to describe the days of demolition that followed. The dust of crushed concrete swirling like clouds. Seeing the gigantic paper machines ripped apart by excavators that looked like dinosaurs, then loaded onto railroad cars and carted away by AIM, the metal recycling company that now owned the property. The sound of metal clanging against metal as the cars rolled out of town.

He tells me this as we sit at a table on Bucksport's mile-long Waterfront Walkway. It is a warm afternoon in September 2017, nearly three years since Verso announced the mill would close. Danny is soft-spoken, friendly, a youthful-looking 55. He says that in the first months after the mill closed, he could not sleep. He was hired as a sander at Hinckley Yacht on Mount Desert Island but developed symptoms of carpal tunnel syndrome. "I never felt old until I went there," he recalls. "They called me 'the old guy.'"

He eventually was hired by a tissue-making mill near the Canadian border, more than 100 miles away, and retrained to run their machines (the man who hired him had also worked at the Bucksport mill). He keeps a small apartment up there and drives home every few days. His wife works as a nursing assistant at Blue Hill Hospital. He has two grown sons who live within an hour's drive: one is a policeman, the other is in the oyster business. His third son, Andrew, was a standout pitcher for Bucksport High, whose winning hit in the Eastern Maine baseball championship was one of the proudest moments of Danny's life. He shows me that on the back window of his Toyota 4Runner, in fact, is a decal with Andrew's jersey number, 19.

A few months after the mill shut down, Danny's mother died. His father followed soon after, and then 10 days later Andrew was gone too. "Time passes," Danny says, "it gets a little easier. But there are days when it hits me." Danny is not someone who talks easily about tears. He tells me that when he and his brother walked out of the mill and through the gate for the last time, with townspeople waiting in the cold rain to applaud and hug them, he held it together. Then he saw Ed and Pat Ranzoni waiting for him. Ed had been his high school baseball coach. Danny did not expect what happened when Pat put her arms around him. He began to cry, for himself; for the end of 35 years of knowing where he belonged; for his friends; for his father, who would sit by the window and look out at the smokestacks without smoke until the day he died; and for the ground giving way beneath his feet.

A DAUGHTER OF THE MILL

Within a few days after Bucksport heard that the mill would shut down, two things happened that would come to be seen as igniting the town's resolve to survive. One was about the future, the other was about the past. They would come to intersect in a way that will undoubtedly change the town forever—but this was impossible to know during that grim October four years ago.

The first thing happened when about 70 townspeople came together at the Alamo for the screening of a documentary about the restoration of a gristmill that now housed the Lost Kitchen, one of Maine's most acclaimed restaurants. The evening morphed into a kind of emotional pep rally: *We have to find our own way. We won't let our town be broken.* People who had arrived somber and in shock, fearful they would be forced to move, left buoyed by what they would come to call their "Night of Hope." One woman whose husband worked for the mill for three decades told me she knew then they would "stay and defend our town, much like a sibling when his brother or sister is threatened. We wanted to help our community go forward in a new way." Within months, there were so many community groups forming in Bucksport that town officials joked they needed a duct tape committee to hold them all together.

The second thing happened when Pat Ranzoni was in her car, crossing the river into Bucksport and looked out on the mill. Earlier that year, the town council had proclaimed Pat their "poet laureate for life." She was known for her bone-deep images about the lives of "my people"—a phrase that encompassed Native Americans, mill workers, and rural Mainers who lived on the edge. In one poem she writes of being a teen, *wanting to accept a party invitation / from friends. Management families. / 'Who do you think you are?' her / bitter father instructed. / She hadn't understood.*

As Pat looked at the mill that day, two words came to her: "Still Mill." And a mission was born in her to create a book with that title, a book that gathered the memories of mill workers and their families—nobody would be able to dismantle and cart *those* away. "I didn't know how I was going to do it," she recalls, "just that I had to do it." Last summer, Pat published the anthology *Still Mill: Poems, Stories & Songs of Making Paper in Bucksport, Maine, 1930–2014.* Of her title, she writes in the preface: "STILL in that it would soon be quieted. STILL in that as long as we live and after, as long as stories are told, the mill and the people who made it what it was—with all its flaws and wonders—shall live on."

Though Pat was shy about talking with me—"I come from a culture that if a stranger shows up, you run and hide," she says—we meet up at her home on a bright September afternoon. She lives with her husband, Ed, about four and a half miles outside town on the rustic homestead her parents moved to when she was a teenager. Even out there in what people called "outback," she could hear the mill's "rumble and roar." She and Ed bought the place in 1970, when her father's body was "breaking down" from his work in the mill.

Pat pushed past 70 a while ago and recently had her knee replaced; there is pain. While we talk, she rests on a cot beside a window that looks out on gardens and fields. Ed knows his way around the woods, and a deer skull from a hunt for the winter's meat adorns the wall in a room dominated by a great stone fireplace. A small red pan hangs from a rafter to catch a leak. "There's some leaks you never can catch," she says.

She sees my copy of *Still Mill,* the culmination of nearly three years of "listening as hard as I could, for as long as I could," Pat says. She signed copies in July at the local bookstore until her hand ached, the line stretching out the door, with proceeds going to the historical society. Wherever she went, people thanked her. One woman said that her father could read only three pages at a time before tearing up. I ask Pat why her readers might react that way. "It's the recognition that somebody values what they have done, that it will be remembered," she says. "Many probably thought they'd have their private memories, but they would be lost [to the world] forever."

To gather stories for the book, she put out a call through newspapers, friends, family, schools, and churches. A modest grant came through to help fund the project. Submissions started coming in, many handwritten. One woman told of hearing blasts of dynamite when the mill site was first cleared. Another woman wrote about the heat—"up to 120 degrees by paper machines"—and added, "Once I broke a finger and didn't say anything, feeling I needed to tough it out and be a man." Another resident lamented that there would be "no more stopping for workers crossing the street, after a long, hard shift. A small courtesy that bound us together as a community." There were also hard truths shared by many mill families. When Pat asked for memories of Thursday paydays, when grocery stores cashed checks, a mill worker's daughter wrote, "Oh, no. Not on your life. Paydays meant a gallon of wine and a bad night for the family, and I won't go there."

When people were reluctant to write, Pat went to them and listened. "People would just start talking," she says, "and keep going." She worked until nightfall, and when sleep eluded her, she would sit up and write more. Pat would pin the pages to clothesline strung across the living room, moving them around until a story unfolded that said, *This is who we are. This is our culture.* Of the finished book in my hands, she tells me, "This is the most important work of my life."

Pat's father, Percy Smith, had been one of the mill's riggers, the construction crew. He would clear snow, drive trucks, repair whatever broke down, load and unload ships. He came from what Pat calls "deep poverty," the kind that compelled him to leave school after eighth grade. Pat herself holds complicated feelings about the mill. She saw the toll it took on her father, but she also knew his pride—his children would not go hungry.

Pat harbors no romantic nostalgia. She tells me about a visit she once made to the mill. "I climbed up these metal stairs, and it got louder and louder, and when I got to the top, there were three of my classmates tending a machine, and it was so loud. I tried to smile. I felt like I'd gone into the diamond mines. And I thought, *They have lived their lives like this.*" And yet. As the hours pass, listening to Pat, her voice soft, gaze steady, I think of what Joan Didion once wrote: "A place belongs forever to whoever claims it hardest, remembers it most obsessively." Every page of *Still Mill* is infused with deep respect for the men and women who walked through the gate day after day, year after year. Pat wants their lives remembered. She frets that the rush to create a new, thriving Bucksport might eclipse what the mill workers' lives had meant. She admits she is struggling with the influx of well-meaning programs, some coming from outside the community.

She has baked me a fresh wild blueberry pie, and as we sit at the table, Pat Ranzoni, poet laureate of Bucksport, wonders aloud if the past will still matter, or simply be swept away. Will there be a place in this still-to-be-determined Bucksport for someone who long ago laid claim to its memories?

EVERY VOICE MATTERS

When I went back to Bucksport last fall to see how the town had kept its resolve, no matter whom I talked with, the conversation always came back to Susan Lessard.

Lessard had been hired in late summer 2015 only as the interim town manager. The energy that had emerged on the "Night of Hope" was still bubbling up but tempered by knowing the town had no control over what the mill site might become. The future rested in AIM's hands. "It was like being tied to a runaway train," one woman told me. Lessard had spent 22 years as a town manager, first on the island of Vinalhaven and then in Hampden, five miles south of Bangor, and was hoping to ease into the role of a consultant. The two previous town managers for Bucksport both left after short tenures, and Lessard had signed only a 10-month contract. "I was the dust-settle girl," she says.

A lot of dust settled—and Lessard stayed on permanently. "I will tell you, at first I was ashamed," she says when we meet in her office in the Town Hall, set on a rise above the river. "I was born and raised 20 miles away in Belfast and had driven the bridge a million times. But I never looked beyond Bucksport as a mill town. And I never looked beyond that to see everything that was here. I had no idea what Bucksport was. And I stopped *to see.*"

When she looked, here is what she saw: a brick-lined river walk, a nationally known film archival center, hiking trails, a tradition of championship high school teams, an ice cream stand that had been a fixture for more than 60 years, a bookstore with a buff-colored cat that cozied on readers' laps, a community that bestowed a "golden snow shovel" to the business that did the best job of keeping the path clear after a storm. And there were townspeople eager to roll up their sleeves to find a way for their town to survive. Their infectious energy gained notice beyond Bucksport's borders. At one community development meeting, a state official remarked, "You guys are the standouts from all towns who have lost their mill."

Less than a year after she arrived, Lessard helped persuade the town council to fund a local director for a project called Community Heart & Soul that originated with the Vermont-based Orton Family Foundation. Its essence—adopted by several other struggling Maine towns—was to connect with people, listen to their stories, learn what they most wanted to see happen in Bucksport. With financial and organizational support from the foundation, Heart & Soul took over the former Rosen's Department Store, which had been rooted on Main Street for nearly a century. Its windows became plastered with note cards filled with the ideas and wishes of townspeople. "It's grass roots," says Lessard. "It's listening to people who don't usually have a voice, like the guys who hang out at Dunkin' Donuts each morning."

Hundreds of ideas flew about like so many birds taking flight. Some were practical: more affordable housing, a long-term-care home, more benches along the river walk. Others were fanciful: a huge indoor water park at the former mill site, for instance. More than just ideas, Heart & Soul came to symbolize a place where people were asserting ownership: *This is the town we want.* Their commitment was palpable. Then, late in 2016, when nobody knew what lay ahead for the mill site, an entrepreneur from Portland came to see Susan Lessard. He was looking for a town that had specific physical advantages. And, equally important, he was looking for a town with spirit.

If everything works out the way people hope, one day historians will look back on how Rob Piasio and Whole Oceans came to Bucksport and built one of the leading land-based salmon production operations in the world, and it will all seem as if it was meant to be.

Piasio, who grew up on Casco Bay in Yarmouth, Maine, had became obsessed with aquaculture while working in Europe as an investment banker. He came back to his home state and founded Whole Oceans in Portland in 2014. He had a plan and backers, but he did not have a location. For several years he scouted sites where he might raise thousands of salmon—not in ocean holding pens, but in special buildings using innovative technology, with clean water recirculating constantly. The site would demand both fresh water and salt water and ready access to transportation lines to bring salmon eggs in and adult salmon to market. He culled his list to about 18 potential places.

When Piasio first came to Bucksport to kick the tires, he met in secret with Sue Lessard and economic development director Rich Rotella and toured the mill site: There was the salty mouth of the bay, there was a pipeline to Silver Lake. There were train tracks. And good access to power. He left. He kept looking. He wanted more than a physical site—he wanted to be sure there was a "cultural fit." When you're about to spend tens of millions, you move with caution.

Then, months later, he read *Still Mill.* In its pages he found a story by the town barber whose father had been badly hurt in the mill. The worker refused to sue, saying the mill had given not only him but his friends good jobs. He read about lunch baskets being passed down from father to son. He read how a town lined the walkway to hug the workers leaving their jobs for the last time. He read that "nothing is impossible when hearts and minds work together as one." He read how Pat Ranzoni looked to the mill crossing into the river and knew what she needed to do. "I was left with profound observations," he tells me. "It's the story of a community and how it changes and how it was formed by its mill. I said, 'Wow! Here's an opportunity to write a new chapter.' " He had found his cultural fit. He told Lessard he wanted to be the town's next 100-year-old company.

On December 17, 2017, the third anniversary of the final shift, the town council honored Pat Ranzoni for the gift she had given everyone with her work. At the time, few people knew about what was coming. One was Susan Lessard. She told Pat that her book had been a way to not forget the legacy of the mill and its people. "This book helps provide closure through understanding," she said. She called *Still Mill* the "springboard to the future." Tears flowed as the past, present, and future entwined in a single moment. Two months later, in early February, Whole Oceans officially announced its agreement to build on the former mill site.

Late one afternoon in early June of this year, I walk north along Bucksport's waterfront, toward what remains of the paper mill. The sun is strong. Rose bushes press against the bank. Water laps against the rocks. Seagulls swerve over the bay and a loon dives maybe 100 feet out in the water. Weeds grow tall along the train tracks. A young woman jogs by. I walk past the year-old art gallery that anchors the downtown; a few years ago it was an empty eyesore. I pass the new Friars' Brewhouse Tap Room, where two Franciscan brothers brew craft beer and make the food. Its "Papermakers Lunch" is a special. I dined there the night before, and Danny Wentworth came in. He said he was glad that soon most of the mill would be gone.

Walking along the pathway, I come to an interpretative panel titled "Looking to the Future." According to one section of text, "the citizens of Bucksport have embraced the reality of 'going paperless' and transformed the mill's passing into a catalyst for new growth and prosperity for the future." Beneath this is a poem by Pat Ranzoni about the "ancient power" of the Penobscot River.

Community Heart & Soul ended its two-year program just a few months before my visit. Now Rosen's storefront stood empty. The hundreds of comments that had been collected were reduced to a final 82 that were given to the town council to consider. They included a desire to start a farm-to-school food program, a community garden, a dog park, cross-country ski trails, community art classes, bicycling and running clubs, a bocce court on the waterfront. The emphasis was on making Bucksport a town where people wanted to live not just because there were jobs, but also because it was where good things were happening and good neighbors lived.

Earlier that day, I saw Susan Lessard. She said that town planners from all over ask to visit, wanting to see what they can graft onto their own communities. Thinking about Bucksport's promising future, "I get goose bumps," she said.

But there were still signs of a town in search of its new identity. One man in his 20s told me that there remained a disconnect between what he called "the gravel pit boys"—the ones who ride their trucks to the countryside and go target shooting—and the "Heart & Soul people." He said they needed to know each other. And with so many action plans to consider, I heard concern that the council would need to find a way to know which ones, or even *one,* they would move forward on.

I visited again with Pat and Ed Ranzoni. Pat said she welcomed Whole Oceans and its promise to be an environmental steward. But her Native American roots made her sympathize with the fish. "Will they ever see sunlight?" she asked. It was clear she hopes a few will find a way to escape to the sea.

As I write this, I'm hearing that the Maine Maritime Academy will likely buy a slice of the mill site to create a safety and offshore survival institute. The expectation is that several thousand young mariners will stay in town while they study, letting Bucksport reclaim a part of its past as a place where great ships left for foreign seas. There is hope that some of these mariners will return to live here one day. I also hear about the prospect of a new inn for travelers who start turning left at the stoplight. The sky, I am told, is the limit.

When I reach the mill, I turn back along the river toward town. I think of the town planners who come here to learn how to turn hardship into hope. I wonder if some things, like the relentless character of people who show up in the winter dark at a paper mill for more than 80 years, belong solely to this place, and cannot be explained with a to-do list. Time and again I'm told about how competitive you have to be growing up in Bucksport—whether it's in football, or wrestling, or softball. Even the high school robotics team made nationals in its first year.

Of all the memories I carry of my time here, the strongest is of the walk I took a year earlier along this path to the mill with Danny Wentworth. I had arranged a tour of the mill site with Jeff McGlin, vice-president of AIM, who was managing the demolition, and Danny had asked to come along. This was already the fifth mill McGlin had taken down. He was taken aback a bit when a former papermaker showed up with me, but he opened the car door and Danny climbed in.

Danny played tour guide through the wreckage, pointing out where various machines had once been fired up. He was surprised to learn that McGlin had spent more than 20 years working for a Wisconsin paper mill, one that had also been closed. Danny showed emotion once, when we came to the walkway between the parking lot and the gate entrance he had once used every day. Now, weeds had overtaken the landscape. "It used to be so cared for," he said.

Twice, Danny told McGlin that "a very good source" had informed him there had been two offers to buy the mill and restart it. McGlin said rumors were always part of the business. "So it wasn't true?" Danny persisted. "No," replied McGlin. (Danny remains unconvinced on this point. "I know we had offers," he will tell me later. "I know we could have kept going.")

As we walked back toward town, Danny shook his head. He had not expected to like the man in charge of tearing down the mill, but he did. "I can't blame him," Danny said. "He's not the enemy. There's probably a better market for former paper mills than new ones." When we parted, he said, "Look around at other places whose mills closed. People are flying out of them. Not here—I'm proud of my town."

Published November/December 2018

Even though the promise of Whole Oceans to create a world-class salmon hatchery on the site of the papermill remains in limbo, Sue Lessard, longtime Bucksport town manager who retired in June 2025, says, "We are still defying the odds. You keep moving forward. Okay, that didn't work out, what can we do now?" A museum dedicated to the paper-making heritage and the people who made the best paper in the world is coming to fruition in the former mill guard house. Pat Ranzoni continues to honor the mill and its workers in her poetry.

Fire on the Farm

Let's start just before the fire. Just before flames tore through the hayloft stacked with 5,000 bales. Just before the smoke billowed through the barn, the cows terrified and men fighting back panic, struggling to get the herd out before everything burned down. Because to understand the loss of a single small family farm, it helps to see what was there before.

It's August 27, 2004. Early evening, about 6 p.m., dinnertime, except farmers don't eat until the chores are finished and there was still the last wagon of hay to get in, and the cleanup after milking. The farm is called Spooky View, named for the cemetery that abuts its land, and it's one of only three dairy farms remaining in Epsom, New Hampshire, a small town east of Concord. A generation ago there were eight. It's an old story —the decline of the family dairy, the land sold to developers for housing lots—but consider: In the 1920s there were more than 14,000 such farms in the state; as late as 1983, there were still 625. On this summer day, Spooky View Farm is one of only 135, and it is one of the smallest.

Inside the barn, Keith Bachelder has just finished milking his 35 cows and feeding an equal number of heifers. Keith owns the cows, having bought them from his parents seven years earlier, but everyone helps out—dad, mom, sister, brother, relatives, friends. It's how small family farms have always made do. Only a few weeks before, he has finally paid off the loan to buy the herd. Outside, his father, Charles, along with cousins and friends, is throwing the last bales onto the hay elevator that trundles to the second-story loft. Charles and his wife, Ruth, bought this farm in the early 1970s when Keith was a baby. Charles is well into his 60s, and he's spent nearly every day of his life on farms.

If you look around, you'll see right away that this is no postcard dream of a farm. Four old tractors and parts lie here and there, ready to give life to another machine. The barn sidles against a garage—the garage to the main house where Ruth and Charles live—all of it useful, none of it especially photogenic. Across the street is the house Keith shares with Sarah, his sister, and just up the road, next door to the farmhouse, lives Brent, their brother. Family and cats are everywhere. A working farm. Home. Where they raised the animals they showed at fairs, and friends came over for Ruth's home cooking and cakes and cold glasses of freshly ladled milk.

Ruth grew up on a dairy farm right here in Epsom. "We did all the milking by hand," she says, "my brothers on one side, me on the other." She and Charles started going together when Ruth was in high school. "He was a farm boy and I was a farm girl," she says. They married in 1963 and built a home together, waiting and looking to find a farm.

"The first time I saw this land," she says, "this fella had lost his wife, so he was selling. The house was half tore up, rain was pouring through the roof. A real mess. We went to the bank and said we'd like to buy it. They thought we were crazy. It was $25,000, and I thought, *We'll be in debt forever.* We started with nothing. But this was going to be our future."

That was in 1970. Every night when Charles got finished working at a nearby farm, he and Ruth came up here and stayed into the night fixing things up. "We've always been a couple," Ruth says. "We milked together. Got sawdust together, hayed together. I only got mad at my husband once. I slammed the barn door and then went back and did chores." They went to auctions together, too, building their herd one cow at a time. "November 12, 1971," Ruth says. "It was Keith's third birthday and we had cake and the milk truck came for our first shipment of milk."

To pay the bills, Charles kept on at the neighbor's farm and Ruth did the milking and chores at Spooky View, hauling 50-pound pails of milk across the barn. She came to the farm with two small children and soon had two more. By then, Charles was staying here at Spooky View. They joined a milk co-op and checks came twice a month. "Always on the 5th and 20th," Ruth says. "That's when you sat down and paid bills. Some years were awful lean. We just had to cut back then. It was just so hard to keep going." But even while farmers all around them cashed in their land, they stayed. "I can't tell you how rewarding the farm life is," Ruth says. "Every kid had chores. Then they'd go off and play, and when dinner was ready, I'd get out in the middle of the road and yell, and they'd come running."

They had only 14 acres of pasture, not enough to grow their own feed. Whenever they had a little money, they added to the herd, building up to 35 milkers. One night, Charles went to the Deerfield Fair to watch the horse pull. He was leaning on a fence and somehow he caught his finger up in a halter, and the horse snapped it right off. When the call came, Ruth gathered up the kids, they got the cows milked, and *then* they went to the hospital. "It's just the way it was," Ruth says. "The cows always had to come first."

Keith saw how hard his parents were working, how tight life was financially after all that time, and he went into welding, working a lot in high-rise construction. But he stayed a farm boy at heart and kept working here and there for other dairy farmers, all the while looking around for his own land. The farm he was meant to be on was right in front of him all along. Ruth took stock of her age and Charles'. She wanted the farm to stay in the family. "I said to Dad," Ruth recalls, "we should see if we can sell the cows to Keith. Dad asked Keith if he wanted to farm."

Yes, he really did.

And that is why on this summer evening, Keith has just finished milking and Charles is throwing the last bale onto the elevator, which is overheating, though nobody knows it. He looks up and sees the flames. "Fire!" he yells, and then everyone starts running for the animals. The next few minutes are gone from Keith's memory: "I don't remember nothing. I still don't and I don't know as I want to," he says.

What he doesn't remember is how the barn seemed to fill with people pulling and tugging at the cows until all but one were out, how the cows ambled about bewildered until they could be herded together in the pasture. Firemen from 13 towns came screaming up Center Hill Road, but the flames fed on that hay and tore through the woodwork until there was nothing left but mounds of ashes. Neighbors came running and carried to safety every scrap of belongings from the house, even Ruth's cookbooks, because it was touch and go for a while as to whether the house would also catch fire.

Ruth had been out visiting with Sarah; driving back, she saw the black smoke rising and she knew her life's work was burning down. "I kept saying, 'Did I leave the stove on? Did I leave it on?'" The finances of a small family farm are always precarious, and Ruth and Charles and Keith had not increased their insurance over the years to keep up with what it would cost to rebuild. The animals were safe, but without the means to rebuild, surely they would have to be sold; Spooky View Farm seemed destined to become one more small-print item in the papers announcing one more auction.

Except the death of this family farm took a twist. Epsom's fire chief, Stewart Yeaton, is also a dairy farmer, and he never hesitated. He told the Bachelders the cows would go to his barn a few miles away, and, in the dark, the air thick with acrid smoke, everyone around who had a livestock trailer drove to the pasture and loaded up the animals. Before dawn, Keith and Charles drove over to the Yeaton farm and milked their cows. "There isn't a farmer around here that likes a handout," Yeaton told a local reporter, "but we've got to help them out. It's just what we do. We rally, pick up, and help the other guy get going again."

Here's what happened next: Everyone, it seemed, wanted to help. Farmers from Pembroke, Bedford, and Contoocook delivered hay. One farmer dropped off more than $2,000 worth of it. All the local stores sprouted donation cans and people filled them up. Keith continued to wake at 4 each morning to drive to the Yeatons' to do the milking and to soothe his cows while emerging from his own shock. "I didn't know I was going to rebuild," Keith says. But it was as though everyone willed him to. He designed a new barn in his head, one that would let the cows have more freedom to roam and mingle. People brought supplies, lent their expertise and muscle. A local company brought a crane and put up rafters. A neighbor came by with a loader and another with gravel to level the land. "People just came to help from everywhere," Ruth says. Slowly the new barn took shape on the land.

For a year and a half, the family missed their cows, as if they, too, were family. "We didn't hear mooing," Sarah says. "It was eerie." Ruth remembers how unsettling it became not to smell manure. "And I always used to hear the chains rattle and the milking machine pump go on and off. So quiet. It wasn't the same."

Then last winter, on February 11, 2006, the first truckload of cows left the Yeaton farm to come home to their new barn. "We were so happy," Ruth says. "We opened the gate and they came running." They put a sign out front: "Cows Are Home." If you go by the farm today, you'll see Keith and Charles on the go from 5 in the morning until past 7 at night. The same chores every day, the days that Keith vows will stretch to months and years, a life that few can understand unless it's in their blood—and if it's in their blood, they know better than anyone that there are some fires that never burn out.

Published March/April 2007

The Bachelders—Keith and his parents, Ruth and Charles—are still keeping the dairy farm going strong. Keith currently milks 45 cows in the barn built after the fire, while tending to twice that many.

The Man Who Writes Nightmares

"At night, when I go to bed, I still am at pains to be sure that my legs are under the blankets after the lights go out. I'm not a child anymore but . . . I don't like to sleep with one leg sticking out. Because if a cool hand ever reached out from under the bed and grasped my ankle, I might scream. . . . The thing under my bed waiting to grab my ankle isn't real. I know that, and I also know that if I'm careful to keep my foot under the covers, it will never be able to grab my ankle." – Stephen King

The tall man is leaning against his Scout, grappling with a handful of 800-page books and a pen, with hands that are slow to unlimber from the cold. The wind whips across the parking lot of the supermarket and finds him where he stands pinned to his car in the school parking lot, writing inscriptions inside the books with the cautious rapidity of someone who wants to say something well, but who is getting colder by the minute.

His denim jacket is badly frayed, and there are holes in the sleeves. Years before, as a student at the University of Maine–Orono, his courtship with Tabitha Spruce, daughter of the owners of a Maine general store in nearby Milford, nearly stumbled on his personal dress code. Once, as a high-school student in Lisbon, Maine, he was preening in front of a full-length mirror, trying to look like his friends. His mother, a tall, thin, but powerful woman who bequeathed her son her Irish blue eyes, threw him against a wall. “Inside our clothes, we all stand naked,” she thundered. “Don’t ever forget it.”

His shirt flaps loose in the back and he wants to tuck it back into his jeans, but that would mean putting the books on the ground, so he finishes his business with the pen and walks quickly past the football field into a side door of the school.

The name of the school is Hampden Academy. It is a small public school despite its highbrow name, located in Hampden, Maine, across the Penobscot River from Bangor. He knows his way around, he thinks, until he opens the door of what he remembers to be the teachers’ room and finds a startled photography student hanging prints to dry in the school’s darkroom.

The tall man is confused and runs a hand through his thick black hair that hangs to his left eyebrow, as it always has, except when it’s groomed by an expensive hairdresser for publicity photographs. The student stares at the intruder, knowing he has seen that face *somewhere.* It is a striking face, with or without the dark beard that appears and disappears each year like autumn foliage. After writing *’Salem’s Lot,* the novel about vampires ravaging a small Maine town that increased his already considerable fame and fortune two-fold, the man remarked ruefully that unlike his vampires, he, “unfortunately, could still see himself in the mirror.”

He opens more doors, sees familiar faces, smiles, says hello, and by trial and error finds the teachers’ room that by 12:45 is deserted. A place for a quick smoke. He has smoked since he was 18, and now, at 31, says he’s trying to quit, as he said the year before, and the year before that. He fights his personal demons one by one, he says, and this one clings to him like quicksand.

Others have described him as hyperkinetic, and he roams the small room restlessly, taking in the titles of the paperbacks used in the English courses. He picks up a well-worn copy of *’Salem’s Lot.* It is a cover that created a sensation a few years ago with its single drop of crimson drooling from the icy blue lips of a child.

The bell rings. In the rapid scuffling of feet past the door he looks up to greet his friend Everett McCutcheon, head of the English Department. “Are you ready?” asks McCutcheon. McCutcheon hefts the book now presented to him. “I knew it would be a big one,” McCutcheon says of *The*

Stand, a book which today [1979] rests comfortably near the top of the bestseller lists. "I've cleared my calendar to tackle it tonight."

McCutcheon has just concluded teaching *'Salem's Lot* to his Science Fiction and the Occult literature class. That class will be joined this period by another class in creative writing to hear Stephen King speak about the success of horror: *Carrie, 'Salem's Lot, The Shining, Night Shift,* and now *The Stand.*

For a moment, as Stephen King pauses outside the door, he realizes that the circle has come around. For the next 50 minutes, the world's bestselling writer of the macabre will stand in a classroom at Hampden Academy and talk about vampires, as he had eight years before. Eight years filled with so many changes, they might well have been 800. . . .

"I was teaching Dracula *here at Hampden Academy. I read it twice and taught it twice to two different classes over a three-week period. I was also teaching Thornton Wilder's* Our Town *in freshman English. I was moved by what he had to say about the town. The town is something that doesn't change. People come and go, but the town remains. I could really identify with the nature of a very small town.*

"I grew up in Durham, Maine, a really small town. I went to a one-room schoolhouse. I graduated at the top of my grammar class, but there were only three of us. We had an eight-party line. You could always count on the heavy breathing of the fat old lady up the street when you talked to your girlfriend on the phone. There was a lot to love in the little town. But there was a lot of nastiness too.

"So I was thinking about Dracula *a lot, and I was thinking about* Our Town. *We were eating supper one night in our crummy little trailer and I was spouting off about* Dracula. *Tabby said suddenly, 'What would happen if Dracula came back today? Not to London, but to Herman?' where we were living. . . .*

"There will always be a special cold place in my heart for 'Salem's Lot. *It seemed to capture some of the special things about living in a small town that I'd known all my life. . . . Maybe it's just that when I wrote the book, we were so poor and the trailer was little and cold and I could go down to my little furnace room where I wrote with a fourth-grade desk propped on my knees. And when I got excited, it jiggled up and down as I hunched*

forward. Maybe that's why I like it so much. I could go down there and fight vampires whenever I wanted."

King's New York agent has said that one of his great appeals is that he places very ordinary people in very scary situations. "People whom you see at McDonald's. People who listen to rock music on the radio and follow the ball teams and go out for beers." The kids in this class look at the big guy slouched forward at the podium, his hands used as punctuation marks, and sense he's really not much different from them.

Their intuition is correct. The big guy, whose book contracts hover near $1,000,000 now, has been a Little League coach; has worked 12-hour shifts in the wet wash of a commercial laundry; has worked in knitting mills from 3 to 11, after attending high school until 2; has pumped gas at an Interstate 95 station; and has picked potatoes for 25¢ a barrel. "I guess the only thing I've missed is blueberry picking," he says.

They open up with questions right away. How about writing? he's asked. How does he do it? He tells them he writes three single-spaced typewritten pages a day. Every day, with only his birthday and Christmas off. To write these pages, he's at his desk by 8:30 a.m. and stays there until 11.

There will be several more hours after lunch, and, if necessary, after dinner as well. He says that at this rate he can almost always complete a first draft in three or four months, a second draft in another three, and have the whole book out of the toaster within a year. To back him up, there are his five published books, and three more novels completed and on the desk of his publisher.

It sounds so easy. But there's not time to tell them about the four long-unpublished novels that will take up space in a dusty trunk forever. Lessons in humility that remind him where he came from in the days when he submitted incessantly to *Startling Mystery Stories,* awaiting their $35 acceptance check, more often than not receiving regrets. When the pulp magazine, the kind that people read on long bus rides, finally accepted one, the editor wrote: "This young man has written many stories for us and we are pleased to be able to publish one at last."

"There were so many times I thought I was pursuing a pipe dream," King says.

His wife, Tabby, says, "Steve wrote before anybody was interested, and he'll write after they've stopped being interested in him. I've never known him when he didn't write. And when he's not writing, he's reading. Even when he worked all those hours in the laundry, he'd drag himself to his desk and write. He's constantly convinced he'll never finish another book," she says. "Or when he finishes, that he'll never write another one. I think," she says, "that if the day comes when he can't write anymore, he would just kill himself."

"My mother brought me and my brother up because our father deserted the family when I was very little. . . . There are good psychological reasons for my attraction to horror stories as a kid. Without a father I needed my own power trips. My alter ego as a child was Cannonball Cannon, a daredevil. Sometimes I went out West if I was unhappy, but most of the time I stayed home and did good deeds.

"My mother worked the midnight shift at a bakery. I'd come home from school and have to tiptoe around so as not to wake her. . . . She was a very hardheaded person when it came to success. She knew what it was like to be on her own without an education, and she was determined that David and I would go to college. 'You're not going to punch a time clock all your life,' she told us. She always told us that dreams and ambitions can cause bitterness if they're not realized, and she encouraged me to submit my writings.

"We both got scholarships to the University of Maine. When we were there, she'd send us $5 nearly every week for spending money. After she died, I found she had frequently gone without meals to send that money we'd so casually accepted. It was very unsettling. When I started Carrie, *I had finished my first year of teaching. After four pages I thought it stank and threw it in the rubbish. I came home later and found that Tabby had taken them out and had left a note, 'Please keep going—it's good.' Since she's really stingy with her praise, I did.*

"When I finished it, I sent it off to Bill Thompson at Doubleday, whom I'd talked to on the phone when I was in college. We were having a really tough time. We had our daughter, Naomi, and our son, Joe. [There is a third child now, Owen.] *Our phone was taken out because we couldn't afford it. . . . When the telegram came saying it was accepted with a $2,500 advance, Tabby had to call me at school from across the street. . . .*

"Later my agent told me the paperback rights were bought for $400,000.

I said, 'You mean $40,000?' He said, 'No, I mean $400,000.' I realized that meant $200,000 for me and I wouldn't have to teach anymore.

"My mother was dying then. But she knew everything was going to be all right. Ah, if my mother had lived, she'd have been the Queen of Durham by now."

The kids don't squirm. The low coughing usually present in an English class is absent—because somebody has asked Stephen King about nightmares, about the unspeakable things that everyone carries around from infancy, like secret moles: the voices no one else hears, the night shadows that take form, the impulses to run past the graveyard, even though they have walked past it hundreds of times before but always in the light. They know this man knows of such things. How else could he have created a Carrie who destroys her high school with her powers of telekinesis? Or the terrifying claustrophobia in *The Shining* when a family of three is snowbound in a malevolent hotel, as a small boy's psychic powers unleash the dry charges of evil? Or the man who gets something bad in his beer and begins to turn into a puddle of goo in his collection *The Night Shift*? Or, finally, *The Stand*, his tale of the survivors of a flu epidemic who converge on both sides of the Rockies, drawn in turn to forces of evil and of good, knowing only one side may endure? And they want to ask him: "How can you write about a man of goo, then sit down upstairs with your children and eat pizza?"

"After 'Salem's Lot *we went to Colorado because I wanted a book with a different setting. And nothing was coming. Somebody said we should go to Estes Park and stay at the Stanley Hotel, a famous old hotel that supposedly was where Johnny Ringo, the legendary bad man, was shot down.*

"We went up there the day before Halloween. It was the last day of the season and everybody had checked out. We were the only guests in the hotel and we could hear the wind screaming outside. When we went down to supper, there were big plastic sheets over all the tables, and the chairs were up on the tables.

"I stayed at the bar afterwards and had a few beers and Tabby went upstairs to read. When I went up later, I got lost. It was just a warren of corridors and doorways, with everything shut tight and dark and the

wind howling outside. The carpet was ominous with jungly things woven into a black and gold background. There were these old-fashioned fire extinguishers along the walls that were thick and serpentine. I thought, 'There's got to be a story in here somewhere.'"

The bell rings, breaking King off in mid-sentence. When the class is over, he is going to the home of his former teaching colleague to listen to music and drink beer, maybe break into a poker game. He works almost as hard at keeping his perspective as he does on his writing. He has seen what eight years like these have done to other writers, seen them mutate into celebrities.

He is teaching this year at his alma mater, for "revenge on my old teachers," he laughs but more seriously admits he needed to rejoin the real world for a while.

But he must juggle demands on his time so that he feels already "a little pawed, like an item at a bazaar." He doesn't get to his lakefront home in Lovell often enough and frets that perhaps he must move, and move again, until he finds the balance of peace and activity that he needs. With something akin to slowly dawning horror, he is beginning to realize that perhaps, for one of the three or four best-selling novelists in the world, there is no such place.

When he lived on another lake, in Bridgton, the police remembered that he would buy his bologna by the case, just as they did themselves. That he went to bean suppers and the meetings at the elementary school. But if somebody asks his neighbors where Stephen King lives, there is the sudden silence of country people on their guard. Because in their wisdom they know something King suspects, that despite bologna and torn denim jackets, he can never be just "the tall man" again.

"I'm very leery of thinking that I'm somebody. Because nobody really is. Everybody is able to do something well, but in this country there's a premium put on stardom. An actor gets it, and a writer gets it. I read Publisher's Weekly *and more and more I see people compared to me. In the review of a horror novel they'll write, 'In the tradition of Stephen King. . . .' And I can't believe that's me they're talking about. It's very dangerous to look at that too closely, because it may change me from what*

I want to be, which is just another pilgrim trying to get along. That's all any of us are.

"We had lunch at the Waldorf with people who bought the movie rights to The Shining. *We sat in leather chairs. Mine was dedicated to George M. Cohan because it was where he used to sit and compose. The waiters are all French. They glide over to you.*

"Then I come back to Maine and pick up the toys and check if the kids are brushing in the back of their mouths, and I'm smoking too many cigarettes and chewing aspirins alone in this office, and the glamour people aren't here. There is a curious loneliness. You have to produce day after day and you have to deal with doubts—that what you're producing is trivial and, besides, not even good. So in a way, when I go there, to New York City, I feel like I've earned it. I'm getting my due."

Published March 1979

I first met Stephen King and his wife, Tabitha (Tabby), in 1976. We lived within a few miles of each other, both beside lovely lakes. One of my first stories for the Maine Sunday Telegram *was to visit the young Maine writer who after 30 rejections from publishers saw his first book* Carrie *and soon after,* 'Salem's Lot, *begin a career that 50 years later has produced nearly 80 books of fiction and nonfiction. Today, he is considered one of the most important figures in American popular culture history. He and Tabby, an author of fiction and poetry, are among the most generous philanthropists in the state of Maine. Their reach includes libraries, schools, arts, historical societies, immigrant organizations, and youth sports. I may be the only writer who not only helped King round up pigs for the market when they escaped, but who also ended up as a character named Mel Allen from the* Portland Sunday Telegram, *in* The Dead Zone.

The Gift

Sandra ("Sandi") Mansi lives in Bristol, Vermont, up a long drive away from the two-lane road, past mounds of timber waiting for her husband's chainsaw and splitter. Lake Champlain lies some 20 miles west, but she rarely goes to the lake anymore—cataracts have stolen her pleasure of sitting by the water and looking out. "I just don't get around like I used to," she says. She's 67 now, her voice cheerful, tobacco-husky, easy to laughter. Her sister lives down the road, her daughter and grandchildren even closer. She grew up nearby, and after living in Connecticut and New Hampshire, she's been home for 11 years now and is here, she says, to stay. She spends her time "puttering" and painting folk-art scenes on wooden boxes made by her husband, Richard Racine.

"I never picked up a paintbrush until I was 60," she says proudly. "It's my time. It's my turn. I brought up my family. I helped bring up grandchildren." From time to time she visits local schools to show a photograph and talk about "Champ," the legendary creature that has riled the imaginations of Vermonters for centuries. The photo she shows is the one she took of a dark, leathery-looking *something* that rose out of the water about 150 feet from where she was sitting on the shore of Lake Champlain.

"The kids always ask was I scared, if I think it's a dinosaur," Mansi says. She doesn't really know what she saw; she has never claimed to be an authority. But this much is certain: All serious discussion of whether something unexplainable lives in the depths of this deep, cold, 120-mile-long lake starts with the single image Sandi Mansi captured in the early afternoon of July 5, 1977.

Her Kodak Instamatic photo was scrutinized by scientists using technology that would detect whether the image had been doctored. It hadn't been. "[She] could no more construct a hoax than put a satellite in orbit," Mansi's lawyer told a reporter. Even the staunchest doubters of the existence of a 15- to 30-foot prehistoric-looking creature living in Lake Champlain can't claim that Sandi Mansi didn't see whatever it was that showed up in her lens. ("Don't call it 'monster,'" she says. "I hate the word 'monster.'") *Discover* magazine called her photo the "Rosetta Stone of Champology."

I went to see her last summer [2010], on the last day of July. I wasn't there to prove or disprove anything. The people who over the years say they've seen an enormous, dark, humped, serpentine creature number roughly 300; among them are dozens of locals who have spent their lives fishing the lake and who tell skeptics they know what sturgeons, otters, swimming deer, and driftwood look like. In 2003, a scientific expedition detected echolocation in Lake Champlain; the only aquatic animals we know of that make those sounds are dolphins, porpoises, and whales. "What we can say for sure," noted researcher Elizabeth von Muggenthaler, "is that there's a creature in the lake that produces biosonar. We have no idea what it is." However, the research done by a team of Middlebury College geologists made an argument that what people observe may be the result of a huge standing wave beneath the surface, called a seiche, which may propel long sunken trees twisting to the surface, startling onlookers. But I wasn't here now for any of that debate. I wanted to know what had happened to Sandi Mansi.

She sat in her pretty yard, bordered by blueberry bushes and apple trees; she relaxed with a can of Pepsi by her side, a story on her lips. Her hair is the color of straw, and behind her glasses her gaze is clear and direct—as is her story. She tells it without drama, pausing only to answer questions. "You know," she says, "nobody has ever asked me how what I saw changed me. Nobody."

On that summer day in 1977, she was showing Anthony Mansi, her then-fiancé and coworker at General Dynamics in Groton, Connecticut, her Vermont roots. Her two children from a previous marriage were with them.

"We started off on St. Albans Bay with my children, Heidi and Larry [ages 11 and 12], and we were just exploring," she explains. "We meandered north, and then the kids started fighting over who was breathing whose air. We were on a dirt road, and we pulled over and walked across a field and down an embankment. It was around noon.

"The kids took their shoes off and waded in. We were sitting there by the water. And Anthony decided to get the camera. So he went back to the car. And I was sitting down the embankment. I was looking out at the lake. And I could see a turbulence, like how a school of fish look.

"I went, 'Wow, that's a big school of fish! Wouldn't my grandfather like to look at this!' Then pretty soon the head and the neck broke the surface. And I thought, Whoa—that's one heck of a sturgeon. I knew what a sturgeon was; they're absolutely huge. But they're not that big. And then the head came up, and then the neck came up, and then I could see the back.

"And then Anthony came to the top of the embankment and he saw it, and he was screaming for the kids to get out of the water. They got out, and he got them back in the car.

"And the whole time I was thinking, *What is that?!* Anthony came to the edge to help me up. And he handed me the camera so he could pull me up the bank.

"I was on my knees getting up, and I picked the camera up, and the creature looked over its back, and I took the picture, and Anthony was like, 'C'mon, c'mon.' I said, 'Wait, wait,' and then we watched it. It never gave any indication it knew we were there. I watched it maybe five minutes. You could see the water coming off it.

"Then the back went down, the neck went down, the head went down. And only then was I caught up in a panic. I heard a boat way off in the distance. He knew a boat was coming. I wasn't afraid; it was more *Oh, my God.*

"When I was little, my grandfather would tell us that if we didn't sit down in the boat, he'd throw us in the lake and Champ would get us. But nobody believed it. Now my mind said, *This must be Champ.* But being a Vermonter, my mind also said, There must be a reasonable explanation for this. There has to be. This doesn't happen to people like me.

"We got into the car, and it was like, 'Okay, what just happened? What did we see?' And my children were like, 'Mom what was that?' I said, 'I don't know.' My son said, 'I know. It was a 2,000-pound duck.' Anthony said we should tell someone. I said, 'Who are you going to tell? Are you going to a state trooper and say we just saw something in the lake?'"

Mansi looks at me and shrugs. She says there have been doubters ever since, because she has never been able to say with certainty where she took the photo. "I know we were north of St. Albans," she recalls. "It was very rural. I'm not sure where we were. I know I was on the Vermont side, close to Missisquoi Bay." But all she has is a single frame—no negative, no roll of continuous shots.

"You know what?" she says, and her voice rises just a bit. "People say, 'Why didn't you take more?' It wasn't a conscious thing. And I've never kept negatives. What good are negatives? I never had any use for them. We just sent it to the Fotomat. I mean, that's how insignificant we thought it was. And I wouldn't even have thought about saving it.

"I know people thought I was lying. But this is what happened. We didn't know what it was. And when the photo came back, it was like Oh, my God. There's no more rationalizing, or trying to figure out what it is. But what do we do with the information? I knew people would say we were crazy. I said, 'Let's not tell anyone.' And Anthony agreed. So we decided to just put it away. Soon we got married, and we slid it behind our wedding photos. And then we hardly mentioned it."

Richard joins us. He's sturdy, with a trim beard; he's handy with tools, at home in the woods. "I've heard her tell this for 30 years," he says. "It's never changed."

Mansi picks up the story after she and Anthony divorced in 1980. (He died a few years later.) Her coworkers were going to Scotland to do submarine overhaul; some said they hoped to go to Loch Ness, see Nessie. "Big-mouth me," she says with a hoarse laugh. "I said, 'You don't have to go to Scotland. We have something like that a lot closer.' And I brought the picture in. I asked them not to say anything—but next thing you know, I was getting calls. It was like opening Pandora's box."

Her photo and her story made its way to cryptozoology experts—people who study "hidden" animals—including Joseph Zarzynski, who would later write *Champ: Beyond the Legend* but whose mission at the time was to persuade Vermont and New York to pass protective legislation against anyone harming the mysterious lake creature. It was only a matter of time before the media pounced. Mansi had the photo copyrighted and gave it to her lawyer for safekeeping.

"I was in fear of it getting exploited," Mansi says. "I wasn't looking to gain financially from it. *National Enquirer* offered a lot of money. I said no. I wanted to keep its integrity. I wanted credibility."

In June 1981, the *New York Times* published the photograph, and Sandi Mansi braced for the response: "I knew I had to have the conviction to say, 'Okay, this is what I saw. You tell me what it was.'"

Dr. George Zug of the Department of Vertebrate Zoology at the Smithsonian's National Museum of Natural History told the *New York Times* in a follow-up story that "evidence was mounting that some creature inhabited the cold lakes of the Northern Hemisphere."

Mansi says that at first the sudden burst of attention drew her in. "I learned that it's so easy to get caught up in one thing and let that dictate your life," she says. "I lost track of my priorities. This was all new. I went on *The Merv Griffin Show.* A limousine picked me up.

"Then reality settled in when I got home. I was living in Winchester, New Hampshire, then; a single mom bringing up two children. I had my children stay with friends for four days. What kind of mother is that? That bothered me terribly. So I said, 'This is my priority—my family. This is something that happened to me, and I will deal with it,' but I never left my children again. I felt God gave us a gift. I've never told anybody that. What we do with the gift will make a difference in our lives."

I ask her, "What was the gift?"

"The gift of witnessing something not everyone has seen," she replies. "And then the gift of weighing it out. I asked, 'What do you want me to do with it, God?' And He wouldn't answer me. So I tried to follow what I thought was right.

"I've learned patience. I've learned humor through it. And I've learned tolerance. If you want to ridicule me, that's okay. It's fine. But I think I opened the door for others to come through and tell. To me that was the biggest success: that people were now comfortable enough to say, 'I don't care if you believe me or not. I'm telling you I saw something.' And that's why we have so many eyewitnesses now. And I'm not taking all the credit.

I'm just saying that it takes only one person sometimes to open the door. And it takes guts to follow through that door."

I ask whether she's had one moment of doubt since that day. "The doubts are that if I hadn't taken that photograph, would it be as big as I remember?" she tells me. "Would it be as prominent? Would I have dismissed it as just something else? The photograph is what grounds me to the fact that this is what I saw, period, the end. Nothing else. This is what I saw."

I ask whether she loves the photo. She laughs: "I don't even have it hanging in my house. I'm not emotionally attached to it. What I have is here," and she touches her eyes and her heart. "That I love. I love that a lot. I know it's there. I will go to God and stand before Him and say, 'God, why me? Now tell me what it was.' The photograph keeps it there. So I know I saw that.

"I know this: Lake Champlain has something—a secret, a hidden treasure. And it's wonderful and it's magnificent, even if you don't believe it's there. Someday I'll be vindicated. And people will say, 'Remember that old lady from Vermont?'"

Published March/April 2011

Sandi Mansi passed away in March 2018. She was 74. Her obituary requested that in lieu of flowers, donations be sent to an expedition to help prove the existence of Champ.

The Two Worlds of Bill De La Rosa

Years from now, when Bill De La Rosa thinks about the morning of May 28, 2016, he'll remember this: the sun blistering down on 460 of his fellow graduates, sitting in their black caps and gowns, the deep green of the lawn, and the trees whose leaves stirred whenever a breeze blew. He's standing on the stage in front of the Bowdoin Art Museum, one of two students chosen to speak at commencement, an honored tradition at Bowdoin College in Brunswick, Maine. The quad is filled with some 2,000 people, but what he'll remember is seeing the faces of his family, eight in all, who sit side by side just behind the graduates. They've come for the first time from Mexico and Arizona to see this campus, one that Bill has described as being so lovely, as if it were an enchanted place from a storybook. They hold their phones high over their heads, pointed toward him standing on the stage.

And he'll remember two who are not here: his father, Arsenio, age 83, too weak to travel from Tucson, his body ravaged from a stroke and years of breathing poison while flying crop dusters; and 2,800 miles away, a woman with a warm, pretty face and dark hair. She's 47 years old. She lives in a tiny apartment 400 feet from the American border in Nogales, Mexico. It's early in Nogales, 7:30 a.m., three hours behind Maine time. She's visiting a friend, one who speaks English. On her friend's computer, Bowdoin's commencement streams live.

Two months before Bill De La Rosa spoke at Bowdoin College's graduation in 2016, he visited his mother, Gloria, in Nogales, Mexico, where he read to her his acceptance letter to Oxford University. Photo credit: Heather Perry

There on the screen stands Bill, handsome, with soft brown eyes. Under his cap his hair is short and neat. A speaker introduces him by extolling his accomplishments, among them earning a Gates Millennium Scholarship, a Truman Scholarship, acceptance to Oxford University, and a month earlier being named the national Hispanic Scholar of the Year. The audience takes this in. In terms of academia, they know they're watching a shining star. Then Bill begins to speak, and soon audible ripples of surprise drift out from the audience.

"I was born in a small border town known as Nogales, Arizona, but raised in Nogales, Mexico. When I was seven years old, my family risked moving permanently to Tucson, Arizona, in search of a better future. We left everything we owned in the small motel room where I spent my childhood. When we arrived in Tucson, we had no money, no place to go, no place to call home. We slept wherever we felt safe—in our car, in alleyways, within trailer parks. . . . My mother earned a living cleaning rooms at our local Motel 6. Sometimes I would tag along and help her clean, so she could come home a little bit earlier. . . . In October 2009, my mother was deported from the United States to Mexico, and she was barred from returning to her home and family for 10 years."

The pretty, dark-haired woman is Gloria Arrellano De La Rosa. She leans in close to the computer screen. Her friend translates Bill's words into Spanish. Bill knows she's watching. And he knows she'll be saying softly to herself, *"Mijo. Mijo."* "My son. My son."

When you meet Bill De La Rosa, your first thought will be how young he looks, how soft-spoken he is. For years his story stayed mostly private; few of his high-school classmates, few of his Bowdoin classmates, knew what was driving him. Both in Tucson, and then in Maine, it seemed that wherever there was a need to help, he volunteered. In his first year at Bowdoin, even while navigating a strange new physical and cultural landscape, he made his way to Portland twice a week to help Spanish-speaking newcomers adjust to Maine, and to volunteer at a legal-aid society. Later he worked with Maine's Somali refugees and then spent summers carrying water into the brutally forbidding desert that separates Mexico from Arizona, where so many migrants have died trying to cross. It was as though he'd looked at a broken world and determined that he could piece things back together one fragment at a time: Portland, Tucson, Nogales, Mexico.

Then, last September, Arizona Public Media and the *Arizona Daily Star* told the story of Bill De La Rosa and his family, and what had happened when his mother was deported, leaving Bill and his family caught in the crossfire of history. They became the compelling faces of a nation divided on the complex dilemma of immigration. The student paper, the *Bowdoin Orient,* picked up the story, and Bill felt the eyes of his classmates pinned on him when he came to the cafeteria or walked to class.

"It felt eerie," he said. "We don't all come from the same place, the same privilege, or shared experience. Here was something that wasn't just happening far away. But this had happened to someone on your campus." A "strange feeling," he said, to be known as the face of misfortune and endurance, but it was his story, and now he embraced it. His story is who he has become.

We met first on a late-February day in Brunswick. We talked while lunchtime throngs passed through the crowded aisles of Wild Oats Bakery & Café. "I remember it was a day full of sun," he said, of Thursday, October 22, 2009, the day when his life changed. He was 15, a sophomore at Pueblo Magnet High School, located in South Tucson, the poorest area in one of the poorest cities in the country. He lived in public housing with his parents, two brothers—Jim, 17, and Bobby, just 4—and sister, Naomi, age 9. They lived tight, but his mother made their home sparkle, and nobody ever left her table hungry. He was a good student, report cards filled with As, a popular boy with an easy smile who ran cross-country.

Every day that week, he'd run home from school, awaiting his mother's call. "My mom was the pillar," Bill said. "Mom was it. She did the cooking, shopping, cleaning, tucking Bobby in. I just went to school." She'd taken Bobby with her across the border to Mexico, seeking papers she needed to live legally; all four children had been born in the United States, all four were American citizens. Her husband, Arsenio, was also a naturalized American citizen. Her lawyer had advised her to cross the border back into Mexico and admit her past, and soon she would rejoin her family.

And it was then, on the Thursday, a day he remembered for its sunshine, that Bill De La Rosa walked into the house and heard the phone ring.

"I rush to answer it," he said, "and it's my mom. And she's outside on a pay phone, and it's pouring. And she's just crying. And she keeps saying, '*Mijo no me dieron. No. No. No. Me dieron diez. Me dieron diez.*' ["They gave me 10 years. They gave me 10 years."] And I just stood there. I looked at a picture on top of the TV. It was a family portrait. It was the last picture we had together. I knew it would never be the same. And I cried. I cried a lot."

Gloria De La Rosa's story contains strands within strands of complexity, but while we sat in the café, Bill did his best to guide me to its core. Years earlier, his mother had crossed into Arizona legally with a visa. She gave birth there to two sons, Jim and Bill. When her visa expired, the family moved back to Nogales, Mexico, where they lived in a single room in a motel owned by a relative.

"My dad would walk Jim and me across the border to go to school in the U.S.," Bill said. "I didn't speak English. My mom was working at a grocery store, earning practically nothing. One day she took my brother and me to the movies. It was the *Pokémon* movie, and it was the first movie we ever saw. Another time she took us to get pizza. It was far away, and we walked. These things were special because they happened only once."

When Bill was seven, the family crossed again to the U.S., making their way to what they hoped would be a new life in Tucson. This time Gloria, whose visa had long expired, came illegally, and she became one more undocumented person blending into a cityscape, as ubiquitous and as invisible as cactus.

As Bill told his story, his eyes seemed to squint as if trying to remember the years of what he calls "the darkness of poverty," when his family "drifted place to place, slept on floors for months." By 2005 they'd found public housing; Gloria worked cleaning rooms, and Bill sold her tortillas door to door. When Gloria left to obtain her legal papers, it was a chance to move another notch closer to her American dream. "She'd tell me she was worried," Bill said. "I kept saying, 'Don't worry—you don't have to worry. You're married with four children. We're all American citizens. Your husband is sick. There's nothing to worry about.'"

But of course there was. Nobody had warned her about a 1996 law called the "unlawful presence bar." What the law stated was clear: If you had entered the U.S. illegally and had stayed for more than a year, and then returned to Mexico, you were barred from even applying for re-entry for 10 years. No appeal, no recourse. And that's when everything changed for Bill De La Rosa.

In a heartbeat, Bill became mother, father, cook, housekeeper, brother, nurse, tireless immigration-law researcher. As often as they could, the family visited Gloria; they brought Bobby back to live with his siblings. Bill's brother, Jim, graduated from high school and joined the U.S. Marines to keep the family afloat financially. I asked Bill how he'd managed to become his high school's valedictorian, earn scholarships, be recruited by the best colleges—all while caring for his family. Bill grew silent for a few moments.

"I knew I had to stay hopeful, so we all had hope, so there's hope also for my mom. If I don't have hope, then she doesn't either. I said perhaps the way I can give her hope is by showing her how I am in school. So I made myself just buckle down and go to school and get the job done. And when semester grades came out and rankings came out, I'd show her and say, 'Look, Mom.'

"I didn't want anyone to feel sorry for me, so I just started wearing different masks. I became a different person in front of my friends, in front of teachers, in front of my dad and Naomi. In front of my mom. In middle school, every day before class, we all had to recite what teachers called 'The Definite Dozen.' There were 12 rules. And I always remembered number 12. It was the last rule, and every day we had to say it out loud. Only then we could take our seats. Number 12 was 'Be relentless. And never give up.' That was always in the back of my mind: 'Be relentless. Never give up.'"

He drew deep breaths when he spoke, as if to make sure his emotions stayed steady. "But there were nights, and my siblings would be in bed, and Jim is off to the Marines, and I'm just with my dad, and he's getting sicker, and they'd be asleep, and it'd be 2 a.m. in the morning, and I'd just be in my room studying, and it's just really me. There would be nights. . . ." He choked up for a moment. "There would be nights. . . ."

We walked down Maine Street toward the library, Bill's second home. Even in late winter, with the trees bare, the campus gave the feeling of old and gracious comfort. Bells rang; students with backpacks hurried on their way. I'd asked about transitions: how one comes from South Tucson to Maine Street. Bill told about coming during a "recruiting" visit in November 2011, when "Explore Bowdoin" hosted the best and brightest of ethnically diverse, often poor, students, who a generation ago wouldn't have been likely to come to an elite New England private college. "That trip opened my eyes," Bill said. "I saw how big the world was. How small my bubble was in Tucson. As we were driving into Brunswick, and we're driving through Pleasant Street, we made a right to the college. I was like, 'So this is what prestigious looks like.' I kept thinking, 'This is New England. The lights. The architecture of the church. It's incredible.'"

Bowdoin got inside him and held on. He applied for early admission. He was accepted. He was awarded a Gates Millennium Scholarship. Bowdoin said, *Don't worry about money.* Soon he found that getting into Bowdoin was the easy part. The hard part lay ahead.

In a quiet private room Bill had reserved for us on the third floor of the library, he spoke carefully, as though he were picking his words one by one from a beach. He knew, no matter how he parsed it, that coming to Bowdoin would mean leaving his siblings and his father and mother behind. "I wasn't sure I was doing the right thing," he said. "There were so many what-ifs. So much uncertainty. I could have simply gone to the University of Arizona. Lived at home, looked after things. But I said, 'How can I best carry on and finish what my parents wanted for us?'"

He met with family friends, his church, his sister's and brother's schools. They all said they'd call if Bill was needed. But the doubts crept in and never left. He worried about having to drop out if his father needed to go to a nursing home, or if he died. Then Naomi and Bobby would be without a legal guardian in the home, and the state would step in.

And deep inside, he wondered whether he was ready for a New England private college. "Yes, I was valedictorian," he said, "but I was from South Tucson. I knew that. I was very self-conscious when I came to Bowdoin. It was intimidating." He took a philosophy class the first semester of freshman year. "The moment I heard everyone speak," he said, "I heard how articulate, how expressive, they were. I crumbled. I was scared. I didn't speak at all the whole semester. Not once. The professor called on me the last day. And he wished me luck.

"Sophomore year was my hardest. At the start of the semester, Jim was deployed. It became mentally exhausting. I'd be in the dining hall with all this food and thinking of everyone at home. It was like I was living in two places at once. I withdrew from a class. I went to counseling."

A friend of Bill's told me that she felt he carried an "invisible bucket. It's heavy, and he carries it everywhere with him. No one can see it, but he's carrying it." Before I left, I asked whether he remembered the last time he simply let go and let himself be a 22-year-old going to school. Carefree. He smiled briefly, and shook his head: No. He couldn't remember.

The next day, a Saturday, we met again at the library, and Bill talked about the fire inside him, the migrants who will risk everything to find what they hope will be a better future, if only they can survive the desert, elude patrols and the vigilante "minutemen" who wait in trucks where the desert empties onto roads. In his library cubicle, which many days he would enter in the morning and not leave until dark, he kept stacks of books devoted to his thesis: why people persist in trying to cross the Sonoran Desert, where more than 2,500 human remains have been found and unknown others simply disappear into the sun-baked sand. Despite the brutal environment, despite the odds, they still try. His thesis probed why. He'd entered Bowdoin to study government and find his way to law school. But in October of his first year, he heard a guest speaker, an anthropologist named Jason De León, talk about his work in the Sonoran Desert, investigating how migrants died there, and how it wasn't an accident but the certain outcome of a border policy called "Prevention Through Deterrence."

"The policy is 'We'll let the desert deter people. People will suffer, people will die, and the word will spread,'" Bill explained. As he talked, his voice was measured, he spoke slowly, and for the first time I felt anger just beneath the soft voice. "When I heard De León, I knew I wanted to get involved," he said. "It seems counterintuitive. I come to Maine, and that's how I find my path."

For two summers he worked at a migrant shelter hard against the desert. His two worlds became three: college studies, worrying about his faraway family, and now, the men, women, and children poised to cross despite the danger.

He became acutely aware that his life in Maine, surrounded by beauty and comfort, was unimaginable to the migrants he studied or to his family. While his fellow students talked about tests and papers, movies, parties, adventures, sports, he kept thinking that "right now someone is trying to make their way across, and they're possibly dying."

When we said good-bye early that afternoon, we made plans to see each other again after alternative spring break, during which he would lead 10 Bowdoin classmates to visit his mother in Nogales, to stand by the wall that he felt defined who he was, to visit the shelter, to meet migrants, and to enter the desert where they might, he told them, encounter human remains. It would be a journey from his world in Maine to his world by the border, and it would be one that nobody would forget.

When Bill led the students into the desert in mid-March, they found the ID of a young man named Danny tangled in a bush. He was only 22. "We saw his face," a student named Jessica told me. "He's our age. He's making this dangerous journey. What happened to him? It was emotional. I don't think I'll ever forget his name."

Bill brought his fellow students to a court hearing in Tucson, where newly captured migrants awaited deportation. They remembered the sound of shackles as one woman tried to wipe away her tears. A forensic anthropologist showed them a photo of a boy, about 11 years old. In the photo, he's playing drums and smiling. He was from Guatemala, and his body had been found in the desert beside his aunt, as they tried to reunite with his parents.

And then Bill brought them to Nogales to meet his mother. She greeted them with "*Mis tesoros, mis tesoros* [my treasures]," and fed them heaping plates of her homemade specialties. "Nobody leaves until it is all gone," she told them. "She was this incredible, beautiful woman who didn't speak a word of English. I had tears," one student recalled. "It was emotional. We hugged and hugged."

When the group returned to Maine, Bill had an acceptance letter from Oxford University, a thesis to finish, two upcoming trips to Los Angeles as a finalist for (and about to be named winner of) Hispanic Scholar of the Year, a speech to deliver to an outdoor leadership school in Wyoming, a speech to write for commencement, and a decision on where he'd go next.

He decided to work at the Center for Law and Social Policy in Washington, D.C. "They do a lot on immigration, inequality, and poverty," Bill said. "Immigration is also a poverty issue. A language issue. I'll learn to see this in a different light." He would ask Oxford to defer his admission to its master's in migration studies for a year. His father was too frail for him to be adding distance.

Which brings us back again to the young man finishing his speech on a sweltering Maine day in late May. "Growing up, my mother would always tell me, '*Hay que sembrar buenos frutos para cosechar buenas cosas.*' 'We have to plant good seeds to harvest great things.' I would add that now that we are reaping the fruits of our labor, it is our responsibility to help others plant their seeds. . . ."

First his classmates and then the audience, which stretched to the outer shady trees, stood and applauded. They didn't stop for several minutes. When the ceremony ended, his family made their way to the field house, where food awaited. In time, Bill found his way to his family. "I had to do a detour," said his professor and mentor, Marcos López, "so many people wanted to hug him and take pictures." A tall man in a suit stopped at Bill's table. He'd listened to Bill's speech and now he looked at his family. "Bill will change the world," he said. "Bill will change the world."

When the crowds thinned, Bill and his little brother and sister took off their shoes and ran laughing through sprinklers on the grass. The next day, Bill would board a plane in Portland, Maine, and fly to Washington, D.C. One professor told me that Bill's legacy will be that all the students of similar backgrounds who come after will know how Bill De La Rosa came too shy to speak in class and left an orator. If you look at Bill's Facebook page, you'll see the expectations that people hold for him. They say, See you when you're a senator . . . a governor . . . see you when you're POTUS.

A commencement is always filled with high hopes for the future. And who's to say what Bill may do in the years ahead? But who'd bet against Bill De La Rosa becoming a man whose vision and words might yet stir a nation into finding its way through difficult choices to make immigration reform unite rather than divide? Who'd bet against Bill De La Rosa being one who could change the world? I wouldn't. Would anyone?

Published September/October 2016

Since I first met Bill De La Rosa, I have thought often of what he had endured, and what he had achieved. He overcame so many obstacles at such a young age and never surrendered to despair or lost hope. Over the ensuing years I followed his journey: He earned two master's degrees from Oxford, in migration and criminal justice studies, then continued with a PhD in criminology. The honors he earned at Oxford could fill a page.

Today he is in his second year at Yale Law School. In January 2024, after 14 years separated from her family, Bill walked his mother, now a legal holder of a green card, across the border to a welcoming crowd who cheered a reunion that was filled with tears of happiness as well as sorrow for the days apart and the death of her husband in 2018. The homecoming was national news, with MSNBC featuring their border crossing. Bill's sister, Naomi, who became the head of the household while Bill attended college, graduated with high honors from the University of Arizona. His brother Jim came home after his Marine tour and is now a father. His younger brother, Bobby, is now in college. Bill is engaged to be married to a woman he met at Oxford.

When he graduates Yale Law School, he says he will devote his professional life to bringing reason, compassion, and fairness to an immigration system that has fractured the country he still believes in. Who would doubt he will not make a difference now?

"An Allagash Love Story" (page 77) tells the saga of Al and Patty Nugent creating a famous wilderness sporting camp from humble beginnings. This photo was taken shortly after the couple stepped onto the banks of Chamberlain Lake. They are standing in front of their first cabin, which was covered with birch bark. "Dear, we were rough looking, weren't we?" Patty said when she handed me the photo that she said few had ever seen. Photo courtesy of Patty Nugent

TWO

THE WAYS WE LOVE

When people tell me their stories of what they love, of their passion for what they do, or where they live, and especially when they are infused with memories of a time they can only recapture in the telling, I feel I am not with them to write a story: I am there to let their story be told.

Scott and Helen Nearing became touchstones for many in my generation who came of age in the '60s and yearned to go "back to the land." So many people I have known were inspired by the simplicity and work ethic described in their groundbreaking book, Living the Good Life. *I attended a number of rural life events where the Nearings were homesteading celebrities and I wanted to write about Scott reaching a century. When I wrote "Leaving the Good Life," I did not know I would be the last writer to see him. Being there as Helen administered to her husband felt like a gift I wanted to let others feel as well.*

In "Taking the Wheel," generosity, caring, and yes, love, led Stony Creek, Connecticut, boat captains to band together. They kept a well-known cruise boat afloat, and then showed the ropes to the daughter of one of their own who had been badly injured.

And here you will see neighbors who came to believe in the most improbable effort you can imagine: making a home for elephants in a mid-coast Maine village. I had accompanied my wife, Annie, to a story she was writing about an environmental college not far from a village named

Hope. We stopped in the general store for a bottle of water. As I paid, I noticed a collection jar with a photo of an elephant and the words: "Bring Rosie to Hope." I asked, and found a profound tale of a passionate cause overcoming so many obstacles, and how it truly took a village to make the impossible happen.

When I am living these stories, they become part of my own life. I think about them during the day. I think about them at night. So when I got word of how this story of compassion ended, I knew that not only did the townspeople grieve but also everyone who had felt buoyed by the impossible quest of a man who loved elephants.

A writer will tell you that when they hear someone say something with deep emotion, those words will linger long after the story ends. In my years of telling stories of New England and its people, Patty Nugent's words as I was about to leave her wilderness camp along the Allagash Waterway were as poignant and lovely as any I have known. When I hear words like these, I want others to hear them, too.

Leaving the Good Life

Helen and Scott Nearing, whose book, *Living the Good Life,* is the bible of the back-to-the-land movement, live on a windswept spit of land on Penobscot Bay in Hancock County, Maine, 20 miles from the nearest stores and banks, in Blue Hill. She is 79; he will be 100 on August 6, and for 50 years they have had little use for towns or stores or banks.

They began homesteading in 1932 on a run-down, 65-acre Vermont farm at the foot of Stratton Mountain, which they bought for $300 down and an $800 mortgage. Scott Nearing was nearly 50 and broke, living in New York City with Helen Knothe, a young violinist who later became his wife. A leading Socialist, he had run for Congress and had sold out lecture halls debating Clarence Darrow. A professor of economics and sociology, he had been fired from three universities for taking stands against child labor and for his pacifism during World War I. His textbooks had been withdrawn and publishers refused his new work. The move to the country was for survival.

They had no electricity and, except for a battered pickup truck, no machinery. They fortified the soil with compost, heated with wood, and built a house of stone. They kept no farm animals and had no children. They ate only the vegetables they raised and the grains and fruits they bartered for. From their sugar bush, they boiled maple syrup for cash. But in 1952, feeling crowded out by Stratton Mountain ski developers, they moved to Maine, to another run-down farm on 140 acres of isolation. He was 70, she 49. They were starting over again.

One cold misty morning late last May, I visited "Forest Farm," now a garden spot that attracts several thousand people a year. I had seen Scott twice, in person, giving talks on gardening at venues filled with hopeful homesteaders. His deeply tanned, wrinkled face atop a straight, sturdy body made me think, somehow, that he would scythe his meadow, chop his wood, and plant his garden forever. But this was a melancholy drive down the Maine coast, for I had just received a letter from Helen Nearing that said that Scott was dying. "He's in no pain," she had written, "just getting ready to leave a worn-out body."

There is a sign nailed to a pine tree at the end of the gravel driveway: "Visitors 3-5. Please help us to lead the good life." They are famous for their stone buildings, all done by hand with stones they have gathered obsessively on walks through the fields, in the woods, or along the shore. When I park, I see a garage, a storage shed, an outhouse, the beautiful balconied house completed when Scott was 95, and a five-foot-tall wall surrounding the garden, all of stone, giving me the impression that I have dropped in at the estate of an English lord.

Instead it is Helen Nearing, a white blouse torn at the shoulder, a faded red sweater, and blue corduroys, who greets me. Scott, her barber of 50 years, has not been able to cut her hair; a few strands stick out from her forehead like quills. She is weary, her face drawn, and when she sits down at the long wooden table in the kitchen to talk, her attention wanders, her ears cocked to the living room, where Scott is sleeping. A fire burns in the cookstove. Herbs and onions hang from an oak beam and a breeze rustles chimes.

"I've never known him a day sick in bed," she says. "Never, never. We've never had a doctor. He was still working outside half a year ago. But one morning he just took to his bed and started to sleep. I think it was November, like he was hibernating. He was restless for a time, shouting out suddenly at night. Now he's contented. He doesn't complain. But sometimes he'll look at me and say, 'I wish I could carry the wood in for you.'"

She walks into the living room. The floor is stone, the walls paneled, and a massive wooden table sits before the picture window that looks out upon their cove. There is a woodstove in a corner, and on the other side of the room where bookshelves span the walls, Scott Nearing lies in a hospital bed with the sides up, like a crib, and beside the bed is a cot where Helen has slept the past several months. "This is my job now," she says quietly. "This is it."

He stirs at her approach. "What do you want, dear?" he says. His face is softer than I remembered, still tanned and weather-beaten but as peaceful as a baby's, and above his lip is a thin white mustache.

"Someone's come to see you," she says to him.

Blinking, he focuses on me. "Well, good," he says. "Good."

I tell him I have found a whole batch of his early books and pamphlets in a secondhand bookstore.

"Thrown away?" he asks.

"No," Helen says. "They've gone to a good person who will keep them."

"I'm going to have them reprinted," he says. He takes a deep breath and coughs. "Sure, sure," Helen says, comforting, and pulls a second blanket over him. He looks out the window to the calm, gray sea. In a moment he is asleep.

They met when Helen was 24. She was a student of Eastern mysticism who had recently returned to the family home in Ridgeway, New Jersey, after studying violin abroad. At her father's request, she invited Scott Nearing, then separated from his wife and living in Ridgeway, to speak at the Unitarian Church. Nearing took her for a drive. Like Helen, Scott had been born to a wealthy family. Raised in the coal-mining town of Morris Run, Pennsylvania, he was the grandson of Winfield Scott Nearing, the superintendent of the coal company. Young Scott sided with the working class. He had a horror of riches and fancy living. When his first wife decorated their home with lace doilies and cut glass, he bought himself a wooden bowl and spoon and refused to eat from anything else.

"That first night he said, 'Do you believe in fairies?'" Helen tells me. "I thought, what kind of guy is this? Of course, I believe in fairies, and I told him so, and he was very interested. I was going with four or five fellows at the time, but I was taken with his integrity, his purpose in life. Even those who disagreed with him responded to his warmth. And he was a vegetarian, as I was. I still tease him that if he hadn't been a vegetarian, we wouldn't have hooked up."

We are in the kitchen, and she laughs. "Can you imagine my parents? A Socialist, a married man, and a man 21 years older. It turned their hair white!"

He told her to live poor for a while before she came with him, so she moved to a slum and found work in a Brooklyn candy factory. He told her to return to the glitter of Europe, to be sure she wanted his life. She did. When he asked her to return to the cold-water flat in New York City and help him research a book on war, she cut her long, dark hair and took a boat home.

Soon she was a subsistence farmer in Vermont, where they evolved a system that would continue the rest of their lives. They worked four hours every day producing their food and shelter, four hours at their professions—his writing on social issues, her music—and spent four hours socializing. The latter was a little tricky in the hill towns of Vermont.

"Our ways amused the neighbors, baffled them, or annoyed them," Helen has written. "That we ate no meat was in itself strange, but during our 20 years in Vermont we never baked a pie."

In 1946, Scott's wife died. "I told him 'I want your name,'" Helen says. "It's a bad name, and I want it." In 1947 Scott and Helen were married. "And we've endured, haven't we?" she says. "And we're so different. His thinking is so pedantic, like he's always at a blackboard: 1, 2, 3, 4, A, B, C, D. And he gets hooked up with me, who sings, plays the fiddle and the organ, and yodels. And he doesn't even like music." She sighs and stands up. "Let's see if he's awake," she says.

"Scotto, open your mouth," she says, propping up a pillow. "I'm giving you some rose hip juice."

"That's nice of you."

"Rose hip juice you made yourself. Picked them and pressed them."

He takes a sip. Then another.

"Would you like some more?"

"Is it handy?" he asks.

"Yup. Right here."

Helen wipes his mouth and smooths his mustache. "He has a mustache now only because I'm too lazy to get in under his nose and shave it. He hates affectation. He heard William Jennings Bryan speak once, and he thought he was such an affected ass that he came home, shaved off his mustache, and gave away his dress suit. And he hasn't had either one since then."

We are speaking in the kitchen about families and the personal price one pays to be Scott Nearing. "People write to Scott," Helen says, "telling him he is a great man, an inspiration. But he had three sisters and two younger brothers who were ashamed of him. They thought he was a failure. We'd send them his books, and they'd come back unopened. He had two children. His son Bob is still friendly, but Scott severed relations with John in the sixties. He worked for Radio Free Europe, broadcasting propaganda to Europe. Scott said, 'You're working against the things I'm working for.' That was it. His son was John Scott Nearing, but then he dropped the Nearing. I asked Scott once if he would have lived his life differently. He said not in the big decisions, but in his personal relations. I think he meant he wishes he could have gotten along better with his son. But John died, so there's nothing to be done."

Past Scott's bed a door opens into a small, narrow room furnished with a desk, a typewriter, a bookcase. On the wall is a painting of Scott from a photograph by Lotte Jacobi. This room is the Social Science Institute, the publisher of many of Scott's 50 social science books. Though *Living the Good Life* was a success, Helen and Scott never touched the royalties for living expenses. All the money went here, to the Institute, to finance the research and publication of *Civilization and Beyond; USA Today; The Conscience of a Radical; Freedom, Promise and Menace.*

"I'd like someone to do a book of the early writings of Scott Nearing," Helen says. "Not just excerpts, but great chunks of writing. There are things in there, *important* things that will never be read by anyone."

We step back into the living room. Scott is sleeping. His right hand rests on his forehead, as though he is deep in thought. She says softly, "I wonder where the real Scott Nearing is now."

We eat lunch in the living room, sitting before the picture window on a bench made from a slab of driftwood dragged up from the cove. There is eggplant soup, an enormous ceramic bowl of popcorn, a bowl of steamed millet, peanuts, peanut butter, honey, apples, and bananas. Helen Nearing's motto of cooking is: "The most nourishment for the least effort."

"Scotto, we have soup and popcorn," she calls. She sits for a moment to crack some peanuts, then leaps to her feet to feed him handfuls of popcorn, returns to the table for more peanuts, then leaps up again to give him soup. I think of a mother bird feeding her nestlings, all that flying off and returning.

"Finish your soup," she tells me. "I'll give you Scott's Emulsion." Into my bowl she drops a couple of spoonfuls of peanut butter and a thick dropper of honey. "Work that down like cement," she says. She adds a scoop of the millet and some apple slices. "We eat this every day." She laughs, remembering a letter from a man who, after reading *Living the Good Life,* insisted on eating from a single bowl. "His wife divorced him. She said she wasn't going to eat like a dog."

A car drives up. It is a nurse to give Scott a bath.

"We were in the hospital for 12 days," Helen says. "I stayed with him in the room. When we got home, I thought I could take care of him, but I fell with him once. When I realized I couldn't, I just bawled because I thought I had to put Scott Nearing in a home. We went to a home for a while. I stayed with him, and they were very nice to us. But this is where he belongs."

Since girlhood, Helen had collected stones with bands of black or white around them. She called them "wishing stones" and felt that with them she had powers of divination. One day, knowing they must leave Vermont, she tied a wishing stone to a string, dangled it over a map of Maine, and closed her eyes. She imagined a saltwater farm, isolated enough so Scott could write in peace, run down enough to be cheap. Over Penobscot Bay the stone circled in an ever-tighter arc. That is where they found their present Forest Farm. And it was then that Pearl Buck, who had wanted to buy their Vermont farm, suggested that they write a book about their homesteading adventure.

"It had never occurred to us," says Helen. "It was just how we lived." They coauthored *Living the Good Life.* It sold 3,000 copies in 1954, then went out of print. In 1970 Schocken Books reissued it to a new generation. It was compared to *Walden,* sold 170,000 copies, and made the Nearings celebrities as Scott approached 90. When the energy crisis hit in 1973, TV networks sent nattily dressed reporters to the farm. Scott would take them to his woodpile, hand them a saw, and put them to work. He'd smile into the camera. "No crisis here," he'd say.

We are upstairs on the balcony outside Scott and Helen's bedroom, so close to the sea you seem to touch it. "I sit up here," she says, "and wonder where I'll go when Scott goes. I think of Switzerland or Holland, where my mother is from. But then I ask myself, what could I get anywhere that I don't have here. I've remade my will so that the house will not go into the real estate market. I want it to be a homestead educational center. People could come and see where Scott Nearing lived."

"Not where Helen Nearing lived, too?" I ask.

She laughs. "I'm just 'Helen and,'" she says. "When we sign books, he signs his name and hands them to me and I write 'Helen and.' If I write my autobiography that will be the title, *Helen and.*"

We walk into the guest room overlooking the garden. It is used by Nancy Richardson, a 32-year-old Pittsburgh woman who made a pilgrimage to the farm seven years ago, remained in the area, and now helps Helen care for the garden and for Scott. Like others in the house, the room is sparsely furnished. The walls are decorated with Japanese prints, a photograph of Helen's cat Pusso (killed by a fisher in October, and for which Helen mourns so much she cannot bear to look at it), and a painting of the stone house in Vermont on which this one is modeled.

"I learned detachment when we left Vermont," Helen says. "I thought if I ever have to leave anywhere again it won't be as hard as this. And when I went back a few years ago and saw that our house had become a ski chalet, well, I said, it's time to build its sister."

Bookshelves fill two walls of the room. "We've never had radio or television," she says. "I'd knit and he'd read to me or he'd shell beans and I'd read to him. If he tried one of his economics books, I fell asleep. He liked Robert Louis Stevenson and anything by Tolstoy. I'd slip a science fiction in sometimes. Or stories about animals. Anything about animals."

She leans down and plucks a book from the bottom shelf. It's a biography, *Scott Nearing: Apostle of American Radicalism,* by Stephen J. Whitfield. She grimaces, "I don't like this at all," she says. She opens it. She has crossed out paragraphs with a marking pen. She reads the words under her lines:

"This is not an intellectual portrait of Scott Nearing. I expect that his thought cannot bear the weight of intensive scrutiny." She shuts the book loudly. "I wouldn't let Scott read it. I said, 'Don't bother yourself with it.'"

In the corner of the room are two boxes stuffed with photographs, letters, notes. She says with satisfaction, "It's all here, a treasure trove. Someday I'll give them to a sympathetic biographer." Stacked on a shelf are metal card files crammed with 5x7 index cards, their headings ranging from "The Future of Civilization" to "Composting." "He took notes on everything," she says. "He taught me his system. 'Don't put information in books,' he would say, 'where you can't get at it.' So I take notes, writing down pithy quotations."

Among her quotations is this one: "No meal is as good as when you have your feet under your own table." Beside that she has written, "Scott Nearing, an opinion, 1970."

We start downstairs. I see four words burned into a plank nailed to the wall: "Sunshine—birdsong—snowfall—trees." She looks in on Scott. "Your eyelashes are growing into your eyes," she says. "Here, close your eyes." She snips quickly. "Thank you very much," he says.

We go through a door into the woodshed. It can hold eight cords. A cord or so is left from the past winter. "He cut and stacked all that last year," she says. "Incredible, isn't it?" A 50-foot-long stone storage shed stands beside the house. Inside, cardboard cartons filled with books are stacked four feet high. "Thoreau had a library of 600 *Waldens*. We have 6,000 Nearings." In a corner are boxes filled with letters from hopeful homesteaders. "The cruel thing was that more than anything he wanted to teach one class with the same students and watch them grow," she says. "And that was denied him. But he had more influence than if he had been a college president, don't you think?"

In the next room are the tools that Scott loves—his axes, including a double-bitted axe he has had since 1900; bow saws, teeth sharp as razors; and wheelbarrows, as clean as if they were in a museum. "Scott has a favorite wheelbarrow," Helen says. "Whenever we were building with stone, that was the one he used to mix the cement." He never left a tool in a field. Even if he were only pausing for lunch, he'd wipe it clean with burlap sacking that hung from a peg in the toolshed. He once wrote, "Order in the woodshed, the woodlot, toolshed, yard, and home are essential. . . . Care and artistry are worth the trouble."

We walk to the nearby farm where Helen and Scott lived for over 25 years before building their new stone house. A few years ago they sold it to Stan Joseph, after already selling many acres to other homesteaders. "We have only four acres left," Helen says, puffing slightly from the climb past boulders. "I wanted Scott to be relieved of the burden of cutting the grass and trimming the trees and weeding the garden." She looks at me. "But I never expected that none of the people who bought our land would stay our friends. We never see them. We were too organized, too methodical for them."

Soon the farm comes into view. A stone wall that took Helen and Scott 14 years to build surrounds the garden. Helen yodels, approaching the house, and we are welcomed inside by Stan Joseph's girlfriend. Helen has come to look at photos of Scott. There is one she would like copied. The two of them are walking down the road holding hands.

Stan Joseph comes in from the garden. He is a large man with a beard, a large hole in his checked flannel shirt. There is an exchange of greetings. He points out a checkerboard hanging on the wall. "Look at that," he says. "I paid only a dollar for it at the flea market. I bet I can get $30 for it in the city."

"You know what you might like to give me is some mint," Helen ventures. "We have lost ours. I kept giving it away and now we have none left."

"Sure, Helen. We could work something out. What have you got to swap?"

We walk back to the house, and at 1:30 the mailman comes. He has a package of blankets sent by a Hollywood producer who is interested in making a movie based on their lives. She scoffs: "Can you imagine?" But she is excited, walking into the house. "Our mailman has read some of Scott's books," she says. "He says he wants more. He wants a list so he can check off the ones he wants."

It is time to leave, and I go to Scott Nearing to say good-bye. I have a friend whose courage to build her own house came after reading *Living the Good Life,* and she asked me to be certain I thanked him for her. So I did.

"You're welcome, I'm sure," he says. "I hope it turns out all right."

We shake hands. His grip is still firm.

"Will I see you again?" he asks.

I say I hope so. I say I would like to.

At the kitchen door Helen presses a dozen book lists in my hand. "Take them to bookstores. Tell them for God's sake to stock this man." She hands me a pamphlet of six pages with "SCOTT NEARING" at the top in bold letters. Beside it in smaller type, "August 6, 1883—" with space for one last date and this brief statement:

"Scott lived a long and purposeful life. He was dedicated to research and to serving. He searched for knowledge and the truth, while he dedicated himself to serve his fellows. From the ideas on death that appealed to him, I have selected some which show the direction of his thought. He undoubtedly goes on researching and learning, and knows more now. This much, at least, we can share of his thoughts."

There would be no ceremony. His body would be cremated and the ashes spread on the garden.

"We planned everything," she says, "but I stupidly didn't expect it. We never talked about Scott going first. He was so vital, so strong. We were equals."

She stands on a knoll while I drive away. In other times she bade farewell to visitors with a ringing yodel, but as I look back, she waves good-bye in silence before she turns back to the house. Later it struck me that Scott Nearing was giving Helen his final act of kindness, leaving the good life as he had lived it, slowly, patiently, one step at a time.

Published August 1983

Shortly after this story was published, Scott Nearing died on August 24. I stayed in touch with Helen. "He had no pain, no doctor, no hospital. It was just time to go," she recalled. "It was ten in the morning. I was on the cot with him. I said, 'It's all right, go, go into the light, you've lived a long and beautiful life, it's time to go on now, and that's all right. We'll get along.' And he just said, 'All . . . right,' and he went." Helen published Loving and Leaving the Good Life *in 1993. Two years later, on an early fall evening, she was alone in her car when it hit a tree near her home. She was 91. Their Forest Farm homestead is now The Good Life Center, which is dedicated to carrying on the Nearings' work and beliefs.*

Taking the Wheel

Sometimes one person's story can seem to contain the whole of human experience—tragedy and triumph, despair and resilience, dreams dashed and dreams made real. And sometimes it is hidden right in front of us. On this afternoon late last summer, the passengers who board the *Volsunga IV* for a leisurely 45-minute tour of the Thimble Islands will hear about the history, lore, and legends that have grown up around these bits of land in Long Island Sound, just offshore from Stony Creek, Connecticut. What they won't hear from the captain is her own story, one that is as enduring in its own right: a story about a father, a daughter, and a village of boat captains who kept a promise.

On this day, as Anna Milne, captain of the *Volsunga,* slowly motors away from the dock to thread her way through the most densely packed group of islands in New England, it is 76 degrees, cloudy, almost dead low tide—a tricky time to navigate, with sandbars, boulders, and chunks of rock that jut above the water like massive turtle heads. She is 26 years old. Her captain's outfit is a black blouse, yellow skirt, and sandals. She wears her long brown hair in braids. Her arms carry multiple bracelets, and her toenails are painted blue. A headset microphone allows her to save her voice and still have her narration carry throughout the boat.

Anna was born a "Creeker," and her earliest memories are of sitting by her father's side as he piloted the *Volsunga.* A lifelong Creeker himself, Bob

Milne was known all along the Connecticut shoreline simply as Captain Bob. For a time he ran both his tourist cruise boat and the ferry for Thimble Island residents, before selling the latter in 2002. When he started his tours in 1987, he was 26, and for years he kept a journal filled with his observations and local knowledge. In 2005, after leading an estimated 12,000-plus trips, he published *Thimble Islands Storybook: A Captain's View.* He wanted his family to know the islands the way he did.

"In my memory," Anna told me, "it seems I was on the boat with him every day, all day." And even when she wasn't onboard the *Volsunga,* young Anna would trail after it in her own small craft, noticing where the rocks lay at high tide, learning the currents and how the wind shifted. (Being a Creeker, Anna told me, means that "you can be 7 or 8 years old and get in your Whaler with the little motor, and nobody bats an eye.")

Over and over, Anna heard the island legends, her father's anecdotes, with his pauses, his inflections, the way he drew word pictures, his voice rising and falling for emphasis. She understood that the stories he told were not just to entertain, but to bring the islands to life. The Thimbles would simply be masses of glacier rock to anyone who didn't know about the families who once lived there or the laborers who cut the islands' famed pink granite—stone so valued it helped build the Lincoln Memorial and Grant's Tomb and the base of the Statue of Liberty.

On today's tour, Anna motors the boat slowly past the Thimbles' neighborhoods. About two dozen islands hold summer homes, and these are the ones that people come to see. Many of the residents have considerable wealth, and some are famous, yet most opt to live a rustic life: kerosene lanterns, outdoor showers, a quietude they can enjoy only 90 miles from New York City. Anna tells her passengers that Stony Creek and the Thimbles were once considered the "Newport of Connecticut," with hotels and ballrooms; they were popular enough that President William Taft, who had become enamored with the Thimbles while at Yale, set up a summer White House on Davis Island.

When the *Volsunga* approaches Cut-in-Two Island, its passengers hear about "a small woman who lived here, Miss Emily," and the famous small man who courted her: General Tom Thumb, of P.T. Barnum renown. "He was smitten," Anna says, "and carved his initials on the kitchen door while declaring his love." She pauses. "Then he found another and left

Emily forsaken." She pauses again, calling up the words her father said thousands of times. "Just like a man," she says, her voice dropping for emphasis. "The scalawag."

As the boat turns toward Stony Creek, it passes by Jepson Island. Here, Anna's tone shifts. She tells about the Hurricane of '38, which without warning battered the Thimbles, huge waves sending cottages into the sea, and seven lives lost. The passengers grow quiet, attentive, as she recounts how one family on Frisbee Island sought safety on the second floor of their home. The father gathered up anything that might float and tied it all to a mattress, which he implored his daughter to hold on to, no matter what. When the family was swept into the sea, only the child, her arms wrapped around the mattress, washed ashore alive.

I am a passenger on this afternoon tour, and when Anna Milne tells us about the hurricane, I think about something she told me earlier, when I first met her that morning. She had been two weeks away from college graduation—her life course set for either law school or a graduate degree in history—and was attending a wedding, when a friend asked her to come outside. He had just received a phone call. "Sometimes," Anna told me, "life just hits hard."

Nobody knows exactly what caused the accident that changed everything. Bob Milne was the only one who could say, and afterward, he would never be able to. It happened on Saturday, May 2, 2015, a week into the new tour season. Just a year earlier, *Yankee* had featured a profile of Captain Bob. In the photo he stands tall and proud on the stern of the *Volsunga IV* against the backdrop of the Sound and the islands.

After Saturday's tours were over, Milne and Mike Infantino, his friend from childhood and the captain of Stony Creek's other 48-passenger tour boat, the *Sea Mist,* met up at the end of the day. Infantino told me he remembers Milne joking, "When is summer over?"

Later that night, Milne was riding his scooter on Gould Lane in Branford, a well-lit residential street close to Route 1. The night was clear, about 50 degrees. A truck was stopped at a red light, and for some unknown reason, Milne's scooter collided with the back of it. He was not wearing a helmet.

When the emergency crews reached the scene, they knew how dire it was. The captain of the fire department called Infantino, who was a volunteer firefighter. "They told me he lost a lot of fluid and he might not recover," Infantino said.

There would be weeks, then months, to come to terms with the limitations of medicine to restore Milne to a semblance of who he was. But Infantino knew what he had to do first. "The *Volsunga* will do her tours tomorrow," he promised the Milne family.

A decade older than Milne, Infantino had seen him grow up in Stony Creek just as he himself had, drawn to the sea. Their boats had competed for the same passengers, summer after summer, for more than 30 years. Sometimes, they had words. "Your competitor is three feet away at the dock," Infantino said. "Maybe you have an issue with each other: 'You left too late,' or 'You came back too early.' Or 'That was supposed to be my group and they got on your boat.'" But, he added, "We always apologized to each other and always before the end of the day."

Infantino knew every licensed boat captain in the area, his two sons among them, and they knew him. Eight of them came together and agreed to run Milne's tours until season's end in October. When Infantino piloted the *Volsunga,* someone else handled his *Sea Mist.* Former railroad signalman Bob Lillquist, hoping to ease into semi-retirement as ferryboat pilot, came on four days a week, and Anna joined the tours to tell passengers the stories she had grown up hearing. Infantino's administrative assistant, Laura Missett, took on all the office work for both tour companies. The captains put family life on hold, and days off from other jobs became time spent piloting the *Volsunga.* Passenger fees were put in a separate envelope for Anna; when she tried to pay the captains, they refused.

Meanwhile, Milne was in the ICU at Yale–New Haven Hospital. "In the movies," Anna said, "you are there when he opens his eyes. It wasn't like that. It's not like the movies. We thought maybe he'd be able to come back. We just didn't know." After six weeks, her father was moved to a rehabilitation center that specialized in traumatic brain injuries. He could not speak, walk, or eat, and gained his nourishment only via a feeding tube. Eventually he was moved to a nursing home. Sometimes Anna felt he knew who she was, other times not. Lifelong friends like Mike Infantino felt bad when they did not visit, and worse when they did.

Anna found a degree of solace in joining the captains aboard her father's boat. She knew the narration by heart. As the captains navigated the Sound, she began to tell about the once-abundant thimbleberries that had given the islands their name, and how an excited scuba diver had brought what he thought was a pirate's cannonball to the surface only to find it was a ball from a long-ago bowling alley on one of the islands. She found a YouTube video of her father's tour, and she perfected the nuances, the tricks of rapport. Each day, she gained more confidence that she could hold her own with passengers.

When the season ended, the captains, along with Anna's mother, Beth, and Laura Missett, had done all they could to keep the business alive. Now it was up to Anna to take the next step. "I knew I had to go to SeaSchool," Anna said, "knew I had to learn to run the boat." For her, there would be neither law school nor graduate school.

In the winter of 2016, Anna enrolled in two months of intensive, all-day classes at the SeaSchool in Freeport, Long Island. She studied everything from navigation and rules of the road to deckhand procedures. The instructor told her there had never been a female student in class before.

That May, Anna started a GoFundMe page to buy the *Volsunga* from the family estate. More than 150 people combined to contribute nearly $14,000, and that season the boat became Anna's.

The Stony Creek captains were again ready to not only pilot the *Volsunga*, but also to mentor Anna, to give her the confidence to one day truly be a captain. Bob Lillquist encouraged her to take the helm while doing the narration, as he stood by to maneuver through difficult areas and to dock. "Anna had to get comfortable behind the wheel," he said. "It's real tricky with reefs and rocks that you can't see at high tide. These are among the hardest waters to navigate on the Sound."

For her part, Anna said Lillquist became a crucial part of her new career journey. "Bob has always been in my life. [Before], I didn't know how important he was. He became my new Captain Bob."

Anna had spent hundreds of hours on Long Island Sound, but the responsibility was different now, the stakes much higher. "I was hesitant," she said. "You put nearly 50 people in this boat, and their lives are in your hands. I had never thought about that before. My dad just did it."

When the 2017 tour season began, Lillquist stayed by Anna's side. Then, one day in mid-June, a group of international students from Yale booked a special trip on the *Volsunga*—and none of the captains could get away to help Anna.

"I had been training for these years and everyone knew I was ready, but I was still nervous to go alone," Anna told me. "My mom came on as my first mate, which made me both more comfortable and more nervous. She asked me if I was ready for her to [cast off]. I just took a deep breath and said, 'Let's do it.' The trip went fine, and when I got back to the dock I told Bob that he could take the rest of the summer off.

"I would have continued to tell myself I wasn't ready if it wasn't for that one trip. I just had to get over that initial fear. . . . But after that trip, I thought, 'I know how to handle this.' "

A few weeks after I took Anna's Thimble Islands tour and met with Mike Infantino and Bob Lillquist—who both declared their pride in watching Anna's seamanship abilities grow—her father was taken from his nursing home to the hospital. Anna was out on her final tour for Saturday, September 8. She was steering the boat past the island where Captain Kidd had his hideout, when the phone rang with the news: Her father was failing. He died the next day, his family by the bedside.

In a way, Anna told me, it felt as though she had her father back for the first time since his accident. She imagined him now being able to finally see her at the helm, his beloved *Volsunga* safe in her hands. Shortly after he died, she said, it rained and then the sun came out. "There was a rainbow," she said, "and it started at my childhood home and ended at his childhood home." She took a photograph of it, which she keeps on her phone.

A few days after that, on a day of rain with no passengers, she took the *Volsunga* out alone because, she told me, "the boat lost him, too." Then she steered back to Stony Creek, where Captain Bob had ended his workdays for so many years, and tied up to the dock with the knots he had taught her.

"It may sound silly," she said, "but I feel like the boat and I finally know each other. She trusts me and I trust her, and we listen to each other."

Published January/February 2019

Anne Milne continues to lead Thimble Island tours from Stony Creek as captain of the Volsunga IV.

An Allagash Love Story

This is about a man called Nuge and his wife, Patty, and a tiny slice of the Maine wilderness they claimed as their own. For nearly 50 years on Chamberlain Lake their names ran together—*Nugenpatty*—like one of the melodious Native American names for these waters. It is an Allagash love story, but the Allagash was always hard on love; so like many stories from the North Woods, this one also begins in mystery and death.

In the summer of 1929, Lila-Beatrice (Patty) Pelkey was 25 years old and waitressing at a sporting camp on Rainbow Lake, where her brother Claude was a guide. One day Claude, enroute to Greenville for supplies, came up missing. His canoe was found upside down, floating by the shore of Chesuncook Lake. There was no proof, but everyone figured Claude had been murdered, his money stolen. He'd been raised along the Penobscot and was too expert a canoe man, too strong a swimmer to simply disappear on a calm summer's day.

Among the men called in to search for Claude's body was a tall, strapping man named Allen ("Nuge") Nugent. He was 26 years old, the head lineman for Great Northern. For days at a time he'd be in the woods with his crew, stringing telephone wire through the wilderness. Patty Pelkey's father took a great liking to young Nugent over those long, hard days of grappling for his son's body, days that ended at a chow line served by Patty. When Claude's body was finally found after nearly a month of searching, Allen

Nugent was invited to visit the Pelkeys at their East Millinocket home.

"Lo and behold, one Saturday Nuge popped in," remembers Patty Nugent a lifetime later. "He came quite a few times before I had any idea he came to see me." She told friends she thought he was the handsomest man she'd ever seen, and she took a job at Kokadjo to be closer. Nearly every night he took her riding over the logging roads in the company truck, hoping to convince her to marry him.

"I thought an awful lot of Nuge, but I'd already been through an unfortunate marriage. My husband had been a hard man, drank an awful lot. So I swore never again. I told him I had other ambitions, although I agreed we'd go together—oh, sure we'd go together—even if it caused a little gossip."

Patty was born the middle child of five brothers and two sisters, inheriting grit from her mother, and from her father, who cooked for lumberjacks along the thundering river drives, an unquenchable taste for the woods. All she ever wanted was to be the cook at her own sporting camp, the deeper in the woods the better. She said she'd save her money for a few years, then they'd find a place for their camps. He already was a noted guide, and Patty reasoned his sports would follow him anywhere. In those days the unorganized townships of Maine were filled with public lots under the jurisdiction of the forestry service. A lawyer told them that if they settled on a public lot, 40 feet from high water, the land would be theirs, and if the state tried to drive them off, he'd back them for free.

Patty knew where she wanted to go. From the time she was a girl listening to her father's tales, she'd been entranced with the name. Sometimes she'd fall asleep saying that name. *Chamberlain Lake. Chamberlain Lake.* Patty picked potatoes and cashed in her insurance policies. With the money they'd saved, about $2,000, they bought supplies and squirreled them away in an abandoned storehouse at Sowadnehunk. Nuge cleared a cross-country trail to Telos Lake, whose waters fed into Chamberlain, hired a horse and wagon, and for days moved supplies to Telos. He cut cedars and pines, the biggest he could find, hauled them into the lake, and with the help of his father and Patty's brother Allie, built a raft 40 feet wide, 50 feet long.

After a week the raft was ready, loaded with trunks and boxes full of clothes, crates of food and tools, and right in the middle, protected by a tent fly, a brand-new Star Kineo cookstove. They had everything they needed—and one dollar—the night they drifted away.

They traveled at night to avoid the wind, Nuge ahead in a boat towing the raft, Patty on the raft with two canoes lashed together in back, in hope they wouldn't swamp. She has lived nearly 20,000 nights since that summer night in 1936, but she remembers that journey up the lake as if somehow it has been preserved under glass for her to admire for the rest of her life.

"It was a pretty moonlit night, about 60 degrees. We moved so slow. If I wanted to see that we were moving at all, I'd take a landmark, a tree, and watch it very carefully. We'd bought a case of canned salmon, and our first meal in our new stove was hot biscuits, baked potatoes, and my egg gravy to go with the salmon, which I warmed in a frypan with onion.

"At quarter past nine the next morning we landed on the eastern shore of Chamberlain Lake. We started up the lake in a canoe, looking for a campsite. Went up one side, came down the other. I looked across and saw a little green knoll, so we came across to look at it. There was a brook and we walked up to it and climbed over a little hill and I thought, 'This is an elegant view.' A little breeze was blowing, and Nuge said it was the prevailing wind from the northwest and would keep the flies away. Nuge put his arm on my shoulder and said, 'Just right, little girl. This is just right.' "

Now it is an afternoon in late February of this year [1986], and Patty Nugent has come home. As always it took some doing to get there. In the morning she left what she likes to call her "city house with all the modern conveniences" in East Millinocket (pop. 2,500), and drove two hours north along logging roads to the headquarters of the Allagash Wilderness Waterway at Chamberlain Bridge. Until recently she would climb onto her snowmobile there and shoot five miles up the lake's eastern shore. But lately she's been making some concessions. On this day the lake is ridged with buckled ice, so Patty allows a ranger to drive her along a winding tote road until they reach a narrow, soft, tree-lined trail where a friend waits with a snowmobile. Attached to the snowmobile is a small trailer on skis. Patty Nugent climbs in. Half an hour later, cushioned with pillows and blankets like a crate of Christmas brandy, Patty is home.

When Nuge died here eight years ago, these were the most famed sporting camps in Maine, among the most famous in the country. It is a life she refuses to give up, and it is likely nobody in America today has run a sporting camp longer than Patty Nugent. The cabins sit clustered on a slight rise back from the shore with sheds for tools and boats and wood, a smokehouse, an icehouse. A tight shoveled path winds through the compound connecting cabins with privies. Built from hand-hewn logs, the cabins are not lovely in winter. Windows are sheathed in plastic; tar paper covers the cedar-shingled roofs. Stovewood is piled high on the porches.

She apologizes over the clutter in the cabin; having just arrived, she explains, she hasn't had time to straighten up. In truth there's not time enough to straighten up these two rooms because the memories of her life here flow from boxes to shelves to drawers. Stuffed somewhere in this room is a pair of trousers she fashioned from an old felt blanket that first winter; somewhere else the enamel plates she brought here on the raft. She had no children, but three generations of children have come to the camps, crowding around her stove in the morning as she fried doughnuts, the hot oil glistening in their hands. They called her Aunt Patty, and the photos of those children, now grown up, romp across a wall.

There's little room to move about, but then Patty doesn't move about too much. Callers come to her. She takes her meals in the kitchen at a long homemade table, looking out a window to the lake. Some days, looking out, she'll see a coyote chasing a deer across the ice, or, in summer, an otter arrowing its way home. Until she slipped a disc ten years ago splitting wood, she served 40 people breakfast and dinner from this kitchen, with full lunches always packed by 6 a.m. for the hunters and fishermen. "I could really step then," she says.

Patty does not live in the past, but if asked, she will float back as light as a tumbleweed. "People are amazed at my memory," Patty says. "They come to me to find out how it was when first we came into the country."

Her visitor asked, so for four days in February she opened her boxes, spilling photographs onto tables like leaves. She took out rifles and drawshaves, and a leg-hold trap that has lain beneath her bed for years, letting her words knit them together into the story of the life they built here. A full moon shone over Chamberlain during those nights, and a north wind tore the breath from you along the shore, but 200 yards back in the woods, out of sight of the cabins, the wind was stilled by the snow-draped trees, and you could remove the scarf from your mouth and nose and look in awe at the piercing, starry sky and think how it must have been once to be alone here with so much forest, to be in love, and to make it work.

Patty sits in her rocking chair, smoking a cigarette and fondling a small, faded photograph that she says few people have seen. The photo was taken a week or two after they landed the raft. They are standing in front of their first cabin, a crude, temporary shelter covered with birch bark. "Dear, we were rough looking, weren't we?" Patty says. "The first time the forest warden saw me, I had a bandana around my hair and a pair of Nuge's pants on. He went out and told people a band of gypsies had settled in." They cleared the land from dawn to dark, butting timber, hauling the logs by hand on homemade sleds; Nuge cut Patty's from cedar so it would be lighter. Patty limbed the trees with her axe, shaved cedar splits with her drawknife, and kept them fed. "I learned lots of ways to fix trout," she says.

She baked beans and bread and befriended Dave Hannah, their nearest neighbor, a tall solitary trapper who lived a mile and a half up the lake. "Dave had no use for us at all. A dam keeper had teased him that Nuge was going to take over his trapline. You should know not to tease a man who lives in the woods alone. He came in here spoiling for a fight. But Nuge said he was here to build camps, not trap. He said, 'Dave, I'll never set a trap in this country as long as you're alive.' And he was our friend from then on. And he never did, until Dave Hannah died and we took over the trapline. And when I ran out of white flour and didn't have any money and was making all my biscuits from buckwheat, Dave Hannah came down, and, God love him, he left me a sack of white flour. The best present I'd ever had."

Nuge taught her to shoot, well enough so she could make an empty tobacco tin cartwheel through the air, well enough so that every year she got her deer. "A new warden came in here," she says, "and saw my deer hanging next to Nuge's. 'One of these yours?' he asked me. I said yes, but I could tell he didn't believe me. 'What did you use?' he asked. I said I used my .38-.40. And if he wanted to, he could take his wristwatch off and set it on the post over there and see if maybe I could hit it. He reddened right up and never bothered me again."

Nuge taught her to fly-fish from a canoe, holding a fish pail over his head as protection from her first wild back casts, and later how to fashion flies from the feathers of wild birds and the hair of deer. She tied her flies on winter evenings, and later they were sold in the biggest sports stores in Maine. He made her knitting needles from telephone wire and copper found at an abandoned logging camp, and Patty readied for winter, unraveling sweaters, using the yarn to knit stockings and mittens. She'd spend hours knitting "Patty caps" that she would line up every fall to sell to hunters. "There are hundreds of my Patty caps in these woods," she says.

In November they had their first paying guests. They each paid $10 a day for Patty's cooking and the privilege of sleeping on a bare cabin floor with their coats for bedding. The business was finally started, but the Maine Forestry Service, which administered the land, wanted them out.

"We asked for a lease," Patty says with a trace of anger lingering through time, "but they just wanted to drive us out. They tried to stop us from cutting timber, but we went right on cutting what we needed for the camps. They didn't know what to make of us. They figured we had some big money man backing us, what with Nuge having guided and knowing so many rich folks. A telephone line ran through the woods back then, and after awhile Nuge got us a phone and hooked us in. At least we could talk to the dam keepers, and it was company. The forestry service kept coming down and cutting us off. And Nuge, he'd just wait a few minutes for them to leave. Then he'd hook right back on. After eight years I guess they thought we were here to stay. They gave us a lease, $10 a year. I told Nuge we'd have them eating out of our hands, and before long all the state officials and the governor were having big to-do's at Nugent's Camps!"

When winter came, Patty sewed parkas from the tent fly off the raft, fished through the ice, and wore double sets of long underwear when she did the wash. Nuge made tables and beds and carved sinks for the camps, and they survived, barely, on small loans from Patty's father.

By 1938 they finished building the camps, including the cabin where Patty lives today. And luck—or fate—dealt them a curious break. For it was then that Dave Hannah died and Al Nugent was freed from his promise and could finally trap the country. "Nuge started me on weasel," she says. "They weren't bringing too much then. He figured if I cut the skin, we wouldn't have lost too much. Then we went to bobcat and fox, and when I mastered those, to beaver. Skinned them right in this room by kerosene lantern and I never cut them."

Nuge ran over 100 miles of trapline. He'd be gone two weeks at a time, living off beaver and muskrat stew, sleeping in tiny, outlying cabins he built along the route. Each day the dam keepers, like worried aunts, phoned Patty. "They needn't have worried," Patty says. "I didn't have a care in the world then. There was nothing I didn't feel I could handle."

She set her beaver traps around the ponds, mink traps around the edges of streams, and bobcat traps back in the woods. There were a lot more trappers in the country back then, but there were a lot more animals, too. Come spring, Nuge hauled the furs to Chesuncook, then to the buyers in Greenville. "We'd never have made it without the trapping," she says. "One year we made over $4,800. That came in awful handy."

One year Nuge told her he wanted to give her a coat of her choice, beaver or otter. "That winter," she says, "we were getting a dollar an inch for beaver and they were all running large. I said I'd take the otter 'cause it was cheaper." They took the skins and a pattern to a furrier, paid $200, and waited. When the coat arrived, a note was attached. The furrier was offering $2,000. "I asked Nuge and he said, 'It's yours. You decide!' Well, I didn't sell the coat. You know what they say about otter? It makes chorus girls' mink look like floor mats." She laughs. "Not that I had as many places to wear it as a chorus girl."

Go anywhere along the Allagash today and ask people about Nuge and the first thing they'll mention will be his strength. He filled the icehouse with 400-pound blocks of ice, hauling them on a sled harnessed to his broad back as if he were a team of oxen. He'd pick up 500-pound gasoline drums, roll them along his leg, and set them into his boat.

She laughs, a congested, throaty laugh always on the edge of a cough. "Nuge was powerful, but when guests got rowdy, I took care of them. You never saw that man without a smile. He'd get up in the morning and it'd be raining or snowing and he'd say, 'It's a beautiful morning.' I'd say, 'Nuge, what's so beautiful about it?' 'Any morning you wake up, darling, is a beautiful morning,' he'd say. That's how he was. No matter what happened, he always said, 'Just right. Just right.' He wouldn't fight with me even when I'd fly off the handle. So I gave in. On the 17th of September 1942 we were married. Just a couple stood for us in Lincoln."

They entertained governors and celebrities and outdoorsmen from around the country. At night, after the meal, everyone gathered in the dining room in the glow of the lanterns and listened to Nuge's stories while Patty rocked and knitted. They were taking in over $1,000 a day now, and they bought a house in East Millinocket and a Winnebago for getaways right after deer season.

"Every day lasted so long," Patty says, "yet time went so fast. People who don't know the woods will never understand. It's the first thing they ask me. And I tell them. We were never lonely. Never. Never."

It is evening now of another day. In the morning, a plane will arrive for the visitor. Eight years have passed, but it is still difficult for Patty to talk about the tenth of February 1978 when *Nugenpatty* became simply Patty. "It was a Thursday, his 75th birthday," she says. "I was frying molasses doughnuts that morning. Nuge was hauling wood and he came back in for some doughnuts. They were his favorite. We talked awhile, then he went back out. After a bit I realized I couldn't hear his tractor anymore. We found him sitting right there in the tractor. It was a massive heart attack. Nuge never had a chance to call for help.

"They didn't want me to fly out with the body," she says, her eyes taking on the memory, "but I said, 'I *am* flying with Nuge.'" It was the biggest funeral they ever had in the church in East Millinocket. Patty wore the otter coat to the funeral, and when it was over, she took it off, put it back in her closet, and hasn't worn it since. People from way downriver and up in Aroostook come to look at the stone Patty got, and as she says, "to call on Nuge." There's a tree-lined pond on the front and a lone fisherman and both their names, one on each side, and their nicknames, and in the middle the words: JUST RIGHT.

"Everywhere I go, people tell me I'm a legend," she says. "A movie man wanted to come and make a movie of me. It don't make me feel any different. It's just my home. You know something," she says, stepping out onto the ice for the first time that week, "I'd give everything back in a minute for just one night to do over, the night me and Nuge pushed off and floated so slow up this lake, and in the dawn I looked across and saw that little green knoll."

Published July 1986

Patty Nugent died August 17, 1990. She was 85. Nugent's Camp has seen three different families operate the camps over the years and they still welcome people who come for the woods, water, and solitude. Though still rustic, the camps have been refurbished. Patty's own cabin where we talked is no longer standing. I had my five-month-old son, Dan, with me on this story, and Patty spent hours talking to me while holding him as she rocked.

Hope for Rosie

Seven miles northwest of Camden, Maine, lies a town called Hope. Some 1,600 people live among its hills and ponds; it's a place where for years a local fundraiser has published a calendar of townspeople's birthdays, so that nobody forgets to congratulate you when they see you at the general store or the post office, which in Hope is the same place. There are farms and orchards, a cobbler, a bagpipe maker, builders, carpenters, artists, and a center for home-schooling information: country Maine with a counterculture energy, a sense of people making their own way. Like so many small towns in Maine, its separate stories patch together into one community. But Hope today is like no other town in New England. In Hope, the children dream of elephants.

The story begins in a small Adirondack town in the 1960s. Schroon Lake, like Hope, held about 1,600 people, with roads that led to forest and water. Jim Laurita grew up there, one of eight children of a schoolteacher father. When he was eight or nine, the circus came to town, and when it left, Jim and his brother Tom, a year older, taught their dog tricks and learned to juggle. Tom joined a troupe of students touring the Northeast; eventually he left college to join first Circus Kirk and then Carson & Barnes in Hugo, Oklahoma. In 1978 Jim followed. "To see the country," he says today. The 25 elephants at Carson & Barnes worked all day, training, hauling enormous tents, pulling trucks out of mud. When Jim first tried to coax one of the elephants to move, the animal swatted him to the ground. "I was told, 'You're on the shovel until you've proved you can work with these animals,'" he recalls. "So that's what I did. I proved I had an aptitude. And I ended up working with them in the ring."

For the past 20 years, Jim Laurita has been the local veterinarian in Hope, caring for his neighbors' pets from his Camden practice; he tells me his story while standing in a spanking-new barn beside the farmhouse where he lives with his wife and two sons. A light morning rain is falling. The barn opens to a fenced paddock, where an apple tree and piles of thick brush stand encircled by greenery. He points out that the barn floor is covered with soft sand, eight inches deep; it will be warmed by radiant heat. In the center a hillock rises, support to help an old elephant stand. And here his story circles back to that young man seeking adventure, and to Rosie, an Asian elephant, orphaned as a baby.

"Rosie was the cleverest one," he remembers. "She was called 'Little Boss,' and wherever she went, the others followed. Rosie and Sis would signal you with their trunks to come over. Then they'd grab your hand and put it in their mouths to pet their tongues. You could lie down on them on cool days, and they just radiated heat. When Sis woke up, she'd lift her trunk and just feel all around you without moving." He shakes his head: "Those kinds of things stick with you."

His story wends its way through summers spent with circus elephants, and at the Bronx Zoo, Wildlife Safari in Oregon, and Cornell's veterinary school; Jim once tranquilized elephants in India to prevent them from entering villages, where they would have been shot. He'd experienced a life with elephants that hardly anyone in Hope knew about. He's 53 now, and when he speaks of elephants, he wants his listener to understand their extraordinary intelligence and how threatened they are—all in one breath.

"You're not sure you're smarter than they are," Jim explains. He tells me about Obert, a male elephant at Carson & Barnes: "I was having a beer, and he kept shaking his trunk, grabbing for the can. It was empty, but he kept grabbing for it. So I gave it to him, and he crushed it and started digging up roots with it. He had formed a tool with a purpose. By the end of the week, a line of elephants were using that can to dig up roots."

Then he rattles off grim statistics: the Asian herd decimated, with only 30,000 individuals remaining; more than 35,000 elephants killed each year in sub-Saharan Africa for their hides, meat, and ivory tusks. "They suffer so much trauma," he says. "Elephants are like the Grand Canyon; they're part of the biological heritage of the earth. We need to make sure that future generations can see them."

Which brings us to a February evening in 2011. Jim and brother Tom, still best friends, both living in Hope, were taking a sauna and talking about a long-held dream to help injured circus elephants. "You do something when you're young and it changes you," Jim says, looking back. "We always wanted to do something for the elephants. It's a long life of work for these guys. And we finally decided that if you wait until everything is perfect, well, you don't do anything." They had stayed in touch with the circus and had seen Rosie five years before, when she was 37, painfully arthritic: "We knew she'd be the first one to help."

Tom, a successful businessman, knew how to turn ideas into action; Jim knew how to make sick animals well. More than a decade ago, another elephant had crushed Rosie against a truck. Her leg had never healed, and she was now hobbling, an old-timer growing older, separated from other elephants. If caring and knowledge and science could give Rosie a better life, the Lauritas wanted to try it. "High-end physical therapy," Jim says. "The kind they do with racehorses: ultrasound, hydrotherapy, acupuncture, nutritional support. It's never been tried."

In early April 2011, they went to a pre-application meeting of the town planning board, a first step, to present a primer on the project. What they found instead were "people there from other towns," Jim explains. "They went right to the politics. Because we're on the wrong side of the PETA [People for the Ethical Treatment of Animals] movement. . . . Anything circus is wrong. I walked out after that first meeting and said, 'We're going to have to do this in a different town.'"

But as word spread about the Lauritas' improbable plan, two things happened. One, the opposition from away intensified. As weeks passed and planning-board decision time neared, animal-rights activists from around the country besieged town and state offices with emails and faxes. Rosie, they argued, shouldn't be isolated from her herd or forced to endure Maine winters. Hope's fire chief received a video showing rampaging elephants.

Here's the second thing: Jim Laurita told his Hope neighbors about his coming of age in the company of elephants, and how he could help Rosie, how they could all help. And the calls began to come: *What can we do?* A former lawyer said he'd handle public relations, fund-raising, regulatory compliance, and other operations. Andrew Stewart, who owns the general store—and is a former safari guide with a zoology degree—agreed to take an intensive elephant-management course. A physical therapist signed on. Others created a website to teach the public about elephants, including how they adapt in northern climes. A video showed Rosie walking, painfully, slowly. She became more than a project. She became real, an animal who needed them.

On a late-summer evening a year ago, more than 100 people crammed into the town hall; the planning board was about to decide yes or no. What members heard were stories of Dr. Jim caring for the town's animals: how he took injured pets home with him so that they wouldn't be alone; how once he had crawled on hands and knees so as not to disturb an old black Lab who could go no farther. The dog was outside, chewing on a bone, unaware of the vet, the softest way out. If Dr. Jim said he could help Rosie, then that was good enough. When the board announced its unanimous approval, the cheers sailed into the night.

Raising money for Rosie became this small community's mission. "Hope Elephants" T-shirts and bracelets flew off the shelves of the general store. Townspeople recycled for Rosie, and they attended concerts for her. Hope became a town with no spare change; everything went to bring Rosie home. Donations reached $100,000, enough to borrow the remaining $200,000 for a heated barn and a double-steel fence. "To build it required a leap of faith," Jim concedes. "We had to build before the state and federal approvals." The barn was completed in three months, and at Christmastime, lights decorated its door, forming the outline of an elephant. Every day people asked Andrew at the store, "When will Rosie come?"

Money could build a barn, but it couldn't buy patience. "Maine is nothing if not cautious," Jim Laurita smiles. Federal inspectors came three times from New Mexico, filled with questions and suggestions, but Jim stayed calm. "Whatever time it takes is what it takes," he said. "If it were easy, everyone would have an elephant." During the delay the circus offered a companion, Opal, a 40-year-old female, also hurt. "We always wanted to have two," Jim says. In May 2012, both federal and state approvals came through.

One day early this September, a large truck from Oklahoma will turn left at the Hope General Store and head down Hatchet Mountain Road. It will stop at the new barn and back up to the paddock, and Jim Laurita will lead Rosie and Opal into their acre of yard. Apples will hang from the trees; bags of alfalfa will be strung from boughs like piñatas. More food will be hidden in piles of brush, so that Rosie and Opal can play and browse at the same time. After a few weeks, children and adults will come to the viewing area and watch, close enough to see elephants blink.

"That can change a life," Jim Laurita says. "When you see them up close, it's a different experience." He hopes one day that this will be a center for learning about elephants, about the need to save them, like the great whales. "*They* were endangered," he notes, "and through awareness they've come back."

Each day Rosie and Opal will be treated for their injuries and eat food from local farms. Volunteers will lead them on miles of walks, around and around the paddock. Hope will settle into being the town where children grow up listening to the call of elephants. And maybe, just maybe, it will be where elephants dream of Hope.

Published September/October 2012

Rosie and Opal arrived in the fall of 2012 and quickly adapted to life in Maine. School field trips to see elephants in this intimate way became a way of life in Hope and surrounding towns. Soon Jim Laurita gave up his Camden veterinary practice to devote his efforts to the Hope Elephants Project to educate people about the beauty and vulnerability of these animals. Andrew Stewart, whose Hope General Store became a hub for the town's support for Rosie and Opal, put the store up for sale to become the director of the project. Then in the early morning of September 9, 2014, Jim Laurita went to feed Rosie and Opal. Nobody knows what happened next. What is known is that he fell and hit his head on the concrete walkway that led to the corral. His brother Tom later said it is likely that

Rosie's instinct was to help her friend and keeper by lifting him with her trunk. She stepped on Jim Laurita's chest, and he died. It was Jim Laurita's love being returned with a tragic result. The town lost not only their friend, but also a part of its communal heart. Soon Rosie and Opal were on their way back to her previous home at the Endangered Ark Foundation in Hugo, Oklahoma. A few months later, Jim's son Henry and Andrew Stewart delivered a van filled with therapeutic equipment Jim had used to treat the elephants. Rosie's best friend Opal died there in 2017, at age 48, and Rosie died there in October 2024, at age 55. When I wrote to Jim's wife, Carrie, that his story would be in this collection, she wrote back. "This is a story that should live on, be told, and remembered. It is a story, however tragic, of a man, a beautiful, wonderful, exceptional man, making his dream come true."

"Everything I Have Tells a Story"

There's a man whose love of history isn't quenched by browsing antiques shops and museums, but whose need to touch and smell and possess the stuff of the past is as real as the air he breathes. His name is Bill Johnson. You can usually find him either sitting inside a large, white-columned building set back from Route 1, about two miles before entering Wells, Maine, or roaming his 15 green acres, bordering the Rachel Carson National Wildlife Refuge. Inside the building (which served from 1923 to 1940 as Elsie Libby's Colonial Tea Room) and all along its broad porch, and strewn here and there along the land, as casually, it seems, as a child's flung-down bicycle, rest the physical remnants of his feverish ambition to seemingly own and in some way preserve nearly every building and artifact that once touched people's lives in years long past.

A quick web search shows that the few people who have stumbled onto the place have felt similarly compelled to tell the world. "You gotta see it to believe it. Best $5 tour ever!" gushed one blogger after a visit this past May 2011. There are photo postings by people who wandered in, not knowing what was there, and who promptly took dozens of shots, some of them strangely beautiful, of tired old buildings and rusted machinery, and curiosities such as a towering wooden moose. So off we went to find Bill Johnson.

The man responsible for collecting all of these buildings and countless hundreds of antiques and relics of cultural pop art (including Elvis memorabilia) sits contentedly in a chair inside the front door. Parked in front of the driveway is a gleaming silver 1937 LaSalle, which he soon points out is the vehicle he uses to chauffeur brides to the unique wedding reception that awaits inside.

"The best dance floor within 100 miles," he boasts, then cautions, "You have to appreciate old junk if you rent the space. Otherwise you go down to the VFW hall."

A sign out front indicates that "Jo Johnson, M.D. Ophthalmologist" shares the space. Another prompts, "Enjoy your pictures. $5 restoration donation. Much obliged." The room is cool and softly lit. I find a round-faced, pleasant man, bearing a passing resemblance to the actor Anthony Hopkins. He's hitting 71, but his gray hair hangs to his shoulders in a pigtail. It's immediately apparent that he enjoys conversation, because "everything I have has a story."

It's Sunday, and he's joined by his wife of 34 years, Dr. Jo Johnson, who's happy to show off her office. "Most unusual waiting room in America," Bill Johnson says. "Probably the world," adds his wife. On a desk rests a device labeled "Complaint Department." There's also a pushbutton that sets off a reaction that ends with a mousetrap going off. "He entertains my patients," Dr. Johnson says. "He's like the cat who brings a mouse home to show you. Only it's not a mouse he's bringing home; it's always something." When patients open the bathroom door, they're greeted by a large painting of a nude woman. Most of her patients like it, she notes: "If they don't, they go to the other office in nearby Saco. It's more conventional in my other office."

Dr. Johnson is trim, with short, dark hair, and at about 5-foot-7 stands taller than her husband by nearly a forehead. She comes across immediately as having the generous spirit of a woman who loves her man and who long ago decided to do her best to make room for what he brings home, much like couples who have learned to live with one partner's need to rescue dozens of stray cats.

"I come from a long line of paper-bag and string savers," Bill Johnson says as we survey a packed front room—everything from Hannibal Hamlin's campaign flag and a statue carved by Union prisoners at Andersonville, to Nantucket baskets, to photographs of Wild Bill Hickok. Each time he swings around, he plucks something to show and tell. "I'm sorry to say I have things I've had since I was 10 years old," he explains. "I've just upgraded in quality over the years. Just the accumulation of a Yankee over the years." He knows the story behind everything he touches, and it's apparent that without the story there's no joy of ownership.

"His mother tells that when he used to visit his grandmother, he'd stand up and look in the china closet, and because he was so little everyone would start screaming at him," Dr. Johnson says. "And his grandmother would say, 'Leave him alone. He won't break anything.' "

Johnson wants visitors to know he doesn't collect these things just to own them, but because they matter, and what matters is the story of where they once stood, to whom they belonged, what was happening in the world when they were once looked at and touched. His family goes back 10 generations in southern Maine, and those ties breed patience. He grew up on a dairy farm and as a boy delivered hay to Elsie Libby, whose tearoom was the fanciest eating place around. Franklin Roosevelt stopped by in 1932 shortly before his first election and complained that her $1.50 lobster was too expensive in a Depression. "Governor," she replied crisply, "this is a short season."

At times, Johnson has waited decades to claim an item he wanted, staking out various antiques shops, using all his gifts of persuasion to hopefully pry something loose from their shelves to his. He waited years to get this place; it had gone just about to ruin since Mrs. Libby had closed the tearoom. She died in 1973, and it took him seven more years to own the tearoom, the ballroom that came with it, and this small parcel of her 1,000 acres, which spilled down to the sea.

Johnson was once one of the most popular auctioneers in the region, with people crowding the lawn here just to laugh at his repartee. "But he'd get upset," his wife says, "when he had to auction pictures of people's relatives. He's very sentimental."

If people come inside and Johnson senses that they view this as a sort of sideshow, a "Ripley's Believe It or Not" in the middle of nowhere, or if they're here to fill their car trunks with a windfall of antiques that he has little desire to part with, he finds a way to quickly discourage their lingering.

But if you stop by with genuine curiosity, you may find that an afternoon slips away. If he senses a spark, he'll lead visitors through his collected life, in words and often song.

He guides a visitor through a jaunty walk around his office and antiques emporium, home to clocks of all sizes and shapes, music boxes, organ grinders, Victrolas, posters, paintings, every this or that you can imagine—and then to the ballroom, with its player piano that he can't pass without playing and singing along. Behind the ballroom is the original kitchen, complete with china to serve 100 guests.

Then he slaps on a pith helmet and heads outside, past a plow and a tractor; an abandoned Depression-era service station and an 18th-century blacksmith shop; a one-room schoolhouse from the 1880s and a faded cabin from the former Sandy Cove nudist colony; a stray cabin, its paint blistered off, from an old Route 1 cottage colony (House o' Comfort: A Dollar a Night); abandoned railroad cars and a railroad depot; 19th-century jail cells from his native Berwick, built by P. T. Barnum's brother; an old-fashioned soda fountain plucked from a Rochester, New Hampshire, drugstore; an ice house, which launches him into a talk on the role that ice exporting played in New England; and a midcentury Spartan trailer. He glides through the Spartan's interior with loving steps, passing his hand over the woodwork, pointing out the original plumbing. "This is a time capsule," he says. "Where else can you find this?"

He stops in front of a caboose. "From 1890," he says. "It was advertised in the Portland paper. I told Jo about it, and she said, 'We don't really need a caboose, do we?' I said, 'Let's go look at it.' So we went, and she saw it and liked it."

And then Johnson may let slip that down the road in Kennebunk there sits an 18th-century former tavern that he restored to a fine dwelling for his wife and son Andrew, now an opera singer in Vienna. Over time the house was awash with his finds, and, rather than fight it, he and his wife moved across the street to a tidy ranch, leaving the house to the lovely ghosts of his obsession.

On a hillside he shows off a parsonage that arrived on trucks. As many buildings as there are standing here, there are more waiting to join them. Each building moved here has put him in some sort of conflict with the town fathers of Wells, who still don't know quite what to think. What exactly is he making here? The structures keep showing up, a village of misfits that to Bill Johnson are beautiful, still filled with the life that once happened nearby.

Every one of his buildings needs care and mending, which he says he'll get to, but judging from his wife's knowing eyes, he may not, not now anyway, not when he has so many other things to do. He talks of building a boardwalk around the land so that visitors can take it all in.

Then there's the 19th-century Baptist church where his stepfather prayed every Sunday. It took him four years to gain a permit that would allow him to disassemble it and move it to his hillside beside the parsonage. Then came one project after another; the months wore on and the permit expired, and now in the summer of 2011 he has to reapply. And 20 miles away is a one-ton steam engine he's bought; he has to figure out how to get it here.

He wants to do so many things, and he could probably do all of them, except for the fact that he rises so early and heads off to flea markets and antiques gatherings, waking his wife up, first when he leaves, and then when he comes back. "He says to me, 'You gotta see this,' and it's like he sees something and he's got to have it," she tells me.

There was a time when Johnson sold as much as he bought. Now, his wife says, "His usual excuse for not wanting to sell is 'You have to ask the boss.' That's supposed to be my clue to say, 'Oh, we can't possibly part with it.'" She sighs softly, whispering, "There are things he doesn't understand. Like there's this little problem: The more buildings he moves here, the more they tax us, and the property's not earning any money. So it's a problem."

I pose the question to the collector himself: "What if someone comes in and says, 'I love this—I want to buy it'?" "They usually don't appreciate it as much as I did when I bought it," Johnson replies. "If you're a collector and it says Antiques, everything has to have a price. But you hang out a sign Museum, you don't have to sell anything."

Smiling, he finishes the tour inside the old railroad depot. On the wall is a sign: Trojan Ice Cream. Beside it, Climax Ginger Ale. "Now, where are you ever going to find another?"

"You know," he sighs, "you can't save everything." I steal a glance at Jo Johnson, and I see in her eyes a truth she knows. Maybe he can't, but that won't stop him from trying.

When I leave, he says, "Be sure to put my telephone number in. I can take care of a busload of people. If they book me ahead, I can take care of them."

Published September/October 2011

Bill Johnson was one of kind, one of those people you write about and always remember with a smile. When I learned that he died suddenly on Saturday, February 1, 2014, at age 73, while bidding for yet more "stuff" that he could somehow cram into a nook and cranny, I thought he would not have wanted to leave this earth any other way than to be in the midst of treasures and the stories they promised. Three years later, after a good deal of renovation, Jo Johnson opened The Tea Room at Johnson Hall Museum to "honor Bill's memory" as one of the most unique venues for weddings and events and company meetings, where treasures from Bill Johnson's life form a backdrop. At a wedding, an antique music box plays the "Wedding March" and Bill Johnson's player piano still lives on.

Keeper of the Lighthouse Keeper

Everyone expected Elson Small would be a sea captain someday. At age 23 he already had his second mate's license and a pilot's license. But after World War I, work was scarce in the Merchant Marines. He was asked instead to be a lighthouse keeper at Channel Light in the swirling waters between Lubec and Campobello, Maine. He took his 19-year-old fiancée, Connie Scoville, down to the rocks by the sea to tell her about the change.

"I felt my heart sink," she says today. "I thought I'd be a sea captain's wife. I'd have a nice home, lots of flowers, a place in the community. Do you know what clinched it? He said, 'Connie, do you love me enough to go on a lighthouse to live?'"

Elson Small was appointed to the Lighthouse Service on November 1, 1920. He married Connie three weeks later. When the children came, they told each other, he would return to the sea. But the children never came.

Connie Small is 81; she lived 28 years in lighthouses in Maine and New Hampshire until Elson retired in 1949. Lighthouses go deeper with her than nostalgia, deeper than memory, into places she cannot explain. She still wakes at sunrise, stirred by tasks that no longer need her doing—extinguishing the lamp, shining brass, baking Elson's pies. When fog moves in, something builds up inside of her; if sleeping, she'll wake with a start.

"There's always the feeling," she says, "that we have to get the bell going. That there's someone out there who needs the bell."

Connie Small at Fort Point Light in New Castle, New Hampshire, in 1982. This is where Connie and her husband, Elson, ended their nearly three-decade life as lighthouse keepers in 1948. A few years later, her memoir, The Lighthouse Keeper's Wife, *brought her national attention.*
Photo credit: Carole Allen

There is little in her one-bedroom apartment in southern Maine that does not touch on lighthouses. She brews coffee in the electric coffee pot Elson bought her in 1946 when, for the first time, they had electricity. She collects lighthouse pictures, stuffing news clippings, postcards, and telephone book covers into a lighthouse-covered album. Even her quilts depict lighthouse scenes.

She talks about lighthouses to church groups, historical societies, women's clubs—whoever asks. "I have no notes," she says. "As it comes, I tell about it. People come two or three times and don't hear the same story twice. I haven't been anywhere where people don't say, 'Why don't you write a book?'" A few years ago she began her book about how a keeper tends his light and how a wife tends the keeper.

"It never can be like it was with us again," she says. "It's an assignment today. But we had a calling."

She is dressed in white with red, white, and blue stripes along her cuffs, and a tiny American flag pinned to her collar. Fresh apple pie and coffee are on the kitchen table. Behind her, casseroles wait for noon company, enough for a crew of shipwrecked sailors. She is telling stories, now and then blurting, "Oh, I talk so much!" and blushing, the color creeping upward against the white like a sunset striking a house.

"I went on Avery's Rock the tenth of October 1922," she says, "and didn't get off until the last of April. . . ."

Avery's Rock, the most desolate station of all, is three miles out in Machias Bay. There was no earth, only a half-acre of boulders and a wooden plank leading from the house to the boat slip. She was 21. There was no phone, no electricity. Rain washed off the roof into cisterns stored beneath the pantry. The lighthouse tender brought coal once a year. If you ran out, there would be no more. Every two weeks Elson rowed to shore for supplies. But the light couldn't be left alone, so Connie stayed. She saw only Elson, and at night while she knit socks or sewed quilts or bedding or clothes, she'd twist the radio dial, hoping to hear another voice, however faint.

The lens was imported from France and they cared for it as they might a baby. It was set in brass, which they polished every day until it shone like gold. "Lots of days we didn't need to," she says. "But we liked going up there to see that lens shining." At dawn they'd extinguish the light, watch the sun creep over the bay, and draw the shades. She cleaned the lens with chamois and covered it with linen. She swept the stairs into a gleaming brass dust pan—"Before breakfast," she says with satisfaction—"and Elson won the pennant for best light station three years straight."

She baked a pie or a cake every day and fried doughnuts in the morning. She canned fish and wild ducks shot by Elson. When the boat slip washed away in a storm, a crew of five was sent to repair it. She did their cooking, their laundry, and on Saturday night heated the water so all the men could take their tub baths.

She found her social life with pen pals, writing to lighthouse families around the world. "I'd wrack my brains trying to write something from off that rock," she says. She put the letters she received in a big box lined with oil cloths. Years later, leaving another island and unable to transport it, she buried it. "I felt better then. I wasn't destroying something that was precious to me."

When Elson became delirious with fever, she tended the light alone through a week of storm. When he recovered, she became ill. "I tried not to give in to it and worry Elson," she says. "I played checkers with him when his face was just a blur."

Once, winching the boat onto the slip, she caught her arm under the clamper, crushing it beneath the cogs. "I walked the floor all night. Next day Elson got me to shore. I had to take the mail team nine miles to Machias while Elson returned to the light. For three months I didn't know I had an arm. . . ."

She blistered the skin off her hands when Elson was away and a storm erupted and the bell broke down. "I untied the ropes we used to ring the bell by hand when we saluted the lighthouse tender. I pulled for an hour and a half—I knew Elson was out there."

After four years at Avery's Rock they moved to Seguin, one of the largest lights on the coast on a clover-covered island at the mouth of the Kennebec. The foghorn blast vibrated against the windowpanes of the house 200 yards away. Once, there were three weeks of fog and the horn never stopped. At night sea birds crashed against the tower; in the morning she buried them. In summer she'd be making beds and find tourists staring in through the door. "I'd hide when I heard them coming," she says. One morning a rap on the door brought her face to face with 25

Gloucester gill-netters, whose approach she'd been nervously watching. They asked if she had a radio.

"They sprawled all over the living room," she says, "but there wasn't a sound. They were listening to the opera." The next day they returned, bringing her a 65-pound cod.

In 1930 they left Seguin as they had arrived—in the fog—moving to Dochet's Island in the St. Croix River, where they lived for 16 years. Elson bought a cow and plowed a field. They went clamming and at dawn they'd catch flounder and cook them on the boat. Elson lobstered, built boats, and taught Connie target shooting. In winter, ice-bound for weeks, they'd shoot icicles. At night Elson played the banjo. They'd spend two weeks in summer at a Portland hotel, and Connie would walk slowly past the shops before going home to the light. Two days after Pearl Harbor, Elson was asked to cut the Christmas tree for the White House. And soon after, he was asked to serve.

"I had three hours' notice," she says, "to get supper, pack, and think what private things I had that I didn't want strangers looking into, then walk out of my house." Connie stayed in Eastport until January 1945. "You never saw such a happy man," she says, "when Elson came to the door to tell me we were going back to Dochet's."

By then the Coast Guard had absorbed the Lighthouse Service, automation had begun, and Elson had only a few years until retirement. He asked for a mainland light. In 1946 they moved to Fort Point Light, or Portsmouth Harbor Light, as it's sometimes called, in Newcastle, New Hampshire. The house lay inside the fort, the towers just outside the walls on a point jutting into the Piscataqua River. For the first time a bridge connected Elson and Connie to the mainland. When they arrived, the fort was occupied by the army. Deactivated bombs were piled higher than her head beside the house.

"I tried to figure out a new mode of living," she says. "I'd never been much with strangers. The light was open to tourists and people came from all directions." She joined a rug club, sang in a choir. It was their first home with electricity and they went on a buying spree: washing machine, coffee percolator, iron, toaster, refrigerator. "It was heaven," she says.

In June 1949, Elson retired. They bought their first home just across the Maine border in Eliot. "I thought the sea was embedded so deep he'd never turn his back on it," Connie says, "but he got a tractor and became a gardener. He had the best garden around, and I had a little stand and sold enough to pay for his fertilizer and these rocking chairs." He built his boats and played his banjo. Sometimes in winter they'd travel to Florida. They had 11 years before Elson died.

"I realized then," she says, "that I'd lived a protected life. I was very naïve. I could always battle the elements, but I hadn't been out to battle the world." In time, after working in a gift shop, Connie became a housemother at Farmington State College, a small teachers' college in western Maine.

"I was so afraid I would say the wrong thing that for quite a while I just listened and watched. Sometimes they'd come in, very upset to the point of tears, and they'd say could I talk with you, and I'd say of course you can—and they'd sit and I wouldn't say a word, and they'd get up and say, 'Oh, you've helped me so much.'

"The girls couldn't understand how I could have devoted my whole life to Elson, how at their age I could have gone off to live like that, without friends," she says. She sits for a moment, reflecting. "My one great desire was to be a portrait artist. If I could have painted you and have somebody know it was you, I would have been in seventh heaven. I had my paints on the lights. But I'd get so absorbed, I'd forget Elson, forget his dinner. I felt I had to make a choice. And the girls could never understand that. Of course," she says, "I don't blame them.

"Elson was never demonstrative, but I knew he loved me. Very few people depend on each other as we did. He's been gone 21 years," she says, "and I haven't found anyone yet I'd want to replace him with."

She calls the Coast Guard at Fort Point and asks permission to tour the light. She had been back just once, briefly, 15 years ago. The house was in disrepair, and she'd felt awkward and shy among the men, so she left quickly without seeing the tower.

From where she parks, you can see the house boarded up with gulls circling above. "Somebody's painted it since I've been here," she says. The house is square, built high off the ground on a concrete foundation, but the stairs are gone. It is late afternoon, and the breeze is nippy, but the sun is out, the sky blue. Several Coast Guardsmen sit on the steps of the station eating pork chops and French fries from plates balanced on their knees. A radio blares, and in the parking lot a man plays basketball alone.

She opens an iron gate onto a walkway over the rocks leading to the tower. Scabs of rust show through the paint on the tower. She notes quietly that the curtains are not drawn.

"When they first brought the crew in here," she says, "Elson went up to the tower. He found the lens cover on the floor where they'd been walking on it. It almost broke his heart."

It is airless and dusty inside the tower. She looks at the stairs twisting upward, plants her hand firmly on the railing, and begins to climb. Her steps echo on the iron stairs. Near the top the stairway narrows, becoming much steeper approaching the lens room. "I was always terrified of heights," she says. "Elson would get behind me. He'd say, 'Look up, never look down.' Whenever I get discouraged, I still repeat that."

She makes her push into the lens room, breathing hard. In place of linen, a plexiglass tube protects the lens. It is a different lens from the one she knew. She bends over it. "Twenty minutes," she says. "It took us 20 minutes to light the lamp at Avery's Rock. We'd time it so it would light just at dusk. It was a vapor lamp and had to be lit just so or it would soot up."

An iron door only three feet high leads to the observation deck. She wriggles through on her knees, her crisp white suit trailing on the ground. The wind is cold, but she stays outside watching the sailboats, her hair blown back, her eyes wide, happy as a colt.

"The tankers would pass right by here," she shouts above the wind. "And there's the bell I used to ring. I used to do the flags, and the tugboat captains called every morning to see how the visibility was." She climbs down, her hands gripping the railing. The door is heavy and shuts with a clang. She walks past the house and pauses beside the wall of the fort.

"I found a starving cat here," she says, "its sides caved in. She was wild as a hawk and would run from me. I put food by the bombs and kept staying a little longer, and soon she came to the dish. Soon she brought a young black cat to the back door, and I knew it was hers. I called the young one Blackie. One day Blackie came over the wall with a tiny kitten in her mouth. She laid it in front of me. Four more times she came over the wall and put them all under the bombs. Each morning I'd look under the bombs and see five little pairs of eyes looking back. It was an icy winter, so Elson built a house for them on our porch.

"One dark morning I heard a terrible yowling. It was Blackie. I swear she was trying to talk to me. I saw right off the kittens were gone. She would go a little ways, holler, and wait for me to come. I followed her all over the place that day and every day for a month. But we never saw those kittens again. We figured wild dogs had run them into the river.

"Blackie stayed with me, but she never let me touch her. When we left, we couldn't catch her to take her with us. I came on the steps for the last time and sat down. I called to her. She came running from around the house and jumped right into my lap! I was so surprised I went to put my hand on her—but she was gone. You know," she says, walking away, "I never once got my hands on her."

She goes home and makes coffee and brings her albums back to the sofa. She shows Avery's Rock, gray and stark, later dynamited by the government to keep vandals away. She shows Dochet's Island, burned to the ground by vandals. "I told them they were making a mistake when they took families off those lights," she says.

It's twilight and her voice is tired, her face flushed from the day. She draws the curtains. She turns on a lamp on top of the television. On its side is a painting of a lighthouse and storm-tossed sea. A tiny light revolves behind the painting. The sea appears to surge, and a light pulses from the tower. She sits in her rocker in the dark and watches.

Published August 1982

A few years after the Yankee *story, Connie Small published her memoir,* The Lighthouse Keeper's Wife. *The book became a bestseller and pulled her from her life in the small apartment into a national spotlight. Every major television network invited her to tell her story. Hundreds of people wrote from across the globe. Two U.S. presidents sent her citations. She gave by her count more than 600 lectures, and when she turned 100, the American Lighthouse Foundation feted her with a gala celebration. When she died in 2005 at age 103,* The New York Times *again told of the life she led.*

THREE

HARD TO FORGET

When you write about the lives of others and you hear their stories for hours and sometimes days, they never really leave you. But there are some stories that long after they go into print, you think about time and again. A doctor's fight against an ancient virus; two young musicians who lived so close and yet so far apart. A lost child. A friend who made a tragic choice. It doesn't matter how long ago.

Even now, I may be taking a walk and see a child playing with his parents, and I suddenly think of Kurt Newton, a four-year-old boy who disappeared in 1975 from a remote Maine campground. Thousands of volunteers joined in the most intensive search in the state's history.

In the summer of 2023, I read about a rabid coyote attacking a woman in Rhode Island. I was immediately back 40 years and sitting with the mother of Kevin Wessell, a young man who fought for his life after being bitten by a dog in Africa. When I revisit "The Fight to Save Kevin Wessell," I am listening again to nurses and doctors, and Kevin Wessell's mother telling me about the days and nights when a medical mystery took hold of their lives.

Over two decades ago, two young musicians, Ranan Rishmawi and Sarah Cohen, let me follow them around for a few days while they prepared for a "Playing for Peace" concert at Apple Hill Center for Chamber Music. Their story was at once uplifting, poignant, and also tragic—they had much to offer each other in their week together, and yet their lives would be irreparably apart. When I listen to the news of their respective homelands, it is impossible not to be taken back to their music studio where they are practicing what they called "A Work in Progress," hearing the melody of their laughter.

Lynn Franklin became my friend when I taught his daughter in my fourth-grade class. Ten years later he flew the small plane he was piloting solo during bad weather into the side of Mount Monadnock, which rises just up the road from the Yankee building. It took days for searchers to spot his plane, and afterwards I hiked with his nephew to the wreckage.

To tell about someone whose reckless confidence made him larger than life, but which had also taken his life, became one of the hardest stories I ever wrote. For "Ode to a Bold Pilot," I had a box filled with his unpublished writings. I had the memories of countless friends who had fallen under his "we will never know if we don't go" mantra. I had a photo of Lynn sitting in the cockpit of one of the bush planes he felt destined to fly. His face glows with a joy so infectious I wanted to show why we were drawn to him.

It was only after his mother wrote to me after the story came out and said how it had helped her both grieve and laugh that I felt I had done my part.

The Fight to Save Kevin Wessell

Shortly after 9 a.m. on Wednesday, January 5, 1983, a pale young man, accompanied by his father, stepped rapidly into the emergency room of Waltham Hospital, 10 miles west of Boston, and with a wild, anxious look in his eyes said that his chest and back hurt, that he could not catch his breath, and that at least once every minute, for reasons he could not explain, he was overtaken by an urge to gasp, as if frightened—a gasp so powerful it made him tremble. He could not swallow without gagging—"I feel like I'm choking," he said—and he added he had been unable to sleep.

His name was Kevin Wessell. His parents lived just down the street from the hospital in the maroon, wood-framed house where he had grown up. He was 30 years old and handsome, remarkably so, dark-haired and mustachioed. His 5'10" frame was lean and hard from grueling eight-mile runs in the Nigerian bush, where for nearly four years he had helped manage a rock quarry for a Waltham architectural company for whom he had worked since high school. He told the nurse that two days earlier he had received booster shots for cholera, typhus, and typhoid—he was due to fly to Africa that night. He reasoned he might be having a reaction to the shots. Privately he thought that what he called his "Nigeria Blues" had gotten the best of him.

He had come to dread the awful heat, the insects, the snakes, and the isolation of the quarry deep in the bush. He was engaged to Mercedes

B., the beautiful daughter of a prominent Boston physician; he called her "Mercy." She had come to Africa that spring, settling down to life in the porter camp. A friend gave them a puppy, a Doberman they named Pepper. Kevin and Mercedes returned to Massachusetts in July for his sister's wedding, and when he went back to Africa, Mercedes stayed behind. In October Pepper died, leaving Kevin even lonelier than before.

"Twice a year, summer and Christmas, he came home," his mother, Dorothea, says. "The week before he'd leave to go back was always the worst. So much anxiety. He'd be gagging. I'd say, 'Kevin, what are you doing it for?' and he'd say, 'Ma, I told them I'd do it, so I'll do it.'"

Besides, he had planned his life with an architect's precision—the payoff for his loneliness was the money he was saving. In 10 weeks, on March 14, he would be leaving Africa for good, coming home to work for the company. This Christmas had been a breathless round of future plan-making. His wedding was set for June 4; reservations were made at the Copley Plaza for the reception. He'd bought land, two acres about 40 miles north in New Hampshire; he and Mercedes had shopped for furniture, and he'd filled a notebook with designs for the house to be built in the summer after the honeymoon.

"It was the beginning of great times for all of us," his mother says. And though she thought he seemed a little jumpy, his eyes a little too big ("kind of bulgy"), she kept it to herself. Then, just before New Year's, Kevin seemed to come down with a cold.

"He complained of being tired," his mother says, "of wanting to lie down, which wasn't like Kevin. He started sweating. His nose ran. He said he must have a bug." He went to Boston New Year's Eve, to the Marriott Hotel, and the next day complained to his mother of a tingling in his arm.

"Which arm?" she asked sharply. He held up the right. "Don't worry," she said, "not your heart arm." The next day he received his shots, and the day after, Tuesday, he awoke with chills. "Must be the shots," his mother said. That night, trying to drink a cup of hot cocoa Mercedes had made him, he brought it to his lips and could not drink. He jerked back as if slapped, holding his throat, which was in spasms, as if a hand had closed around it and was squeezing it tight. He was awake all night. By morning his heart was racing and he was gasping for breath. Alarmed, his father drove him to the hospital.

In the emergency room, the nurse saw he was breathing too rapidly, hyperventilating—a classic symptom of an anxiety attack. She gave him a paper bag, made him sit down, and told him to breathe deeply, nice and slow, into the bag. Then she summoned the doctor on call.

Dr. Douglas Butman was making his morning rounds when he answered his page. The son of a Waltham druggist, he was, at age 68, one of the hospital's senior physicians. "Just an old-fashioned GP," he likes to say, "who still makes house calls." In four decades there was little he had not seen in medicine, but he was stunned when he saw Kevin Wessell in the emergency room.

"I'd given him his shots on Monday," Dr. Butman recalls, "and except for the jitters he always felt before going back to Africa, he said he was fine. Now here he was, obviously in great distress—and he had a plane to catch in a few hours! Kevin asked if it might be a reaction to the shots. I doubted it. Then he wondered if his not drinking milk for several years might be the problem. I said I didn't think that too likely either.

"'Then it must be my Nigeria Blues,' Kevin said. And I thought of a syndrome discovered in World War I, neurocirculatory asthenia. Doctors called it 'soldier's heart,' or sometimes, 'nervous heart.' It was caused by emotional stress and gave soldiers all the symptoms of heart patients—shortness of breath, palpitations, chest pain, feeling of faintness. It reminded me of Kevin. So I gave him an injection of Valium. But to be safe, I ordered an electrocardiogram. I found aberrations in the electrocardiogram that were just unreal. Nothing diagnostic, but dead wrong for a boy in his physical condition. I couldn't let him get on a plane that night. I said, 'Kevin, I've got to put you in the hospital. I don't know what's wrong—yet.'" At about noon Kevin was wheeled into room 412 on the Nichols medical-surgical ward.

At dinnertime Dr. David Duhme, covering for Dr. Butman, received a call from a nurse that tranquilizers were not helping Kevin Wessell. He seemed extremely anxious. He was spitting copious saliva into a basin and kept saying he was choking. He refused to eat or drink.

"I saw him about 7 p.m.," Dr. Duhme recalls. "These were strange symptoms. He described it as trouble breathing—but it was not what anyone else meant by trouble breathing. He said it was a sudden urge to take a gasping breath, and that certain things stimulated it. Water, for example.

"He said the sight of water made him have trouble breathing. So I brought a glass of water and his whole body recoiled in spasms, with sheer terror on his face. The same thing happened when I took out my throat stick. It certainly seemed like a severe anxiety reaction. He was so tense, so fearful. I had the feeling he was ready to go off in any direction. But something didn't figure, because while we talked, he remained calm and reasonable. You don't see that in many patients who have to be hospitalized for anxiety.

"He admitted he got nervous before going away, but this didn't feel like that, he said. So we just sat there talking, and I was asking him about his life in Africa, frankly stumped, when out of the blue, and very calmly, he told me about his dog Pepper."

One day in October something curious had happened. Pepper, standing by the edge of the camp, ignored Kevin's breakfast calls, then loped away and did not return. Searching for two days, Kevin found his dog caught in a steel leghold trap set by native tribesmen. Though bleeding and weak, Pepper wagged his tail and whimpered a greeting. Kevin released him then and knelt to check the leg. Without warning and before running off, Pepper attacked. "His teeth went through my arm like butter," he wrote Mercedes.

Bleeding badly, Kevin drove an hour to the nearest medical help, a German clinic, figuring the pain of the leg wound had driven Pepper mad. He had vaccinated the dog for rabies, so he was not worried about that; nevertheless, the doctor gave Kevin two shots. One, Kevin figured, for tetanus, the other for rabies, with boosters a week later.

Dr. Duhme asked Kevin's family, who were in the room, to find his vaccination certificate. He examined Kevin's right wrist. Only thin, white lines, barely discernible, remained from the perfectly healed wound. "And Pepper?" he asked.

"I found him lying in the grass, dead," Kevin said. "I buried him." Quietly Dr. Duhme scanned the vaccination chart. He expected to find a notation for rabies serum; he found instead, on October 8, the words "tetanus" and "tetanus immune globulin," both vaccines repeated a week later.

"I had this sudden sinking feeling," Dr. Duhme says today. "The old image of rabies—hydrophobia—struck me. Here I'd been trying to evaluate his fear of drink!" He told Kevin he wanted some other doctors to look in on him. Then quickly he stole away to the medical library.

David Duhme was 37; his specialty was internal medicine. He was recruited by the hospital in 1979 from a Boston neighborhood health center and asked to join Dr. Butman (who hinted at retirement) in his practice. Hurrying down the hall, he was excited, fascinated, though fearful. "Sometimes I'd wondered what it would be like to treat rabies," he says. In the United States it ranks as one of the rarest (averaging one to five cases a year) and most hopeless of human infections. Its symptoms are, perhaps, the most frightening and bizarre in medicine. The madness, the frothing, the violent reactions to water, end inevitably in death. (Only three survivors worldwide have been recorded.) If Kevin Wessell had rabies, David Duhme wanted to whip the curtain off the ancient scourge and see its face. This morbid curiosity, he figured, had been kindled at age three. In St. Louis, a city then rife with rabies, he had been bitten by a cat and had undergone the traumatic series of 21 shots—three rows of seven beneath the skin in the abdomen—which left him swollen and badly bruised.

Dr. Duhme was unsure that Kevin's problem was rabies. In fact, he was inclined to believe it was not. The word comes from the Latin, "to rage," and Kevin did not seem sick enough. "My image of a rabid person is someone who would need restraints," he says, "and we had just had a perfectly cogent conversation." There were other possibilities. Diptheria was remote, but had to be considered, as did a host of tropical infections. Once he had had a patient who had swallowed a test-tube cap, causing spasms in the throat. Something lodged in Kevin's esophagus could perhaps explain his inability to swallow. There might be pathology in the neck, or it might be a thyroid problem.

Probability too weighed against rabies. A human is naturally resistant to rabies virus—a person bitten by a rabid dog and left untreated still has only a 15 percent chance of being infected. Simple washing of the wound with soap and water reduces that risk to only one percent. It had been 50 years since the last case of human rabies in Massachusetts; it seemed unlikely that it had turned up here in Waltham. Yet, as he perused the literature, he felt he was reading symptoms right from Kevin's chart.

". . . the intervals between the bite and the appearance of symptoms range

from nine days to over a year, but in 90 percent of cases it lasts between two weeks and three months, tending to be longer after bites on the limbs than after those on the face. . . .

"The first sign is often a vague feverish illness resembling influenza, a common cold, or a sore throat. A feeling of tension, inability to sleep, have all been described. None of these features is particularly suggestive of rabies. . . . The majority of patients develop a symptom which is, however, highly suggestive of impending rabies. They feel an abnormal sensation radiating from the site of the bite wound, which by now will have healed. A tingling . . . lasting for a few hours to a few days."

To Dr. Duhme it was all there on Kevin's chart, like a light trying to penetrate the fog. He called Dr. Donald Thompson, a neurologist (rabies attacks the nerve endings in the brain), and Dr. Susan Aoki, infectious disease specialist, and asked them to see Kevin.

"The neurologist said that Kevin had been able to spell 'world' backwards," recalls Dr. Duhme. "And a person with dementia could not do that." Dr. Aoki noted that Kevin, when he relaxed, seemed to be swallowing normally. An Iraqi doctor who knew rabies also came in. "He said emphatically that this was not rabies," Dr. Duhme says. "He was too well."

Nevertheless, late that night, Dr. Aoki phoned the Centers for Disease Control in Atlanta, the nation's clearinghouse for disease information, and asked for advice. "Close observation" was the reply. As a precaution, nurses were told that there might be a problem; Kevin's secretions were to be double-bagged and incinerated. Still, when the Wessells asked what was wrong with Kevin, Dr. Duhme admitted that, while rabies had to be considered, he just did not know.

At 6:30 a.m. Thursday morning, Dr. Duhme found Kevin smiling, calmly sipping water, wondering if he could jog in the hallway to stay in shape. Dr. Duhme's internal debate continued. Rabies ravages the nervous system so severely that the average patient, without heroic lifesaving procedures, is dead within a week. So Kevin should be getting steadily worse, but, if anything, he was improving.

Only a few hours later, when Dr. Duhme was off, a lab technician asked Kevin to swallow barium for a throat X-ray. Kevin flung it away, shouting, "You're trying to kill me," and this time there was no calming him down.

He began crying out continually, “I don’t want to go back,” and “Mercy, Mercy.” A doctor changed his sedatives, thinking perhaps they had backfired and excited Kevin instead. He sat shaking on the side of the bed, now up, now down, unable to rest. His thrashing pulled out his intravenous needle, but he was too agitated to have it reinserted. His mother watched his wide, staring eyes and thought they reflected not just fear, but fury and shame, as the saliva he could not swallow frothed down his chin. The room had become a nightmare, and his roommate was removed.

Mrs. Wessell was confused and angry with the doctors, who still seemed to think that this was a nervous reaction. She knew her son was no psycho. But she knew something inexplicably horrible was happening to him. “That’s not my son,” she told a nurse.

“He was delirious,” she recalls. “I said he had to have a nurse stay with him all night. They said it wasn’t possible, it had to be arranged ahead of time. I said, ‘Okay, but no way am I going to leave my son until I know what’s wrong.’ He was burning up. I wet a cloth and put it on his face, when all of a sudden he stands right up on the bed. Now I’m screaming for a nurse because I can’t hold him. The nurses come in, and Dr. Butman, and everybody’s trying to calm him down, to get him to lie down, but I know my kid is in another world. The next thing I see he’s not breathing, his eyes are back. I hear ‘Dr. Blue, Dr. Blue’ [code for respiratory arrest]. Then everyone came running into the room.”

It was at 10 p.m. and about a week after Kevin had first complained of “catching cold” that the doctors’ debate ceased. No longer was there any question of this being a case of anxiety. Kevin had just suffered a grand mal seizure.

“I’m afraid,” Dr. Butman told a distraught Mrs. Wessell, “that what we fear may be true.”

By midnight a web of tubes and catheters probed his body; Kevin lay in isolation in the intensive care ward, semiconscious, with ice packs beneath his arms. His temperature read 106 degrees. A call was made to Atlanta’s Centers for Disease Control.

“The CDC said to take a tissue sample from the base of the neck. That’s where the virus would be, exploding outward from the brain,” Dr. Butman says. “No one wanted to do the biopsy. People were afraid. There was no surgeon around, but being an old GP, I’d done an awful lot of surgery myself. And, anyway, I'm an old crock, so it made no difference to me. I said, 'Oh, hell, give me the knife.'

"Dr. Aoki and I drove the sample packed in dry ice to the airport. It was 4 a.m., like when I delivered babies. What flabbergasted me was how quiet Logan was, just some cleaning men getting ready for morning. And I had this eerie thought—if something happened to the plane and an animal got into the box, we could start a rabies epidemic right here. I felt that I was sending a time bomb."

Waiting in Atlanta for the lab reports was a soft-spoken, 35-year-old physician named Ken Bernard. An authority on diseases transmitted directly from animals to man—Q fever, typhus, rabies—he was the CDC's medical epidemiologist, Division of Viral Diseases, charged with overseeing the care of rabies patients anywhere in the country. At 4 p.m. Friday word came: Kevin Wessell had rabies. Immediately, Dr. Bernard phoned Waltham Hospital—extreme caution must be taken because Kevin's saliva was potentially lethal. (Within hours, Mercedes and a doctor who had been splashed in the eye with saliva began immunization with a new $500 vaccine flown in from Florida, so potent it required only five injections in the arm. In addition, the hospital identified 132 people who had had contact with Kevin. Though no doctor or nurse had ever contracted rabies from a patient, 30 asked for immunization—mostly to still their fears.) Then Dr. Bernard booked a flight to Boston and went home to pack.

Ken Bernard knew nearly everything about preventing rabies. The science was little changed since July 6, 1885, when Louis Pasteur saved the life of a child, mauled by a rabid dog, with his untested vaccine. But he did not know how to cure it. In that, he was heir to a fragmented history. For centuries, doctors all but drowned their patients, thinking that if a patient could but endure four minutes underwater, his hydrophobia could be cured. One doctor, hoping to extract "the poison," put gunpowder on the bites, then lit it. Bezoars sold for great sums; found in the stomachs of sheep, goats, and deer, they were said to have great powers on the bites of mad dogs and thus were called madstones. But the most common treatment was euthanasia, "to stifle the poor wretch between feather beds."

In 1970 in Ohio, on the night of October 10, a six-year-old farm boy woke up screaming, a rabid bat clinging to his thumb. Two weeks after completing rabies shots, he lay comatose in a hospital. Rabies experts at the CDC theorized that if intensive care could keep a patient alive long enough, perhaps the body itself could provide the cure. Until then rabies victims died within a week; the immune system needed more time to fight back. Skunks and raccoons and foxes sometimes survived rabies, so it was possible. Young Matthew Winkler was given anticonvulsants, fluid was extracted from his brain to relieve pressure, a respirator helped him breathe. After a week he began to emerge from the coma; weeks later he was discharged, hailed as the first human rabies survivor. But hope for intensive care as an answer proved premature. There have been only two more recorded survivors since.

The last time Ken Bernard had treated rabies was in August 1981. An American living in Mexico had been bitten by his dog. Several weeks later he was seized with terror at the sight of water, "so that I wanted to drown the fear out of me," and came to a hospital in Tucson, Arizona. Soon afterwards the CDC diagnosed his condition as rabies.

Dr. Bernard put his hopes on interferon. Extracted at great cost from human white blood cells, interferon seemed to fight any viral infection, much as some antibiotics kill any bacteria. At the time it was being hailed as the wonder drug of the eighties, possibly even a cure for cancer. After 10 days of interferon, the man had died.

Saturday morning Dr. Bernard stood by Kevin's side, a soda straw hidden in his hand. Some Waltham doctors, having seen Kevin grow alert enough to write notes to his family, remained unconvinced of rabies. Dr. Bernard trusted lab tests, but he trusted his own test more. Lifting the straw to his mouth, he blew a gentle stream of air onto Kevin's face. The reaction was spontaneous and violent, as though Kevin's whole body were a raw, inflamed nerve.

Dr. Bernard said to the surprised doctors watching, "Aerophobia. More diagnostic than hydrophobia." He knew Kevin's was an advanced case of rabies. The only hope he could offer was another go at interferon, already on its way from California. He sensed the family and the hospital had great hopes for the drug, but he harbored no illusions; he felt nearly as helpless to save Kevin as if all he carried was a handful of madstones.

That afternoon a hole was drilled into Kevin's skull, and a tube passed into the brain which would drip every evening five million units of interferon (twice that would be injected into his arm). Kevin could neither swallow nor cough; every few minutes a nurse would suction his foam. A few feet outside his door, at the nurses' desk, the rhythm of his heart beeped across a screen. A respirator sighed beside his bed. IVs dripped like rain. There were no windows, only a glass door curtained against the curious. Lights were dimmed to perpetual dusk. There were drugs for blood pressure and fever, convulsions and sleep, and fear. There was a specialist on call to monitor every organ. Kevin's family wore gloves to hold his hands, looked at him through goggles, spoke to him through masks. Late at night a nurse asked if he was afraid. He nodded yes. She asked if he wanted not to be left alone. He nodded again. She sat down, took his hands, and held them for an hour, two hours. Before leaving she made certain someone would be there when he awoke.

The next morning Dr. Duhme exulted, "He looks remarkably well; he's making use of sign language." Nearly everybody, including Kevin, seemed buoyed by the change.

Kevin's family and friends stayed by his side. They murmured to him, "You've got things to do, you've got things to do"—as though incantation could throw into retreat the virus that hour by hour was canceling all plans. By Tuesday Kevin's kidneys showed signs of complications. An infection began in his eyes. The eye drops terrified him. "It's as if he can't help resisting," a nurse wrote. "He appears to be trying very hard to cooperate."

The days passed, as if by metronome, filled with the routine of critical care. Kevin, hallucinating, would smile or wave, shake a fist at the ceiling, bang on his chest with both hands, grimace at eye drops, snatch at lights constantly shined in his face to monitor the eye infection. He would clamp down hard on the suctioning tube, teeth clenched in a tug-of-war with nurses trying to relax his grip, until, reluctantly, Dr. Duhme ordered a powerful paralytic, rendering him helpless, unable even to blink. A week after beginning interferon, Kevin needed his first blood transfusion. Every day, like gradually encroaching winter, Kevin lay quieter, slept longer, until on Sunday, January 16, he was caught in the long, solid grip of coma.

Kevin's story had become terrible but irresistible news to reporters throughout New England. They were drawn by the contrast, the modern wonder drug versus a disease that seemed, as Dr. Duhme said, "out of the Dark Ages of medicine." He told reporters, "We have to be optimistic. The few who have survived went into coma, too. All his organs are functioning well. Improvement with interferon should come within two weeks. January 24 is the critical date."

The eye worsened, the infection perforating the cornea. "The worst I'd ever seen," says Dr. Duhme. "He was going blind." Despite Kevin's coma, failing kidneys, and beginning pneumonia, on January 21 he received a cornea transplant. "If you're going full blast to save a life, you must do everything," explains Dr. Duhme. "We couldn't have him survive rabies and say, 'Sorry, you're blind because we lost hope.'" Wherever the doctors looked, they saw crises; no sooner would one be quelled than another broke out; treating one problem often worsened another. His white-blood-cell and platelet counts were becoming dangerously low, possibly a side effect of interferon. It was unclear to Drs. Bernard and Duhme whether Kevin was being helped or harmed by interferon.

"We debated," recalls Dr. Duhme. "One theory was that the immunological response to rabies is just as lethal, maybe more so, than the virus. The antibodies attack the disease in every cell of the body, in every brain cell, until the body dies. Some autopsies find no rabies virus at all. And the hypothesis was that interferon helped temper the antibody response. So that could be good. On the other hand, Kevin had the dubious honor of being the first person to culture rabies virus from his cerebrospinal fluid. It seemed the virus was going wild without antibodies to kill it."

Shortly after midnight on Thursday, January 27, an exhausted Dorothea Wessell left Kevin's room. He was bleeding from his nose, mouth, and breathing tube; she kept cleaning his face. His hands lay on pillows, his heels, turning blue, lay elevated on water balloons. At 1:10 a.m. the heart monitor at the nurses' station sounded an alarm. As if in response to his cries for "Mercy" of three weeks earlier, this time there were no attempts at resuscitation. The autopsy found virus everywhere. A hospital spokesman said it had been decided not to go into detail. The report stated only that Kevin Wessell had died of rabies on January 28, 1983.

A week later, in Michigan, a five-year-old girl said her right arm hurt. Diagnosis was a sprain. She grew irritable, stopped eating, and the arm grew weak. By February 17 she was comatose, and her parents remembered that late one August night she had screamed that a bat was biting her. "Only a nightmare," they had reassured her. Her death from rabies came March 9, the first human rabies case in Michigan since 1948.

In the summer Ken Bernard flew to Kenya, where a 23-year-old Peace Corps volunteer was dying. She had been bitten by her puppy in May. "He's been acting strange," she wrote in her diary. "I hope he doesn't have rabies." In neither case did consulting physician Dr. Bernard choose to recommend interferon.

David Duhme thinks back to one missed signal—when Kevin asked if he could jog. "I took it as a healthy sign," he says. "It was only later that I realized he was about to go mad. You don't jog in a hospital."

One of Kevin's critical care nurses needed time off after his death. "You see a lot of people die," she says, "and you're not supposed to get involved—but he wanted so much to live." When she returned, she found she was more sensitive and kinder to her patients. She still walks in the cemetery behind the hospital, following the path along the river to where the new graves are, and places a fresh flower by Kevin's stone.

Dorothea Wessell works for a florist down the street from her house, making arrangements for weddings and funerals. "I don't make plans anymore," she says. Though it is extremely painful for her to speak of Kevin's death, she feels she must. She tells of an epidemic of raccoon rabies 500 miles to the south that experts predict one day will reach New England. She hears of people who live nearby with unvaccinated dogs and cats; her face tightens and very quietly she says, "People don't understand what happens. I thought it was only a dog bite. But it changed everything."

Published July 1984

Soon after this story appeared, I heard from a few medical professionals who wanted to be sure the readers knew some important facts about a disease that, while extremely rare in humans in the United States, still claims thousands around the world. They wanted people to understand that anyone bitten or scratched by an animal in a country where rabies was endemic should receive immediate medical attention. The great danger, they asserted, is ignorance of the disease; that if Kevin Wessell had received the needed vaccinations, his life could have been saved. While Kevin Wessell was the first person to die of rabies in New England in decades, he would not be the last. In October 1995, a 13-year-old girl who complained of shoulder pain and tingling was initially diagnosed with Lyme disease. She became the first person to die of rabies in Connecticut since 1932. It was suspected that a bat that was flying in the house while she slept had infected her. A year later, a 32-year-old woman from New Hampshire died in a Massachusetts hospital from a dog bite she received while travelling in Nepal: she had not sought treatment. In 2012, a 63-year-old Cape Cod man also died from a suspected bite from a bat. His was the first confirmed case of rabies contracted in Massachusetts since 1935.

Ode to a Bold Pilot

"There are old pilots and there are bold pilots, but there are no old, bold pilots." –Anonymous

Looking back, it seems appropriate that word of Lynn Franklin's disappearance should come like a summer storm, late at night without warning, while I was sleeping. It was how he always arrived. It was Thursday, June 30, 1983. Phoning from Maine was Lynn's companion, Sharon Townshend.

"Lynn was flying solo to Connecticut," she said. "He's two days overdue."

"He's always overdue," I said.

"There's a forest fire up north. Maybe," she said hopefully, "maybe he went there."

"Maybe he started it," I said.

Sharon was worried, but she laughed. She knew what I meant.

I met Lynn in the fall of 1972 when I was teaching fourth grade in Gorham, Maine. In my class was Lynn's only child, a wide-eyed girl named Petra. Each day after noon recess I would try to calm the class by reading aloud. On this day the children finally were settling, as quiet as embers, when a man burst in clutching a parakeet in one hand, a small cage in the other. He wore a leather coat and baggy pants held up with suspenders. His eyes, deeply set in a lean, handsome face, glowed with excitement. It was Lynn.

"I've brought you a bird!" he cried. "You need *life* in here!" And then—whether on purpose or by accident I never knew—he set the bird free. All I could do was stand by, spellbound. The children climbed over desk tops as they swarmed after the bird, which screeched as it flew about the room. Finally, in terror, it dashed against the window where, mercifully unharmed, it was captured. Lynn had disappeared, taking with him my plans for the afternoon. As I read aloud for two hours, 30 children eyed the door hungrily, hoping he would return. The next day Petra brought me a note: "I knew kids would love the bird. Am searching for snakes. And rabbits. Have many afternoons free!—Lynn."

It was always like that with Lynn, as easy as it was to be angry over some disturbance, it was nearly always easier to forgive his exuberance, and it was not long before we became friends. I had never known anyone quite like him. He was at once exhilarating and exhausting to be around. He possessed no sense of time, or rather, his sense of time seemed unchanged since infancy. When his fevered energy was exhausted, he'd nap, awaken refreshed, and not understand my reluctance to join him, whether it be at 10 at night or three in the morning.

One night he insisted he could read Joseph Conrad's *Typhoon* aloud through the night. At its heart the book is about a man who allowed nothing to deter him, and as friends staggered off to sleep, waking and staggering back into the room periodically, they'd find Lynn at his post, eyes bloodshot, voice a whisper, reading on.

He lived by impulse and tried to pull everyone into his world. Driving with Lynn, I could never be certain when he might turn off and head elsewhere because he'd "been on the road long enough." He raced sailboats and once, while en route to a race in Nova Scotia, he stopped at the house of a friend of a friend, a man Lynn had never met. He came in, said, "Hi, I'm Lynn Franklin. Can I sleep on your couch for a few hours? And I'm off to a race. I need to leave my daughter here for a few days."

He was this paradox. He was free-spirited, yet he began every day by writing a letter to his mother. He greeted friends with the cry, "Cameradós!" and a bear hug, then he'd go for weeks at a time into the woods and nobody would know where he was. Because he was always escaping from some tight spot, I called him "Coyote" after the cartoon character, Wile E. Coyote, that Road Runner was always exploding into smithereens or chasing off a cliff, only to have him reappear moments later; and Lynn would laugh, pleased with the image. In time I realized my image of Lynn as Coyote was more complex, that he was also Road Runner, setting his own traps.

Lynn was 36 when I met him, a freelance photojournalist who found his stories in Maine, mostly among the fishermen along the coast and among the people in the North Woods. "Until you know a woodsman well," he'd say, "it's almost impossible to get a straight answer." So he returned again and again until he became like family to the hermit trappers, bush pilots, river guides, loggers, and deep-sea fishermen.

He'd sell his oral history stories to the *Maine Sunday Telegram* under the title, "Profiles of Maine," where readers met Joe Kelly, the foreman of the log drive on the St. John River. He sat beside the river and said to Lynn, *What could a man give in exchange? What could you give in exchange for your soul? What could you get?*

He drove an ancient, battered Saab that he was always fixing up, using parts from more battered Saabs that littered his yard. He'd set off with a dozen rolls of film and a half dozen tape recorders that were crusted with sea spray and clogged with sawdust, confident at least one would work. He'd wake his editor, Eddie Fitzpatrick, in the middle of the night. "You've got to hear this!" he'd say, and then press the tape recorder against the phone. He was always just arriving from or departing for somewhere and when asked about his trip he'd invariably say, "There were a *few* incidents."

"When we set off with Lynn," said a friend, "we never knew if we'd return. But he made things sound so exciting. How could we refuse?" Said another friend, "He drove us beyond our capacity to be rational."

Said Lynn: "My zeal replaces judgment. But then I love zeal!" There were sailboats wrecked on sandbars, others wrecked on rocks; unrunnable rapids that somehow were run; and when he became a pilot, so many close calls that even those who loved him found excuses not to fly with him. He seemed blinded to danger by his own boldness and by his overwhelming love for the outdoors. He refused to believe that something he loved could ever harm him. I often resisted his entreaties to adventure and I never joined him at sea, on an expedition, or in the air, and he never poked fun. But once when he was learning to fly, he sent this note: *"And so cautious people wither and maybe never bloom—unless caution is a flower. And what would it look like? Maybe a walnut is a caution flower."*

Miraculously, he was almost never harmed, as though fate regarded him as fondly as did his friends. He loved mythology and one of his favorite myths was that of Achilles. Sometimes I suspected he thought himself invulnerable, as though believing he too had been dipped by his mother into a charmed river.

And why not believe? His mother told him how she had fled on the last boat out of Barcelona with her three other children just as the Spanish Civil War erupted; how he had been born four days later, July 28, 1936, in Marseilles. Word had come that his father, the acting U.S. Consul-General, had been killed in Spain, but the report had been in error. His father had survived and soon joined them in France.

Lynn was named for his father, who he described as a hard man with a harsh temper, who had scratched his way from the lead mines of his youth to a life as a United States Foreign Service diplomat. He demanded order and discipline. The family moved from France to Sweden to Canada to the West Indies, which Lynn found "interesting only before hurricanes." By age six Lynn had been rescued twice from drowning by his mother, from the tracks of an approaching train by his sister, and had run away from home in three countries. In desperation his mother tethered him to a harness attached to a clothesline where he could dash about without disappearing. "He was always looking for something wonderful that wasn't at home," she would later say.

When Lynn was seven, the family moved permanently to his mother's ancestral home, historic Fall Hill, built in 1720 on the banks of the Rappahannock River in Fredericksburg, Virginia. It was where George Washington, a cousin, once played; where Civil War cannonballs lay hidden among the shrubs. At nine he was sent away to school, the first in a succession of schools, each one charged with the task of "shaping up" the precocious but rebellious lad. At the end of the trail, after his father had died, after aptitude tests by the score, and after a fair fortune spent, Lynn left academia degreeless for a shepherd's life in Ireland.

That was followed in due time by an attempt to farm Fall Hill ("A mistake," his mother admits, "but he made the neighbor children happy giving them rides on the tractor") and a stint as a clamdigger in Long Island

Sound where he lived on a sailboat sunk in a sandbar and the fishermen would watch, incredulous, as he clambered up and down the boat as the tide rose and fell. Then he met a young art student, Patt Robbins. ("Our first date he took me to a plush restaurant where a waiter stopped him. He had no tie. 'Then give me a tie,' Lynn said, and he threw it around his neck like a scarf and strolled into the dining room as if he owned it.")

It was 1962. Lynn was 26, Patt was 22, and a year later they married. They moved to New Orleans, where Petra was born, where Patt studied art, where Lynn worked the docks, posed for art students, and eventually, after abandoning plans to salvage a sunken treasure, talked his way into a reporter's job with the *Times-Picayune.* In the summer of 1971 they moved to Maine where Patt taught, and soon Lynn began finding his stories and his adventures, and I doubt even Lynn knew which one he chased the most.

In the spring of 1977 Lynn went to Greenville on the shores of Moosehead Lake, hired by the heirs of a timber baron to document their family history. Except for the long, slow breakup of his marriage that eventually led to divorce, and his perpetual penury, it was the best of times for Lynn. A collection of his articles was published as a book, *Profiles of Maine.* And a collection of his stories and tapes became part of the permanent collection of the Northeast Archives of Folklore and Oral History at the University of Maine.

"Think of it," he said. "The archives may last 1,000 years. The great-great-great grandchildren of the people I interviewed will be able to come and hear their ancestors. Think of that!"

Greenville is the bush pilot base for the Northeast, and all day Lynn could see and hear the seaplanes being loaded, taking off, and returning. He wrote his nephew, Ken Macdonald, for whom Lynn had become a hero: "I've just got to fly with 'em, Kenny. I've got to understand it, understand what it is to fly with them."

He hung around the pilots, and they let him climb aboard whenever there was room to spare. He went with them to drop sacks of groceries into snowdrifts for hermit trappers. Later, when Lynn had his license, he'd buzz his friends' houses and drop sacks of paper plates with advice on all subjects written upon them, thinking himself in a fine tradition.

He flew to Labrador and saw the endless migration of caribou running across the snow. He flew to Alaska, three days crammed behind the pilot, pushed against the wheels and tail assembly and extra freight. He was publishing interviews with the pilots, but he wanted more than a story, more than just their respect. When a friend of his mother's who often helped him out financially sent money for a new typewriter, he rented one instead. And with the money he paid the pilots to teach him to fly.

Flying with a bush pilot by his side, instructing, Lynn found rapture. "I curved and dove and climbed and tilted the wings. . . . I dove into the craters and lifted on the upsurge, dove and looped, the sky upside down, like tossing Petra into the air and spinning her and catching her, holding her tight, and tossing her again." He sent me a card with one line written upon it: "Here I am, where I ought to be."

Lynn left Greenville in 1979 to write his bush pilot book, and he brought back to Gorham not only a pilot's license, but a personal myth that he, too, was a bush pilot, as though their experience, their sixth sense about weather had been transmitted to him like magic as he wrote their stories. He liked to think that he, too, could take a road map and go from Maine to Alaska without a hitch. However, he frequently got lost.

"We took off for the Allagash," said a friend, "and when he said we were over Rumford, I looked down and we were over Colby College in Waterville." Sometimes he'd drop precariously low over highways, neck craned, peering out the window for road signs. Once he saw windsocks waving below, and thankful that he'd found the airport, he came in for a perfect landing—on the fairway of the Kearsage, New Hampshire, golf club.

He was also trying to find his way as a writer, abandoning the oral histories that for nearly ten years had made his reputation. "I want to hear my own voice," he said. But it was a difficult transition and there were few successes.

He spent a year writing a book about a psychic, certain he had a bestseller, but it sold poorly and was soon remaindered. He found no publisher for *The Baseball Book, A Fan's Guide to the Greatest Game on Earth*, which he co-wrote with a painter friend. "Who's going to buy a baseball book by Lynn Franklin and a painter in Maine?" sighed one publisher.

The unpublished manuscripts piled up in his small, cold office where to start his day he put a heating pad beneath the typewriter, and when the machine warmed up, he placed the pad beneath his feet. His bush pilot book grew so long and so entangled that he'd compared it to "a dismantled engine." He'd send it to editors, packed in cartons, hoping that one could make sense of the parts strewn around. None could.

By now our friendship had changed somewhat—I was his editor at *Yankee.* We bought six stories but turned down four times that many. "Why is it," he asked, "that when I write for money I don't do it as well?" And I had no answer.

Whenever things became too much for him, he'd set off on a wilderness trip in a canoe. He'd take only the barest of provisions, certain he could catch fish and forage in the forest, and he took no tent, sleeping beneath his overturned canoe like a traditional Maine guide. And it was there, writing in his trip journals, that he wrote in a voice as clear as a mountain river. And nobody ever saw it.

"The way to cross a lake is at night when (and if) there is no wind. If the moon is full, the experience must resemble traveling through outer space. The canoe seems to fly over the water as if one stroke could propel it to the other side of the lake. The moon becomes six moons or twenty in the ripples off my paddle on the water. Fog forms and drifts away and forms again. It is not unusual for fog to form to a depth of five feet. I can stand in the canoe and see over it. The experience is that of flying over the clouds. Only the ache in my shoulder tells me the length of time I have been at work on my crossing. And then, as if suddenly I am close to shore, trees and rocks take on definition. The landing seems always to be a surprise like the end of a dream."

At 8:30 a.m. on Tuesday, June 28, 1983, Lynn drove to Stan Harmon's airport in Limington, Maine, to rent a Cessna Skyhawk. Harmon liked Lynn, but he was always nervous when Lynn took one of his planes. He was never quite certain where it might turn up.

Once Lynn had rented a two-seater Cessna, promising to return by 4:30. At 4:30 Lynn had phoned. He was being detained. He was at LaGuardia. He'd always wanted to land at LaGuardia. Unannounced, without permission, he'd scooted like a gnat past rows of jetliners before being accosted by the authorities.

He had told Harmon that day that he was going to Connecticut for *Yankee* to write about a former teacher he hadn't seen in over 30 years. "I still love him," Lynn said. It was warm and hazy in Maine, but the forecast along Lynn's route called for possible rain. Lynn was certified for visual flying only.

"Marginal weather," Lynn remarked before taking off. "I love it."

Stopping for gas in Concord, New Hampshire, he took off knowing unsettled weather lay ahead, knowing he would break the bush pilot's first rule: never chance flying blind in unfamiliar terrain. But he had always been forgiven, except this once, when at 10:01 a.m. Lynn Franklin flew into the side of Mount Monadnock. There was no charm to protect him from that.

He had not filed a flight plan. Nobody knew where to search anymore than if Lynn had been a wild bird that had not returned to the nest. On Saturday a pilot on a sightseeing tour of the mountain spotted the wreckage. Searchers found Lynn, 400 feet below the 3,165-foot summit, strapped into the plane that had broken in two and burned. Lynn had died on impact. It was how everyone expected Lynn to go, probably the way he would have chosen. It was just too soon. He was 46.

Lynn would have enjoyed his memorial gathering. We shared Lynn stories and laughed at his foolishness and his recklessness and his eccentricities, like his penchant for going into Howard Johnson's with a thermos and asking people for their leftover coffee. He had been everyone's naughty boy, everyone's Peter Pan. I think it was why we loved him. It was a lot more fun growing older with Lynn around to remind us to be young.

I climbed the mountain with Lynn's nephew Ken and his friend Sharon. The plane lay there crumpled among the trees and rocks. We stood quietly on the rocks looking down at the lakes glistening below. At 21, Ken resembled the youthful Lynn. He was tall and wide-shouldered. He was a falconer, a mountain climber, a white-water canoeist, and had decided to be a writer. He looked at the plane and then he laughed and you could hear Lynn in that laugh.

"He'd be so angry with himself," Ken said. "I can just hear him. He'd say, 'Next time, Franklin, next time we fly *over* the mountain!'"

Published May 1984

Lynn had told me he was going to visit his favorite teacher, William H. Armstrong, the author of the classic young adult novel, Sounder. *Sometimes Lynn would suddenly appear at my home in Keene, and I have always wondered if he was trying to land at Silver Ranch Airport in Jaffrey, just a few miles from the* Yankee *office, which was located near the base of the mountain. His older sister, Bess, published a memoir for her family in 2013. She wrote, "During the many years since Lynn died, I have learned to be so much more nonjudgmental. I mark it with Lynn's death because I regret so deeply that I surrounded my opinion of him with "shoulds," like he should earn more money, he should take better care of his family, he should avoid danger, rather than thoroughly enjoying every encounter with him and relishing his exuberance, his joyous outlook, and his incredible creativity. . . . That little boy who was born when I was seven and tried to run away even as a toddler, using my doll stroller to hold him up, supplied more joy in my life than I ever knew. He was so beautiful. His life continues to enhance mine today."*

A Work in Progress

When people say Apple Hill isn't the real world, we say this is *the real world. Our job is to take the stage and tell our story. It's a high-stakes game. If we don't take the stage and tell the story, who will? Our job is to make the rest of the world understand this is the real world.*

–Eric Stumacher, founding member of Apple Hill Chamber Players, home of Playing for Peace

On a blue-sky Sunday afternoon in late August, the old barn with its makeshift stage seems too small to hold the stories that will play out in the next few hours. Outside, a breeze ripples across meadows and woods of this southern New Hampshire farm, home to the Apple Hill Chamber Players, five world-class musicians whose mission has become to tour the troubled spots of the world.

They give workshops, audition young musicians, and offer scholarships to about 30 to come to a hillside in East Sullivan, New Hampshire, to play beside people who have always been strangers and enemies. Apple Hill is part intensive music camp, part bridge for friendship. "The pebble is located here," says Apple Hill executive and artistic director Eric Stumacher, "but the ripples go out and out."

On this day, known as Playing for Peace Day, the concert barn is packed. Irish Catholics will play beside Irish Protestants. Inner-city Americans will play beside rural New Englanders, Cypriot Greeks with Cypriot Turks. Armenians with Azerbaijanis. Arabs with Jews.

After several short recitals, two women, both in their early twenties, both wearing black dresses, walk together to the front of the room. Look at them. They could be sisters. They both stand 5'4". Their eyes and hair are brown, their skin olive, their smiles pretty and shy. They both want to spend their lives playing and teaching music.

Ranan Rishmawi sits at the piano, her fingers touching the keys ever so slightly and waits. "There's not an hour in my life without music," she told me a few days earlier. She said her friends at home chide her for not playing Arabic music. "They don't understand my love for classical music."

Sarah Cohen places her fingers on her cello and waits. Her ambition is "to play all over the world. I hope my music can change minds." Their eyes meet, they smile slightly, they nod, and the first notes of a Bach sonata drift through the barn.

Ranan is a Protestant Christian who lives in Beit Sahour, traditionally thought to be the Field of the Shepherds, where angels appeared to shepherds to tell them of the birth of the infant Jesus. Sarah is an Israeli who lives in Jerusalem. They live so close together, they feel the same sun, the same rain. But they know the truth of their lives: They live so far apart. They come from different worlds.

Ranan lives under Israeli occupation. Sometimes she cannot leave her house for days on end. She says her life is as bleak as if lived in a cell. She has all but lost hope for an end to the cycle of occupation, Palestinian suicide attacks, followed by curfews, bulldozers, more soldiers. Every day she fears violence and reprisals. She says she does not have the words to convey the anger she feels about her life, and the life of her family. "Not for one minute here do I forget what's happening in my home," she says. "I can't."

She says that when her plane landed in Boston, the first people she met on the way to Apple Hill were Sarah and a horn player named Shachar Ziv, only days removed from the Israeli army. After an Israeli nightclub was destroyed by a suicide bomber, Shachar wrote a song with these lyrics: "I'm going to sleep now, I'm seeing only what is beautiful." Ranan did not want to look at Sarah or Shacher. She did not want to speak to them. "I know they're not responsible for the trouble," she said, "but their people have taken everything from me." She could not imagine one day sitting beside one of them on a stage.

In Israel, Sarah lives with a tentativeness, a wariness, not knowing when or where a suicide bomber might target next. When a bomb blew apart the cafe where every day she drank her morning coffee, she said, "I shivered for days. When I met Ranan, it was awkward. She was the first person I met at the airport. But you can see in somebody's eyes if they're nice, and she is. Now with Ranan, I see her as a person. I talk to her. There's nothing to fear. What Ranan goes through is not my fault. What I go through is not her fault. I just want peace."

So they share this too: They are young and musical, and they live every day with fear.

Now in this barn on a soft summer day, on a green hillside in East Sullivan, New Hampshire, they will play the third movement of J.S. Bach's *Gamba Sonata in D major.* This is a dance Bach wrote to be played at solemn state occasions—a sad, mournful piece of music, yet somehow meant to be uplifting and spiritual. For three minutes, 20 seconds, they must depend on each other's ears and eyes and sensitivities to play it well and to play it so that everything in the barn stops except for the music.

They live together in a small cabin tucked away on a dirt path. They never speak of the troubles at home. "There's no point in talking about these things," Sarah had said. "We can't change how it is." So they talk about music and tell jokes, and they both know that it is what stays unspoken that allows them to smile as they begin to play. For the next 200 seconds they must be one voice.

"My personal belief is if we could solve these problems by talk, we would." -Eric Stumacher

Eric Stumacher is a large man, as if his body has expanded over the years to allow room for his vision and idealism in the midst of a world grown increasingly dangerous, with hatreds seemingly more potent than ever.

He grew up in a socially conscious home in Pennsylvania. "I was a child of the '60s," he says. "I was taught it's not enough to just pursue dreams, but you want to make the world a better place. I was taught to make a difference."

He studied music at Juilliard and always knew he wanted to use his music to bring harmony to people at war. He came to the farm 31 years ago, and even as the Apple Hill Chamber players received acclaim, there was a larger task in mind. The first Middle Eastern students came 15 years ago, and today Playing for Peace has become known throughout the world.

"Pursuing ideals in a beautiful place makes sense," Eric says. "People interact with people every minute of the day. Walking, hiking, eating, playing music, playing soccer. We place people in cabins so they'd be living with people they think are their enemies. People who would never in a million years sit at the same dining table become close friends. Everyone pulls for everybody, whether they are Israeli or Palestinian. I feel I'm passionately pro on both sides. I say, 'You're both right. Now what do we do?' "

He heard Sarah Cohen, one of Israel's bright young music prodigies, play a few years ago on a kibbutz in Israel. He heard Ranan in a conservatory in Ramallah. "We look for people who play from the heart," Eric says. "It's a direct window into who they are."

He chose the Bach sonata for Ranan and Sarah because he knew Sarah was much more advanced. The slow tempo, he hoped, would help Ranan. When Apple Hill chose Ranan for a scholarship, they sent her music to practice. "I tried to practice," Ranan said, "but I couldn't. My piano was too bad. The piano tuner could not reach my house. He couldn't get through the blockades. When I came to Apple Hill, I had not played for months."

When she arrived at Apple Hill she found a small rehearsal room and stayed there alone, practicing scales. "I didn't want to talk to anybody," Ranan said, "I just wanted to play."

"When Eric told me I'd be playing with Sarah I said no, I cannot do that. I called my father. I said I don't want to do this. 'You care for music,' he said. He told me this was an opportunity for me to play with her. He knew she was good." –Ranan Rishmawi

Sarah has played cello since she was five. Her mother took her to Switzerland to live when she was a child, and she later studied in a German conservatory. She played in Moscow. She became a polished, seasoned performer.

Ranan has had no professional teacher for several years. She no longer knows if what she plays is correct, or if she is simply repeating mistakes. "When I play alone," she said, "I only hear me. Just me. Now I feel I lose all music. I lose my school. When an American or German musician is practicing, I'm in my room, waiting. I feel that." But on this day, a few days before the recital, Sarah and Ranan are holed up in a rehearsal room with Eric, looking for cohesion.

"We're going too fast," Ranan says. "I'm not good now. I cannot follow." Eric tries to buoy her confidence. Earlier, he had told me, "Ranan is struggling. But it's important that she do this." Now he sits beside her at the piano and places a hand on her shoulder.

"Ranan, I want you to feel a smooth, steady beat," he says. "Your ears are open. Your eyes are moving. Don't just play notes. When you make a mistake, don't let that stop you."

Again Ranan and Sarah go through the movement.

"It's beautiful," Eric says. "Beautiful."

"You like it?" Ranan says.

"It's beautiful."

"Me, too," she says.

They play again. Ranan watches Sarah's bow. As soon as her hand finishes, Ranan takes her hand off the piano. "Don't rush," Eric cautions. They play again. Ranan misses a note. Sarah laughs softly, not unkindly. Ranan joins in. They laugh together. Sarah had said earlier that she knows what Ranan is going through. "Ranan is very musical totally. I went through that level, too," she says. "You're just worried about playing the right notes. Playing in front of people. For me as her partner I have to get her to enjoy it. She's working on her technical end, so it confuses her when hearing me. We'll do rehearsals together without Eric just to try out some things. It will give us confidence that nothing can go bad in performance. Now we're a work in progress. We have to open each our ears and play over and over again. When we get it together, it will be one picture."

In the concert barn during the Playing for Peace recital, Eric sits beside Ranan. "I knew she was nervous," he said, "and needed reassurance. Only time I've done that with a performance." The sun streams through a window, lighting Ranan's music. The music is lovely and haunting, and though few in the audience know Ranan's and Sarah's story, they applaud loudly as the two young women touch hands ever so lightly and bow.

When the concert ends, Eric has final words. "This is the real world," he tells everyone. "We must have the courage to take the stage, to be expressive, go with courage."

The next day, Ranan and Sarah leave Apple Hill. They hug one last time. But they are honest. There are no promises to write, to call, to visit. "It won't be possible to see her," says Sarah. "I don't think it will be possible to stay in contact with Ranan."

"It's not her fault," says Ranan. "Sarah is a good person. But I won't see her."

While the war in Iraq raged, I emailed both Sarah and Ranan to see where their lives had gone after Apple Hill. Sarah responded immediately. "At the moment I'm in Switzerland concentrating on my repertoire in quietness and without tension. I believe that for the time being, I can do more for my beloved country abroad than struggling for bread and water. I have not seen Ranan, nor have I talked to her, but I have thought about her a lot. I hope she is fine."

After my four emails to Ranan went unanswered, Apple Hill staff gave me her phone number in Beit Sahour. When I got through, I was first told I had the wrong number, then that there was no one there named Ranan. Finally, in late April, Eric had an email from Ranan. "I'm fine," she wrote. She told Eric she should be finishing her last semester at school in June. "I don't know what I will do after that, but I will tell you if something happens with me."

I remember what Ranan had said one day at Apple Hill as we sat in a gazebo and listened to laughter coming from the barn. "It seems a fantasy. My home and the trouble so far away. But they're not far away. I feel no hope. It's a bad life, worse than bad. I will not marry unless I know what kind of life I can bring my children. My father, he always has hope and he gives me hope."

This September, Sarah will come to New England on a Playing for Peace scholarship to study and play her cello. Her world stretches ahead, a world of achievement and applause. She has earned it through rigorous work and wonderful talent. I wonder if Ranan has played at all since her moving sonata in the barn. It is as if history and fate have snatched her away to a place of silence. I wonder if, for Ranan, the days at Apple Hill are like a dream, that each day becomes more difficult to believe it ever happened.

Published July/August 2003

Playing for Peace continues bringing young musicians together in New Hampshire. Sarah Cohen has performed around the world with chamber ensembles, orchestras, and as a soloist. She lives in Switzerland, where she plays her music and also teaches at music schools. When I contacted Apple Hill asking for assistance in finding Ranan, Sam Bergman, executive director, wrote me, "I've now confirmed that we don't have any contact info for Ranan, and no one here has had contact with her since that summer many years ago as far as we can tell. . . . I hope she's okay, but I don't think we'll have any success in trying to find her." What I found online was an Instagram account with no posts. And a Facebook entry from February 2024. Ranan had posted a photo of a hand on a piano keyboard with "MuNa Khoury Awad: The best, most wonderful and kindest piano teacher."

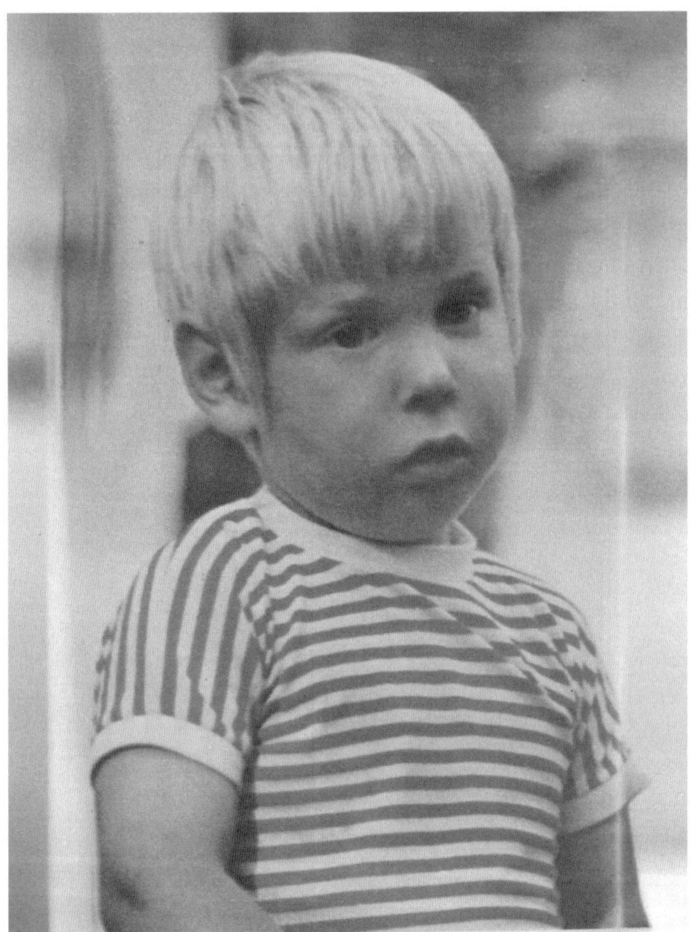

After four-year-old Kurt Newton disappeared from his parents' northern Maine campsite over Labor Day weekend in 1975, the most extensive search in state history failed to turn up a single clue as to what happened. This haunting photo appeared on missing-person posters across the country.

The Day Kurt Newton Disappeared

Even now, four years later, Ron and Jill Newton will sometimes let their minds drift back and silently relive that Labor Day weekend, hour by hour, trying to snatch it all back and hold it still at 10:00 a.m., Sunday, August 31, 1975.

It had been a grand weekend, camping with their children, Kimberly, age six, and Kurt, age four, and three other families from their home in Manchester, Maine. Natanis Point Campground was small and remote, its 58 sites cut from a paper-company forest 1,300 feet above sea level in Chain of Ponds, a wilderness township six miles below the Canadian border at Coburn Gore. Campers fished from two ponds that were deep and cold. When a fisherman landed a salmon from the small wooden bridge below the thread of beach, he would yelp with pleasure and a crowd would gather. Mountains loomed over the ponds, and when at night a loon wailed and the forest pressed close on all sides, you knew you were away.

That Friday the Newtons arrived first. It was their first trip with the recently acquired secondhand tent trailer, what Jill called "our luxury." They gathered wood along an abandoned logging road nearly a mile from their campsite. "It isn't camping without a bonfire," Kurt said happily. On Saturday their friends arrived, and Kimberly raced her bicycle through mud puddles while Kurt furiously pedaled his big-wheel tricycle after her, trying to keep up. It was the end of summer, and there were huge meals and laughter and quiet, chilly nights by a roaring fire. To Jill Newton things felt "just right," which was not unusual.

"We'd been married eight years," she would say later, "and everything just seemed to work right. We got along so well. We had saved for four years to buy a house, and when we were ready, there was our house across the street from the elementary school. From before we were married, we always said we'd have two children and no more. We had a girl and then by a stroke of luck we had a boy, just what we wanted. It became a sort of joke between Ron and me. We'd say, 'How did we get so lucky?' "

Sunday broke with a heavy mist over the ponds. Ron took the bite off the morning, using the last of the wood to light a fire. Kurt slept until nine, fighting off a cold; when he awoke, he shivered. "I'm so glad Daddy built a bonfire," he said. Ron dressed Kurt for the damp, chilly morning: red jersey, navy blue sweatshirt, speckled red-and-black corduroys. Kurt tugged on dark brown shoes over mismatched white socks and topped off his outfit with a favorite navy blue jacket decorated with baseball emblems.

Jill called Kurt "a head-turner," a striking child with an impish sweet face, bright blue eyes, and platinum blond hair. "The loveliest, sweetest towhead kid you ever saw," said a neighbor. Though he was rugged, Jill worried that Kurt was "tied to my apron strings." He was painfully shy and afraid of being alone, even for a few moments. "Sometimes when grocery shopping, I'd walk around the corner and he'd stand there, and I'd come back and find him almost in tears," Jill said. "I could put him outside to play all day and he would never leave. He always made sure I knew where he was."

Kimberly would often spring into the shallow woods behind their house and implore her brother to join her climbing the trees or playing hide-and-seek. As Kurt quivered on the edge of the lawn, she would tease, "Kurt's such a baby." Once Jill asked him why he wouldn't go with Kimberly into the woods. "Momma, there's monsters in there," he answered.

After a hearty camper's breakfast—fried potatoes, ham and eggs, toast, and juice—Kurt put a doughnut on a stick and warmed it over the flames, then threw the paper plates into the fire. Jill gathered the mud-soaked sneakers from the day before and with her friends walked to the bathhouse 50 yards away to wash them. Kim began playing a game and assumed Kurt would ride his tricycle around the campsite. Ron climbed into his Bronco, ax in hand, and drove off to get firewood. This is where their minds halt, confused and troubled, where Ron and Jill Newton try to snatch it all back. For then a friend from her trailer heard a plaintive "Daddy, Daddy," as Kurt apparently ran to his tricycle, a determined little boy trying to catch his father, and pedaled away—into a mystery as deep as the forest that seemed to swallow him without a trace.

From the campground, a rut-strewn logging road runs north, parting the forest, which gives way reluctantly. An abandoned horse hovel sits back from the road, nearly obscured by undergrowth, about a quarter-mile from the Newtons' campsite. Here, 12-year-old Lou Ellen Hanson, returning from a walk, was startled to see the small boy churning past on his tricycle. "Hey," she called out, "do your parents know where you are?" but the boy made no reply as he pedaled on, and she turned toward the campground.

The road continues another quarter-mile, then forks. To the left it leads to a small campground dump on a knoll, past a shaky bridge over a stream. To the right it continues for a mile, then gives way to heavy undergrowth. For the next several miles leading to Route 27, the road is nearly impassable to all but four-wheel-drive vehicles. The road and its "back-door" access to his campground was a source of irritation to campground owner Lloyd Davidson. Fishermen would use it to fish his waters, or to use his showers. He would grumble that if it were his land and not leased from the paper company, he would have bulldozed it long ago. It was on this road, about a half-mile past the fork, where Ron Newton went to chop wood, the sounds of his ax barely audible from the dump.

Jack Hanson, Lou Ellen's father, who served as a volunteer caretaker for the campground, found the tricycle just before the steep rise leading to the dump. It was off the road, at the edge of the woods, a position that reminded a state police investigator "of a little boy who's been told never to leave his things on the road." Thinking it had been discarded, Hanson carried it over the rise and heaved it atop the trash heap, then drove back to the campground.

"We hung the sneakers on the line," Jill Newton recalls. "We'd been gone at the most 10 minutes. We saw no Kurt and no tricycle, so we started walking around asking campers if they'd seen a blond boy on a big-wheel tricycle. I began to think he must have gone with the men to get firewood, but then they rounded the corner and no Kurt. We met Jack, and he told us he had found the trike at the dump. We raced to the dump, and there was Kurt's big-wheeler, but no one in sight, not a sound to be heard.

"'My God, someone's taken him!' were my first words." The men quickly reassured her that Kurt must have thought his father was just a little ways into the woods and had wandered in after him. They would find him in no time. "How could a boy who won't even go into the woods with his sister around his own home go into these incredibly wild woods?" she asked. But it would be only the first of many baffling questions with no answers.

Duane Lewis, Maine Fish and Game warden inspector, was patrolling near his home in Phillips, about 75 miles south of Chain of Ponds, when the call came from the regional game warden that a child was lost. A small search party had already been organized from campers to comb the logging roads. Lewis, at 39, was a veteran warden with 14 years and nearly 75 searches under his belt. No search of which Lewis had been in charge had failed to find a person missing in the woods. Because the missing boy was only four and the temperature was expected to drop into the 20s that night, Lewis called area wardens for assistance even as he sped northward.

A woods search strategy can never be haphazard. Its plotting is an intricate balance between intuition and science. With grown-ups the contour of the land, or the presence of streams, can be weighed against the age and expected endurance of the victim. But a search for a four-year-old changes everything. Usually, the will of a child lost in the woods is fragile, easily broken; he will sit by a tree and cry, and within a few hours searchers will find him. But on rare occasions, a child's stamina outlasts that of an adult. Propelled by an inward trembling, he will outstrip his methodical pursuers, and all bets are off. Duane Lewis was convinced that "it's much harder to plan a search for a small child," but he was equally convinced when he arrived at the scene at 4:00 p.m. that with the 29 searchers already at hand, the boy would be home by nightfall.

Soon a warden service helicopter and a search plane augmented the ground search concentrating on tote roads near the dump. Kurt had always been fascinated with the National Guard helicopters that whirred over his house, and Jill was certain he would respond to the warden's calm voice calling him on the loudspeaker from above the trees. "Kurt, I'm up in the helicopter. Your mommy and daddy are waiting for you, and I want you to follow me back to the camp. Walk toward the helicopter. Don't sit down. Don't be afraid. Just stand up and walk, and I'll take you back." Later, Jill would consider that first day's efforts and say, "Even if he'd somehow gotten out of the prime area, that helicopter would have brought him back."

The temperature dropped to 26 degrees. Jill thought, "How frightened Kurt is. How he must wonder, 'Why doesn't my mommy come get me?' "

Manchester, Maine, heard the news at 7:00 p.m. Ron Newton had grown up beside the firehouse, and neighbors could remember the tall, thin boy racing frantically after the fire truck at the first blast of the whistle, being pulled aboard with his shirttail flying. He had joined the volunteer fire department at 17. He was hometown and had never left, becoming a supervisor for the highway department. Soon streams of cars from Manchester headed north.

Jill had grown up 18 miles away in the small town of Wayne. She had been the only girl in her one-room schoolhouse, and she lived above her father's general store. Everybody knew Jill Lovejoy. When word spread that her little boy was lost, the cars from Wayne joined those from Manchester on Route 27. When they poured into the campground late at night, an eerie sight awaited them: Ron and Jill calling into a loudspeaker at the edge of the woods by the dump, "hoping in the still of the night we'd hear his cry." Wardens probed the darkness, their lantern beams flashing among the trees.

By first light on Labor Day, a bloodhound team scented on Kurt's pajamas. A year earlier the same bloodhounds had been instrumental in tracking a two-year-old girl lost in the New Sharon woods. As the search party, now swelled to nearly 200, waited, the hounds bolted from the dump, ran ten yards, then whirled in confusion, apparently overwhelmed by the conflicting scents from Sunday's heavy search.

The weather steadily worsened, becoming, as one searcher said, "dark, dank, and miserable, with the fog settling in and everybody soaking wet and chilled to the bone." The searchers began to realize the enormity of their task. The woods were filled with holes, "some bigger than a man," as Duane Lewis said, and piles of rocks and boulders covered with moss, and enormous root cavities. Years of windstorms had taken their toll. Briars scratched at the searchers' faces as they crawled through the blow-down looking in vain for a small boy's footprints, or bits of clothing torn as he stumbled past. Holes under boulders were tediously checked, then rechecked by other searchers, each check indicated by a marking slash, until the forest was pocked with their grim graffiti. The search grew into what officials described as "the most intensive woods search in the history of Maine."

Nothing grips the hearts and minds of people as does the specter of a lost child wandering helplessly in a woods, waiting for rescue. Radio and television appeals touched Mainers from all walks of life. Buses brought workers from paper mills and factories from throughout northern and central Maine. College students, crusty woodsmen, and an elite six-man mountain rescue unit joined together at Natanis Pond. Cars lined Route 27 for more than a mile, the feet of bone-weary volunteers poking through the half-opened windows. To feed the searchers, who one day numbered 1,500, women from the Kingfield-Stratton area solicited food from their neighbors to stock their civil defense kitchens, until soon donations poured in from across the state.

The Newtons were determined that nothing would be left to chance. When Jill learned from a searcher that a top-secret plane had been used in Vietnam to find guerrillas in dense jungle, she ran to the wardens. "I don't care what it costs or how it works," she said. "I just want it to tell me where my son is." And late Monday night the $10 million C-130H gunship lifted off from Eglin Air Force Base in Pensacola, Florida, with her nine-man crew, the first time it would be used in a civilian search. The plane was equipped with infrared sensors and low-light television-sensor equipment for nighttime use, equipment so sensitive it could detect the heat differential between a white median strip and the blacktop road at ten thousand feet.

Jill was "wildly excited" when she heard the plane was on its way. But Ron, who was "very protective about letting me get my hopes up," cautioned, "It's just a machine, don't put too much on it."

Even veteran woodsmen were in awe of Ron Newton's quiet endurance as days and nights passed with him refusing to rest. "The responsibility was ours," he'd say quietly. "The burden is ours to get him back." On Monday, returning wearily from the woods at dusk, Ron tripped and fell heavily in a deep gully. His ankle turned bright purple and swelled to twice its size. Though ordered off his feet by a doctor, he continued to end a day's woods search at his familiar post in front of the loudspeaker, calling his son's name into the forest. In desperation, friends laced his coffee with tranquilizers. Wednesday night, his fourth night without sleep, the drugs finally took effect. His speech slowed and he sat gripping the loudspeaker close to his mouth, unable to speak, until finally his head dropped as he gave in to his shattering fatigue. "He was the toughest man I've ever seen," said Duane Lewis. "Just unbelievable stamina."

The C-130H gunship flew a three-hour mission Tuesday morning, failing to detect a trace of Kurt. The plane was hampered by low-hanging clouds and heavy rains that grew so bad searchers could not see their way in the woods and had to be pulled out. Hovering over the search area in the helicopter, Jill would call, "This is Momma. I want you to go to where you can see the sky. Come and wave to Momma." As the rain and fog continued into the fourth day, hopes dimmed that Kurt could be found alive, and the strain on Jill was growing unbearable.

"If someone had asked me beforehand how I would have acted," she would say later, "I would have said I'd go to pieces. But something happens to keep you going. You find reserves you didn't know you had. I kept telling myself it wasn't going to do Kurt any good if I wasn't able to function. It seemed that every time I turned around, the wardens were pulling Ron out of the woods because I was upset. Finally I said, 'Look, I'll tell you if I need him. But I'm going to cry. There's no way I'm not.' "

She preferred to search on her own with a few friends, "going on gut instincts. I kept thinking I'd find him whimpering behind the next tree." One day she found some holes by the horse hovel that bothered her, one in particular large enough for a child to have crawled through and way down under. Lacking a flashlight, she began clawing at the ground, desperately trying to see in. Looking up, she saw a group of National Guardsmen recently activated to search. " 'I've got to have help,' I said, and three or four of them started digging. I was panicky by then, saying, 'Oh, please, God, he's got to be in there.' And I looked down and this guy crawls out from the hole and he says, 'There's nothing there,' and I said, 'He's got to be,' and he said no and tears rolled down his face."

As days passed and absolutely no trace of Kurt was found, a sense of unreality flooded Jill. "It seemed it was someone else's child, not mine. Not our Kurt," she said. At night, "the worst time," she'd rest fitfully, listening to strangers bellowing her son's name into the dark, and the thoughts crowded in. "If he panicked, if he heard a noise, if anything the noise would have kept him out of the woods . . . even if he ran into the woods why haven't we found tracks . . . he'd surely have taken off his jacket that first day when it warmed up . . ." and, as always, the questions kept turning because there were no answers. At night she faced terrible thoughts—"How does a four-year-old face starvation?" but in the morning searchers were buoyed by her dauntless optimism.

"You walk beside people you've never seen before, and they're poking and searching, hunting, and calling his name," she said. "With all this drive and all these volunteers, we're going to find him. And even though he's four, he's very sure-footed. I know he's scared, but I'm still optimistic we'll find him safe." Ron quietly vowed, "I won't give up until they find him."

On the fifth day of the search, the governor of Maine, James Longley, flew to the scene. He promised the Newtons, "Anything in my power I'll do." He called the search, which had moved into the extraordinary stage of a shoulder-to-shoulder combing of more than 2,000 acres, "the most impressive experience I've ever had."

The C-130H aircraft returned and flew another mission, again failing to detect a trace of the lost child. The bloodhounds tried vainly to pick up scent pools, places where Kurt might have lingered, and which under some conditions may last for 10 days. The woods search grew so intensive that although Ron Newton twice lost his pen in terrain called by Warden Supervisor John Shaw "the roughest I've searched in 19 years," it was twice returned.

Psychics from throughout New England offered their help. Later, in frustration, Duane Lewis would say, "One says east, one says north, and another tells us west or south. There's only so many points on the compass." The horse hovel was dismantled, as was the ice house next to the camping office. The dump was bulldozed, and workers sifted through clumps of dirt. Teams of volunteers with shovels dug along the tote road. Finally John Shaw and Duane Lewis, haggard from constant 22-hour days, announced they were no longer appealing for volunteers. The search would continue, they said, until Wednesday, September 10, 13 days after Kurt Newton's disappearance. "We've done just about everything we can think of," they said. "Everywhere you go, there's marking tape and our footprints."

The day the search was to end, the governor extended it two more days. "It's the perplexity of the situation," he said. "When you've searched that long and hard, there's always the hope that this time we're going to hit it." It ended officially at dusk on Friday, September 12, in the woods by the dump, with 12 wardens, six state troopers, and 75 volunteers making a final, mournful shoulder-to-shoulder sweep. At the end, over 3,000 searchers had taken part, and absolutely nothing had been found.

Ron and Jill Newton stayed two more weeks before returning to Manchester to put Kimberly, who had stayed with friends, into the first grade. They began weekend journeys to Chain of Ponds, two people in a woods that might as well have stretched forever. Duane Lewis returned as well, a solitary figure on overgrown tote roads that he hoped might still yield the most elusive tracks of his career. Years later he would be unable to spot a sneaker thrown carelessly on a river bank, or a torn shirt discarded on a roadside, without thinking about Kurt Newton. "Every now and then in the history of mankind the incredible happens that we can't make sense of," he would say. "We should have found him—but we didn't."

The Newtons posted "Missing" signs deep into the woods, warning hunters to report any unusual signs. And then the snow came, and Ron had his snowmobile to take him deeper into the backcountry until winter grew raw and even he was forced to say *enough*. By then they had decided that Kurt was not in the woods, that he never had been, that somehow he'd been taken and probably was still safe. With the tenacity they had shown from the beginning, Ron and Jill determined that if Kurt were to be found, it was up to them.

"From the beginning we never discounted the possibility that Kurt was abducted," said State Police Lieutenant G. Paul Falconer, who headed the initial investigation, adding, "but there are no facts to indicate he's not in the woods." A team of investigators interviewed everyone known to have been at the campground, using polygraphs when in doubt. One camper reported that she had seen a white station wagon roar out of the campground leaving a cloud of dust in its wake shortly after the time Kurt disappeared. But no such car was registered at the campground, and nobody else reported seeing it. Upon further questioning the camper hedged: perhaps she'd been mistaken.

Experienced trackers reported they could find no evidence of recent vehicle traffic on the logging road beyond where Ron Newton had been cutting wood, the only road available for a "back-door" abduction. "With so many children available in the cities, why would a kidnapper come to one of the most remote campgrounds in the state, hoping to find a child riding a tricycle alone down a deserted road," asked State Police Detective Richard Cook, who assumed charge of the investigation, and who heads it today.

There was a grim report that a captive bear, often teased by local children, might have been released a few miles from the campground shortly before Kurt disappeared. A bear could have carried Kurt swiftly outside the area, experts conceded, but it was highly improbable that there would be a complete absence of signs.

The police sent teletype descriptions of Kurt throughout the United States and Canada. Soon Kurt Newton stared hauntingly from post-office walls in hundreds of cities. A call came from a man in Connecticut. He had returned from camping in the Canadian Rockies. There he had noticed a small blond-haired boy staring at him with a quizzical expression. He said he was struck by how nervous the boy and the man with him seemed with each other. He saw the same boy, he said fervently, on a Kurt Newton "Missing" poster. That same week a call came from Vermont. Two waitresses were sure they had seen Kurt in their restaurant. Detective Cook drove to Vermont and found that boy. It wasn't Kurt.

There was an electrifying day four months after Kurt was lost. A call came from New Orleans that a small blond-haired boy of perhaps three or four had been found wandering in the French Quarter. He was very shy. He responded only to names with a k sound, like Kenny or Kurt. The Newtons raced to Boston to view a videotape of the child. But even as they watched it, certain he wasn't their Kurt, the boy was identified as the abandoned son of an itinerant Missouri woman who was hitchhiking out west, and his name was Clifford.

Jill would wake up and admonish herself, "You're being ridiculous. You've got to make up your mind. Either he's in the woods or he's with someone." She went to Laconia, New Hampshire, for an interview with famed psychic

Jeane Dixon. Dixon told Jill she knew about Kurt's disappearance and had been meditating on it.

Jill said, "I told her the police felt very strongly he was in the woods. I was trying very hard for her not to tell me what I wanted to hear. She said, 'No, I feel your son is alive.' I said it was unbelievable to me that in 10 minutes on a deserted road, anyone would have had the time or the inclination to take him. She asked me if I had other children. I said, 'Yes, a six-year-old daughter.' She paused, then said, 'No, I'm picking up your son's vibrations. But he's going to have to be missing you a great deal for me to pick up a direction. And it's very easy to appease a four-year-old.'"

It became Jill's singular determination to "get Kurt's picture to everyone in the United States and Canada." At first the Newtons went "door-to-door, like traveling salesmen," driving to Quebec City and stopping at every gas station and store to pass out posters. That experience exhausted them, and they returned convinced they must mount an unprecedented mailing campaign of mind-boggling proportions.

With help from friends in the printing trades, their basement soon overflowed with more than 75,000 posters stacked into every conceivable space. They sent for telephone books from major metropolitan areas in the United States and Canada. Every night friends gathered, 20 and 30 strong, in the firehouse to confront a mountain of Yellow Pages. Ron bought stamped envelopes by the thousands. "Our home resembled a paper factory," Jill said. Pictures of Kurt left the tiny Manchester post office for department stores and restaurants thousands of miles away.

Jill was troubled by the memory of her own response to such posters when she was a girl. "I'd see the pictures of wanted criminals and I'd say to myself, 'Today I'll see him for sure,' and then I'd forget what they looked like. No matter how much you stick a child's picture in front of people," she fretted, "they can't remember."

Eventually, the Newtons considered the fact that soon Kurt would be school age and somewhere he had to go to school. After six months of nightly correspondence, they had compiled a list of every superintendent in every school district in the United States. "I couldn't believe how many schools there are," Ron said. Tables were set up in the firehouse, and again friends pitched in. They worked state by state, sending a letter asking that the picture be posted for two years, and including five posters to the superintendents. It took six months of nightly gatherings to finish, and then they began anew with Canada. Two years after Kurt pedaled away, their incredible campaign was over. They had spent well over $5,000 on mailing costs alone; by the end only a stack of 1,000 posters remained in their basement. "When the last envelope went, we had the feeling we'd done everything we could," Ron said. "Then all we could do was wait."

Letters came back from everywhere, filled with sympathy and prayers, and many enclosed photographs of children in local schools. "We got some awful close resemblances back," Ron said, and police in far distant places checked them out. Time passed, and the Newtons realized that soon a picture of Kurt at four would mean little to a teacher meeting him at six or seven. "Sometimes I think, if Kurt walked by me, would I know him?" admitted Jill. "It's a weird, panicky feeling." They were left with the hope that Kurt would tell a teacher that he used to live in Maine and he used to have a sister named Kimberly and that one day he was taken away.

Four years after Kurt's disappearance, a visitor to the Newtons would be struck by how normally they are living with this most abnormal of burdens. Jill has opened a beauty shop downstairs in their home, and has a growing number of customers. Ron works 14-hour days for the highway department and on weekends putters around in his shop, planning improvements to their home. Kimberly is a bright, winsome girl of 10, who swings from the weeping willow in the yard, loves baseball, and complains that her mother doesn't allow her to ride her bicycle in the street like her friends do. "Ron's constantly telling me I've got to let her do more," Jill said.

There are changes, of course. They have sold their tent trailer and no longer go camping. There is laughter in the house, and there was a trip to Disneyland, but Kurt is always on the edge of things. "Kurt's name is always around our household," Jill says. "We say things like, 'Kurt had a pair of pants like that,' or 'Wouldn't Kurt have liked that.' A boy moved next door after Kurt was lost, and he kept asking Kimberly, 'Well, who is this Kurt? And where is he?'

"People who don't know me say how many children do I have, and I say two, a ten-year-old and an eight-year-old, and I don't think about it because I will go on expecting that someday he'll walk through that door, even at 50 years old—until somebody proves to me that I'm wrong. I think your mind has to rest. Now we can take a big gulp and say, 'Okay now we're going to forget about it for a while and have a good time.' It's never, ever forgotten, really. I know it's there, and I know I'll come back to it, but I've learned to glide around it. To keep on going."

On Sundays there are picnics outside, or at the lakeside cabin two miles from their home. "We were extremely close before," Jill says, "and we're closer now. Ron was quiet before, and he's quieter now. It's still hard for the two of us to talk about it a lot. It's like we're careful not to rile too much up. We've accepted and are coping with the way things are. But isn't it incredible that after all that's happened during these four years, we don't know any more than we did when we first missed him?"

They speak about plans to convince the president to establish an agency to help parents whose children are missing. They think their experiences in distributing Kurt's picture would be invaluable to anyone in a similar dilemma. And they still seek ideas. "If anyone can come up with anything and give me an address of how I can do it, that's what I want."

After spending a weekend with Ron and Jill and Kimberly, two images remain, as bright as Kurt's blue eyes that seem to burn from his pictures. It is a Saturday night, and Kimberly is sitting cross-legged on the old brown sofa in their lakeside camp. She is dressed in a pink bunny suit, and her lovely brown hair is brushed down her back. It is late and the light in the cabin is dim and she is sleepy, but she wants to finish reading her book. The name of the book is *Donn Fendler, Lost on a Mountain in Maine,* the dramatic true story of the 12-year-old scout from Rye, New York, who, against great odds, survived a nine-day trek to safety from mist-shrouded Baxter Peak. "I wonder if that's how it was for Kurt," she says softly, and when she is finished, the happy ending tucked in her mind, she is ready to sleep.

On Sunday the table is set outside the Newtons' home for a traditional Sunday dinner of roast pork and potatoes. It is sunny and a wind is blowing; there is debate whether to eat indoors or out. Their garden is planted and staked out, and Jill sits in the warm grass of late spring. "I really enjoy watching things grow," she says. "But I'm so impatient waiting for the produce." Across the yard Kimberly is laughing as she sails on her rope swing. Ron, who is camera shy, is finding things to do to keep from being photographed.

"You know," Jill says, "in a way I feel fortunate. I have a prayer. And I have tomorrow. And tomorrow may bring Kurt."

Published September 1979

I met Ron and Jill Newton when I first wrote about the search for Kurt while I was a freelance writer for the Maine Sunday Telegram. *Though we were close in age, in our early 30s, I had no children. I sometimes wonder if I could have written about their heartbreaking search for their son if I had been a dad at the time. It was during my first story on them that I told them I had once taught fourth grade, and if every teacher in the United States could see his picture, maybe one would see him in their class. And they were undaunted in their quest to do just that. Shortly after my story in* Yankee *appeared, I received a call from a doctor's office in Georgia. A nurse said a couple had just left with a little boy who closely resembled Kurt's picture. They seemed to have no knowledge of his health records. I contacted Maine State Police, but the couple apparently was never found. When* Yankee *posted this story on its website in 2018, reader comments came from people who had helped serve meals to the searchers along with those whose fathers had been game wardens on the search who still felt the anguish of not being able to return Kurt to his family.*

FOUR

HERE IN NEW ENGLAND

Everyone who lives in New England knows this region in their own way. For some, New England may be Boston, Providence, Hartford, Portland. For others, it may be the northern towns that tuck along the Canadian border, or the ports where fishing boats leave the harbor before dawn.

New Englanders fly from international airports, and they also fly on the small planes that are the lifeblood of islands miles out to sea. They walk the ivy campuses of Harvard, Yale, Brown; they go to schools that struggle to stay open. In the public eye, New England can seem to be one of the least diverse places in the country. In Lewiston and Portland, Maine, more than 40 languages can be heard today in the school hallways.

When I give talks, I often ask attendees what New England means to them. They say changing seasons, miles of ocean, farms, history, lakes, forests, valleys, orchards, sun-soaked Fenway Park. When Emily Dickinson writes, "I think New Englandy," no matter where we live in these six states, we know what she means.

I feel "New Englandy" the most when I am home, watching my wife in the garden while I tend to the wood. When I first moved to Maine in 1970, my wood came in eight-foot lengths, $25 a cord. I was young and reading We Took to the Woods *by Louise Dickinson Rich, so splitting cords of wood with saw, ax, and maul made me feel kinship with the hardy souls* *who were here before me. Now my wood arrives cut and split, and our task is to stack and carry and burn.*

My woodpile stretches across the back of the yard, at least 50 feet. I have dry wood from last winter piled in the woodshed and on the driveway, a stack just shy of a cord gets the morning sun. My wood weathers by the week, cracks appearing as it dries, nature's art as time slowly ages the once-blond maple and oak; by winter it will be brown. The woodpile tells a story from the future: months from now it will burn bright in our stove as the night presses down.

We live along a river. Geese stop by through the summer and fall, and we see the goslings grow up. A moose wandered into the yard once, and heron fly above the current, and one day I watched a deer with three legs make its way slowly along the bed. There are rocks in the river, and the deer, with its missing hind leg, stumbled along, but when it reached an embankment, it scrambled up and soon left my sight.

I am rooted to this house by the river, but because the region is so compact, within a few hours' drive, I can be talking to Lela Anderson about her life as a sardine packer ("It Takes a Woman with a Strong Back"), or Joe Lentini, who knows as much about mountain rescues as anybody alive ("A World Apart"), or any of the people and places that you meet in the pages that follow.

I think this feeling of "New Englandy" is what Jud Hale ("Yankee's Yankee") understood was his magazine's most powerful connection with readers, just as Edie Clark made her life on a country road in an old farmhouse touch thousands ("Leaving Mary's Farm"). All of us can feel heartened when we watch a three-legged deer climb out of a river; all of us can see what Edie Clark sees from her window where she writes about the wind blowing and leaves flying like sparrows. We can all feel the sorrow of leaving a home we cherish.

Here in New England we live so close together, we share the weather, the food, the past, the future. I can talk wood and geese with whomever I am with.

When the Red Gods Call

We did not always know fall as the time when we chased the color, as if it were an elusive animal that we could somehow corral. Our grandparents knew a time when the leaves turned color without fanfare, a process as natural as the wind, the southward flight of birds, and the gathering cold. The beauty of our autumn filled the towns and villages then no less than today, but we stayed put, tending to the life in front of us.

Arthur Tauck, Sr., was the first person we know of who envisioned the commercial possibilities in chasing the fall colors. He had invented the aluminum coin tray for use in banks, and he crisscrossed the region selling the trays. He had an eye for beauty and an entrepreneurial spirit. On a fall day in 1925, he loaded his seven-passenger Studebaker with customers who paid $69 and embarked on a journey along the Mohawk Trail; he had made arrangements for overnight lodging and meals. He carried on lively conversation with his passengers, telling them the history (as well as legends) of the places they were seeing. Word of mouth brought new passengers, new trips. The guided-tour industry was born.

A decade later, Kodak introduced color film, and yearly improvements brought color photography into the hands of more people. By 1970 Americans had purchased more than 50 million Instamatic cameras. Nothing brought out the hunger to capture beauty on film like a New England autumn—the time when, as *Yankee* writer Ben Rice wrote more than 50 years ago, "the red gods call."

Now fall arrives full of hype and hope, a singular New England sport, an intricate guessing game filled with leaf "scouts," charts, schedules, and statistics from past seasons. Our New England states compete for the right to claim "best viewing." We argue about the glories of past years. "You should have been here in 1997" is a common refrain. "That was the best color I've ever seen." The fall of 1999, once expected to be the runt of the litter following a long summer drought, surprised everyone with its comeback.

New England is an understated region. We have no special festive weeks, no Mardi Gras, no Kentucky Derby. What we do have to set us apart has always been with us—fall. The color marching up the hillsides, the morning snap of cold that gives way to warm afternoon sun, the startling sight of leaves blowing across our path, giving bounce to our step. Feeling so alive, we enjoy spending money: hundreds of millions of dollars flow into our states in a few short autumn weeks. Our towns and villages have long prepared for the tourists. The inns are fully staffed. We hold harvest suppers and crafts fairs, pumpkin festivals and classic-car shows. Apple orchards, where we once came simply to pick fruit, have become family entertainment centers—a carnival of mazes, hayrides, and hot doughnuts fresh from the deep fryer. If summer days are carefree, autumn is when we feel most alive.

Many visitors are lured here because there is genius behind the marketing of our fall colors. To not be here, say the tourism campaigns, is to miss out on something rare and special. Every Columbus Day weekend, typically the season's final hurrah of peak color, more than half a million visitors squeeze into New Hampshire. Locals call them "stall-and-crawl" leaf-peepers. But we feel pride that so many people want to see what we live with every day.

Yes, fall foliage is hyped. But know this: all the hype is valid. There are hundreds of white-sand tropical beaches in the world, hundreds of ski mountains, many great cities. But nowhere on Earth can you duplicate the duration and the intensity of color we see in New England. We know the season is fleeting, we sense that urgency, our hearts race a bit faster driving northward into the color. Be there, our hearts say, or it will be gone. It is our most intimate love affair with nature, a few weeks each year when we can do nothing but admire what the sun and soil and cold offer to us. All of our technology cannot alter nature's way with our leaves, and we love it all the more because of that. You never know exactly what you will see. Each tree, each bend in the road, each pond, each meadow—each brings the possibility of something new.

It is the time when we really notice what's around us. When people ask me the secret to enjoying these weeks, my reply is simply *notice*. Pay attention. If one tree lacks fire-engine red—the prima donna of our colors—notice the variations of color: the russets, the pale purples, the soft yellows, the tinges of green. The magic of a New England fall lies in the shadings, all the colors in between the exuberant scarlets.

I write this in late October. The full foliage season in the North Country is gone. The vacancy signs have returned outside the inns. When I drive my sons to school in the early morning, I see more bare branches than I do trees with color. But there, in the heart of town, on the lawn of a bank, stands a sugar maple—with barely a leaf missing. It may be the most beautiful tree I have seen this year. Tomorrow it may be different, and I know that soon the leaves will lie in thick mats around its trunk; the gray threat of winter cannot be stopped by this single sugar maple in town. But as long as that single tree holds on, then I will, too. If you're chasing after peak color, I'd say, come today. It's all here, on this one tree by the bank in the center of town.

Published in Yankee's *special edition "Seasons," 2003*

In fall we say the foliage explodes, erupts, pops, bursts, blazes—and sometimes it is hyperbole, but every autumn there is that week, sometimes two, when it is not. I think of a drive my wife and I took during the first autumn of the pandemic. It was late September. We drove west on Route 101 through Dublin, past the Yankee *offices, past lake and mountain, and after a few curves we came to a pull-off by a reservoir. Outside a car with New York plates stood a woman holding a small child; from across the road her husband bounded over, camera in hand. "It's spectacular," he said. I told him it was early because of the dryness, and that usually it doesn't look like this until Columbus Day weekend. He shook his head in amazement. "It's spectacular," he said again.*

Yankee's Yankee

When your world narrows—as it did for me in late March 2020, when many of us retreated to our homes—then narrows even more with each passing week, you think about people you once saw nearly every day who now might as well live in another country. And in a sense they do. Which is why yesterday I phoned Jud Hale, *Yankee*'s longtime former editor, under whose watch the magazine became an icon of New England. When I asked how he was, he said he was okay. "I'm not supposed to," he said, "but I've been sneaking out to go to the post office."

Jud lives in a retirement community only two miles away, with his wife, Sally, in a pretty cottage set amid woods and by a river. He is stepping gingerly into his later 80s now, and the past few years have forced him to shed some of the most important fixtures in his life: the island home on Lake Winnipesaukee, where his three sons and later his grandchildren felt a summer day had no end; his home in Dublin, where he wrote in a tower room; his "House for Sale" column, which he penned longhand as "The Moseyer" for decades; his long succession of golden retrievers, various mutts, and finally Murphy, a long-haired dachshund, whom Jud carried with him on journeys until Murphy, grown deaf and blind, could not hang on any longer.

Before the pandemic sent us all home, Jud still came to the office nearly every day. In winter, the parking lot can get dicey, no matter how urgently it is plowed and salted. For several years we have urged Jud to park in a reserved spot by the front door. The more we asked, the more he dug in and refused, deliberately, it seemed, choosing to park as far away as possible. He once spent three years as a tank commander in Germany, and whatever residue remained from those days roared back at our efforts to tell him that we worried.

He'd arrive around 10:30, give or take a half hour, chat for a few minutes with Linda, our receptionist who has been with *Yankee* for more than 50 years, before climbing the stairs to his second-floor office, clutching his wicker basket that held a *Boston Globe,* a mug of coffee, and pieces of mail. We could hear him walking down the hall as he called out to each person in their office: "Hi, Janice . . . hi, Tim . . . hi, Ian . . . hi, Heather . . . hi, Joe. . . ." If the New England Patriots had played the day before, he would linger outside the office of Joe Bills, a former sportswriter, and deconstruct the game. Which was notable, since Jud cared so much about the team he could rarely bring himself to watch. He'd then sit at his desk, drink the coffee, read the newspaper, open his mail, and make a few phone calls, his voice booming down the hall.

After an hour or two, he'd walk back down the hall, basket empty, down the stairs, and out the door. To an outside observer, he had achieved little. To those of us in the office, he had shown us how what we do stuck to him like a burr, how the meaning of this work remained, and he just wanted to be part of us, even on days of ice when we looked out the windows as he made his way across the pavement.

He attended our Thursday morning editorial meetings, and we began each one with what I called "Jud's Three," during which he would read or talk for three minutes about some quirky or historical New England tradition or tale. He has been with *Yankee* since 1958, when he joined his Uncle Robb's magazine as a do-everything assistant editor, and he had a lifetime of anecdotes to pass down. He was—and remains—a storyteller. He wrote three books, and his best, *The Education of a Yankee,* makes clear where the stories began.

Though born to Boston wealth, his parents moved the family to the wilderness village of Vanceboro, Maine, on the edge of the Canadian border, where they lived on 12,000 acres of both farm and timberland. His father employed every logger for miles around, and his mother started a

Waldorf school based on the teachings of Rudolf Steiner. "When I dream, I always dream of Vanceboro," Jud once said to an interviewer.

He always told his writers that storytelling mattered above all else, that we had to make readers *feel.* Make them laugh, or cry, or be amazed, but they could never be bored, and if they felt emotion, they would want more. You wanted to write for Jud the best story you had in you, because he believed you would.

I would not be writing this letter if it were not for Jud. When I met him in 1977, he had taken over the reins of both *Yankee* and *The Old Farmer's Almanac* a decade earlier. John Pierce, the new managing editor of *Yankee,* brought me to Jud's office after softening him up a bit by saying that he had read stories I had been writing for Maine newspapers and that Jud should get to know me.

Few people enter Jud's office without getting a tour of what he calls "Jud's Museum," and so before I talked story ideas, I was brought into a small world that is best described as something akin to one of those strange roadside collectible places, except this curator was a tall, blond-haired man, educated at Choate and Dartmouth, who took delight in setting a banana peel on a shelf to see how long it would take before it dissolved.

He showed me a safety pin from the first flight over the North Pole, and a piece of cloth from Lindbergh's *Spirit of St. Louis,* pebbles from Red Square, a photo of Red Sox legend Ted Williams, and a letter rescued from the *Titanic.* Over the years, I never learned of anything that was removed from the museum, just more "treasures" he wanted us to know about: seats from Fenway Park that were removed during renovations, and a humble jar labeled "Einstein's Brain."

When Jud read that the doctor who had performed Einstein's autopsy had kept the brain to study, he wrote asking if he could have it in his museum. He added he would respect it and care for it. The doctor wrote back. He had promised Einstein's family it would not go on display. Jud wrote once more: He would keep it out of sight in a drawer. The doctor never answered. Undaunted, Jud created "what his brain would have looked like," as he'd tell everyone who looked at the jar in wonder. In time it became hard to know whether the museum reflected Jud's idiosyncratic tendencies, or whether in his efforts to keep himself entertained by all that surrounded him, he became its most original artifact of all.

That day when I met Jud, I came with a list of 28 story ideas. He said he wanted 25 of them. He said that had never happened before. He and John Pierce assigned me a story each month, $600 apiece. To make my life easier, they gave me a contract so a check would arrive early each month. To a freelancer, this was like finding a hidden door.

A year later, my dad, who had retired to Florida, discovered that the back pain he had complained about after taking up golf for the first time was lung cancer. The more time I spent seeing my dad, the more I fell behind to keep up with the monthly stories. John and Jud then told me they had retroactively changed my story fee to $800, so I was caught up. There are gestures one does not forget.

A few months before my father died, Jud asked me to join *Yankee* full-time. I told my father as he lay on his bed, his eyes glazed by pain-killers. The lessons of the Depression had burned into him, and he had long fretted that my freelance life was a precarious way to live.

"I'm going to *Yankee* full-time," I told him.

"Benefits?" he asked.

"Yes," I said. He smiled, one of the last I can remember, said, "Good," and then he closed his eyes and slept.

It is easy to look back on my years with Jud and to play the game of where I would be if he had not wanted so many of my stories; if he had lost patience with a young writer who could not fulfill the deal he made. Sometimes I give a talk to some group that wants to know about *Yankee*. I like to warm up by saying, "This is a story I heard from Jud Hale."

He and his wife, Sally, were somewhere around Tamworth, New Hampshire. Sally had an upset stomach. At a general store Jud stopped to get her some Tums. As he entered the store, he noticed an old fellow sitting quietly in a chair next to the door. Jud walked up to the counter and asked the proprietor for Tums.

"I'd like the cherry flavor, please," Jud said.

"We don't have the cherry-flavored Tums," the man replied.

"Well, do you have the orange flavor?"

"No, we don't," said the man.

"Well, then," Jud said, a little exasperated, "I'll just take the plain Tums."

After paying for it, he was walking out the door when the old fellow in the chair looked up at him as he was passing by and said . . .

"Looks like you're gonna have to rough it."

The audience always laughs, and I bask in Jud's light for a while. We are all roughing it now, and we don't know when life will smooth out. But it will, and when it does, I'm going to ask Jud to make it five, not three minutes, and to make us laugh, maybe cry, to remember the power of a good story to pick us up no matter how often we fall.

Published in the June 18, 2020, edition of "Letter from Dublin," a regular column I wrote for Yankee's *website during the pandemic. Jud Hale is now in his 90s. He still cares passionately about Boston sports teams, and we still talk about* Yankee *stories.*

The Perfect Lobster

"Our notes about Nunan's Lobster Hut are written on butter-stained paper towels. Just as you save the ticket stubs from a great play or a petal from a sentimental corsage, you want to keep something of Nunan's. . . ."

– from Jane and Michael Stern's Roadfood, A Guide to the Best Down-Home Cooking in America *(1978)*

From the weekend before Memorial Day until the last weekend in September, Bertha Nunan, perhaps America's most famous lobster cook, begins her days at dawn in the tiny fishing village of Cape Porpoise, Maine, not with crustacean but with crust.

This is when she begins the first of her 25 daily pies. In the corner of her house she calls "my pie shack," she bakes apple, blueberry, and chocolate cream pies. She has started her summer days like this since 1956. Sometimes she wonders "what all my pies would look like stacked together."

When the pies are removed from the oven and set to cool, she starts work on her brownies. And when the brownies are cool, it is time to think of the evening ahead, when the pastries, along with their maker, will go to Nunan's Lobster Hut, a nondescript clapboard building sandwiched between Route 9 and a salt marsh in Cape Porpoise.

The kitchen is small, filled with the sweet fog of lobsters and clams steaming in blue enamel pots. A tank is filled with local lobsters, many caught by Bertha's 19-year-old son, Richard, who begins his days, as his father and his grandfather once did, hauling traps from the icy waters offshore.

From this humble setting emerged one of only three four-star ratings awarded by traveling gourmets Jane and Michael Stern to restaurants in New England. To the regulars who forsake the fancy lobster houses in the Kennebunkport environs for the hard wooden booths of Nunan's, the recognition came as a mixed blessing. It's never been easy to get into Nunan's in summer. Now they had to compete with the entire country.

In a good year (and the definition of a "good year" in the lobstering industry is revised downward each year) Maine lobstermen will sell some 20 million pounds of lobsters. Only a tiny fraction of those will be cooked the way lobstering families have cooked lobsters for generations. It is the way Bertha Nunan learned from her father-in-law, Captain George Nunan, the way she cooks lobster today.

"When people ask me what I do," Bertha says, "I tell them. Then they look at me and say, 'But we don't cook them that way.' And I think, 'Well, they will now, I bet.'

"The secret to cooking lobsters is not to murder them. Give them a nice, slow, respectable way out. Don't drown them in too much water. Boiling them in a lot of water just boils their flavor out and too much water waterlogs them. I put in two inches of water. Whether I'm cooking two lobsters or 14, I take a salt container and with the spout open I pour it three times around the pot, then, plop! at the end [about three teaspoons]. When the water is boiling, put in the lobsters, put the lid on, and steam them for 20 minutes. Not a minute less or a minute more. That's how Grandfather [Captain George Nunan]showed me and I've done it that way ever since.

"When they're done," she adds, "draw up your butter and serve the lobster with a dish of vinegar as well. Now the next step is what a lot of people, and practically all restaurants, ignore. It's why people tell me our lobsters taste the best of any they ever had. I always wash the pot after cooking each lobster. Lobsters are scavengers and they can get pretty greasy from the bait. Look in the pot the next time you cook them and you'll see a sediment from the shell. So I always put in fresh salted water for every batch of lobsters."

Cooked lobsters are placed on trays next to a bag of potato chips and a hard roll and butter. "We're not frilly," says Bertha without apology. There are few frills inside the eating area either. Heat is provided on cool summer evenings by ancient gas space heaters. There are several sinks along the walls with a roll of paper towel for butter-smeared hands. The refrigerator filled with cold drinks and beer sits in the open, and newspaper stuffed into a crack above a wooden ledge is dated June 13, 1973.

But no matter. The spartan atmosphere inside reinforces the impression, felt immediately upon entering, that dry land has been left behind at the door; inside the Hut you are afloat in the seafaring legacy of generations of Nunans. The wooden lobster buoys dangling from the ceiling are emblazoned with a slash of crimson against white—the Nunan trademark for three generations of lobstermen. Strong, thick netting from the days when Nunan men gillnetted off the Grand Banks is stapled to a wall, and faded photographs of sturdy men in fishing togs line the walls as though the restaurant has become their public album.

The painting of the *Sadie Nunan* draws the attention of the customers, who, in this informal atmosphere, roam about, bibs beneath their chins, tracing the yellowed history of their hosts. The *Sadie Nunan* was the greatest in a fleet of seven Nunan schooners that Bertha describes proudly as "making Cape Porpoise prosper."

If they look closely at the photos, people will notice the short, sturdily built man standing beneath a stately elm tree. The tree, which was in front of the present restaurant, is gone, and there is no way for the curious to know that the meal and Bertha Nunan's methods of preparation really began under that tree, when Captain George Nunan decided one hot summer's day to sell some lobsters, the way kids sold lemonade, from his front yard.

"Captain George left gillnetting and came home to Cape Porpoise to go lobstering in 1932," relates Bertha. "About 1951 he just set a kettle and cooking stove beneath that elm tree and cooked up a batch of his lobsters the way I do now. People passing by stopped. He'd sell the first one for $1.25, then 80¢ every one after that. People told him they were the best lobsters they'd ever eaten. Pretty soon he had more people stopping by that elm tree than he could handle.

"In 1953 he converted his garage into a kitchen, where we work today. He built a tiny dining room with benches lined up along the walls. I came along," she says, "in 1956 when I married his son Clayton. He fished 200 traps and in summer brought all his catch here. I started working at the Hut that summer. I scurried around so much Grandfather called me 'Hoppy' and the name stuck. Even today when people come in and ask for Bertha, my girls will say, 'There's no Bertha here.' "

Her son Richard, now finishing his final year of high school, will soon marry his high-school sweetheart, who has worked at the Hut for five years. He got his own lobster license at the age of nine. Fishing with his grandfather and father, he learned the seal-dotted waters off Cape Porpoise, and when it was necessary to fish in earnest, he was ready.

"We lost Captain George in 1972," Bertha says, "and two years later we lost Clayton, too. It was on Father's Day and Richard was 14. He was determined he'd take his father's place. *The Little Roxanne* became his boat then, and he would leave the house at five, fishing for the Hut. My friends told me I had to open up. They said if I didn't open up within a week, that I'd probably never open up. I guess they were right. It's a good thing Captain George taught me everything he knew about cooking and Clayton taught me about the business. He must have known something."

Published June 1979

When you walk into Nunan's today in its 73rd year, still "no frills," you will dine on lobsters caught by Bertha's sons Richard and Keith, who prepare lobsters exactly as their mother, who passed away in 2009, taught, the way she had learned from their grandfather Captain George. Their wives, Terri and Kim, are fixtures in the dining room, and Kim has been baking pies with Bertha's original recipe since 2003.

Caribou

The wind that swirls the snow in northern Aroostook County is like no other in Maine. People of the prairies would know it, for it is a farmer's wind, driving across the northern plateau into the valleys of the St. John and Aroostook Rivers, unfettered by trees. Loggers came long ago to take the white pine and the spruce, and on their heels followed potato farmers who cleared the rest. From Houlton to Fort Kent, miles of potato fields stretch into the distance, their boundaries marked by thin stands of trees in place of stone walls.

The visitor's strongest impression of northern Aroostook is of distance—he cannot believe he can see so far. The land lies open on all sides, with horizons that remind you of being at sea. Perhaps it is the nakedness of the land, at once so utterly subdued by humans yet so vulnerable to nature, that knits people to it. For it can be argued that nowhere else in New England does home and a sense of place feel more ingrained, more tenaciously guarded, or longer mourned when it is lost, than here in the Aroostook River Valley, which for its hub has Caribou, a city of 10,000, named for an animal last seen here in 1908.

Caribou is called the melting pot of Aroostook. Officially a city only since New Year's Day 1968, it is where the rich and varied lives of the region—the Scots and Irish, the Acadian French, the Swedes and Lebanese, and the indigenous Aroostook Micmacs—merge and blend like so many tributaries. And it is where the age-old family farm of 100 acres or less bucks up against agribusiness operations of several thousand acres.

Once Caribou was the largest shipper of potatoes in the world, a boom town with endless potential, but there are worries here now, as there are throughout the potato belt. Farmers lose money when the weather is poor or the demand falls off; the town is losing its young, and anger over the influx of Canadian potatoes threatens to explode into violence. Intermittent rumors rumble like thunderstorms that Loring Air Force base, a prime civilian employer six miles east, will someday be closed.

But in Caribou people do not panic. Endurance is learned early by children working in the fields during fall harvest. The people are open and friendly, as gregarious a populace as will be found in Maine but made of more than a little steel cultivated through generations facing tough times and coming through. And more than anything, it is winter that tempers that steel.

Stories of the cold pass along through generations like heirlooms. Clara Piper, lifelong Caribou resident, recalls her parents talking about Friday the 13th of February, 1861. "They called it 'Cold Friday,'" she said. "It was 36 below with a vicious wind, and it was unusual to have the wind with that cold. People who went out for just a few minutes had to struggle to make it back inside. But the mailman was determined to bring the mail. His name was Bubar, and he was known for his size and appetite. He was always glad to be invited in for a meal. He went on snowshoes 12 miles to Presque Isle, got his load of mail, and started home. But the wind got him, and he cut down a cedar tree and kept a fire going all night to stay alive. The next day," she said with pride, "he brought the mail."

In 1939 the National Weather Service established its northeasternmost station in Caribou, lending authority to the old stories. Except for the summit of Mount Washington in New Hampshire, it has the lowest daily mean temperature of reporting stations in the Northeast (38.8° Fahrenheit). Throughout the winter Caribou gains a certain notoriety when, more often than not, it is reported to be the coldest town in the nation.

How cold? On February 1, 1955, Portland shivered at two below. That day Caribou set a record at 41 below, rising to a toasty 26 below the next day. Those are official temperatures. The weather station is located on Caribou's highest point, 600 feet above sea level, and amateur weather observers say that the cold air drains into the valley below, where it is at least ten degrees colder on Main Street. Two years ago, the first five days of January told this chilling story: -9, -5, -24, -27, -20; still it was a mild month compared to January of 1957, when the mean temperature for the whole month was 1.3 degrees. But there is grudging affection for the cold and for the wind that creates whiteouts with the dry, drifting snow; there is scorn for those who surrender to the elements.

Two years ago, when windchill hovered around 100 below, a Caribou minister canceled his Sunday services for the first time. I was told some of his congregation were astounded and disappointed. They reasoned there were storm windows in the church and ceiling fans to circulate the heat; anyone with any sense had plugged in their engine block heater and the plows were clearing the drifts.

At 20 below the city is bathed in a kind of frozen mist escaping from the streets. Water vapors from chimneys freeze across the valley and the blue silence of the Arctic descends. People walk the streets breathing through scarves, and twice a day they scan the sky for the weather balloons recording it all. At 100,000 feet the balloons burst, mini parachutes float the instruments to land in a nearby field it is hoped, though sometimes they arrive across the border. When found, farmers are asked to return them, like hotel keys dropped in a city mailbox. Every hour the temperature is updated, windchill noted, the better to advise schools and farmers, as well as the power company in case their workers need to climb poles that day. Firemen pay attention, knowing that a combination of cold, dry air and overworked furnaces and woodstoves could create a tinderbox should a fire begin, and winds arrive.

The harvest ships in winter, and farmers take precautions that potatoes accustomed to the 40-degree storage house are not ruined in a stiff northwest wind while being moved from barn to waiting truck. Even with care, cars sometimes won't start, and you would no more leave the house without jumper cables that you would without a coat.

Even so, the people of Caribou insist they'd rather see 41 below in Caribou than 10 above on the coast with all that moisture biting through. There are many who insist that winter is their favorite time. There is cross-country skiing, snowmobiling, and the seasons ahead are laden with the anxieties of seeding and harvesting, and besides it is so beautiful with these rolling hills covered in snow. Winter is when Aroostook catches its breath, the psychic conditioner for the laborious months ahead. When the people of Caribou have faced another winter, they know they can meet the spring.

Published June 1979

More than four decades after this story appeared, much has changed in and around Caribou, but much remains constant. Young people have left, and the population has dropped to about 7,400. Loring Air Force Base closed in 1994, taking with it military families as well as 1,100 civilian jobs. But with the resilience that northern Aroostook is known for, a year after the base closed, the Maine School of Science and Mathematics opened at the high school that once educated the Air Force children. One of the country's only funded charter schools focused on STEM, the school attracts students from throughout the state who live in dorms fashioned from a former elementary school, and is rated one of the top high schools in America. Aroostook remains the third-largest producer of potatoes in the United States, but the traditional fall harvest break today is down to only two of the 14 districts in the county. What has not changed is the pride in being winter's hometown. Weather balloons still float over 100,000 feet above the land; parachutes still descend with their baskets of instruments. Caribou remains one of the coldest cities in the country. In 2015 I asked a writer to return to Caribou in winter. There a weather observer boasted that while Boston sees, on average, only a single morning of subzero temperatures in a year, he was proud that "we get about 41."

The Shad Always Come Back

The shad and I arrived together at the mouth of the Connecticut River, heading inland in the first days of spring. They had migrated in great schools from the Gulf Stream, compelled like salmon to spawn in the shallows of the river they left in infancy four or five years before. The cry, "The shad are running!" follows them on their journey to spawning grounds that once reached as far as Bellows Falls, Vermont, 170 miles from the mouth, and that will reach that far again next season when the final fish lifts are built at Vernon Dam. The fish are spring's most bountiful gift to those living by the river, and the word "shad" pervades the language here: in the day you see shadbushes in bloom, and swat shadflies from your head. Their presence seems reassuring: in a world in flux, the shad always come back.

These Connecticut River shad are the most famous in the world. To be taken from this river is the imprint of quality in a shad. I was told it's the cold water that preserves the flesh and the fragile roe better than anywhere, and that sometimes fish markets in New York, eager to please impatient customers, label shad from the Chesapeake Bay or the Hudson as "Connecticut River Shad," before a single one has entered the river.

I came to the small river towns to join for a while the sometimes intimidating world of the commercial shad fishermen. They work at night when their drifting gill nets are invisible to the fish. From the riverbanks south of Hartford you see only the lanterns, attached at the ends of the net, bobbing downriver, the quiet only broken by motors revving when a drift is done, the net hauled upriver to begin again.

This is how their grandfathers and fathers fished, nearly always in the same stretches of the river, regarding it as their legacy. Once this river turned black with shad, perhaps six million racing northward. I heard tales of hauling seines being torn from fishermen's hands by enormous schools of shad; bunkhouses were built on fishing piers so that men could haul fish all day from the nets spanning the channel. In time, dams, pollution, and overfishing decimated the shad run, so that only a hatchery program begun a century ago could restore it. Pound nets and set gill nets were outlawed, and seining became an impractical way to catch the reduced number of fish. Today half a million shad remain while 100 men drift their gill nets in the dark.

Shad fishermen call their fishing areas "reaches," as fixed in their boundaries, a few miles long at most, as city neighborhoods; they would defend a reach as they would their homes. Every fisherman has a tale of violence on the river. A fisherman in Old Saybrook said bluntly, "If you came into my reach without permission, acting like you owned it, I'd let you fish that night. Then I'd sink your boat."

I joined fishermen on three boats on three reaches far apart, from Old Saybrook to Rocky Hill. Near the mouth of the river, the men studied and struggled the most with tides and currents; nearly all were full-time commercial fishermen and the shad, like lobsters and oysters, were but one species in their yearly cycle. Upriver they fished in the dark, often drifting until dawn when they would deliver their catch to a wholesaler before going off to a regular job. "We're cranky the whole season," a Rocky Hill man said, and often they must snatch their rest between drifts, dozing in the boat. To all of them shad fishing marked the turning of the year—it was what they had prepared for since January when they began stringing their nets; they were the last of their generation, growing smaller each year, and it was easy to think that when they rowed their net downriver they were responding to the spring as surely as the fish they hunted.

On a soft night without stars I met Ken Swain on the Old Saybrook–Old Lyme reach. In the distance we could see Saybrook Point Lighthouse marking the river where it spilled into the Long Island Sound. He was

54 and had fished here all his life; one of his earliest memories was lying curled up in a shad box while his father fished.

He told me to be ready by 5:30, though darkness would not fall until 8. By his reckoning these would be the best conditions of the season: moonrise an hour after sundown with a downtide. "The fish will be moving!" he exclaimed, and he meant to be the first boat on the reach, which by shad fisherman's law would reserve him the first drift. Others have the same idea, of course, and the time that they plan to be on the reach they guard from brothers, even sons, if they are fishing in competing boats.

Toward evening you can stand on the railroad bridge in Old Saybrook and watch the shad boats racing to the abandoned fishing piers where they anchor until dark; it is a scene repeated everywhere on the river. What they are chasing is money. The previous week a boat drifting 1,000 feet ahead of Swain netted 120 shad; Swain's catch was 18.

On this night we came early, but another boat was already anchored off the pier that Swain favored. A few nights before he had chased a boat into the Sound, trying to ram it into oblivion after the fisherman had defied his claim to first drift. There seems no greater wrong on the Connecticut than defiance of shad-fishing protocol.

By nightfall the boats were scattered on the reach, making ready to fish. They were lit dimly by lamps powered by car batteries placed beneath a seat. The boats are Brockway sculls built by Earl Brockway in a small boatyard in Old Saybrook. They're not pretty and aren't meant to be, but they can take a pounding. Squat, open, 16- to 20-foot plywood boats, the sculls are used by nearly every shad man on the river. Swain, in his 28-foot fiberglass boat, is an exception.

In silhouette I could see the men in the boat ahead of us throw their net in the water. The river is widest here at the mouth, and Saybrook fishermen will use 1,200 feet of net, 20 feet deep, double that used in some reaches upriver where the banks close in. The net, buoyed by corks placed six feet apart and weighted down by metal rings, has lanterns floating on the ends to guide the men as they play it out across the channel. The size of the mesh will let the smaller fish glide through safely, but the larger shad will be trapped behind the gills. While the net drifts downriver, lights are out and it is quiet. We could be in a cave, except for the lanterns moving with us, 1,000 feet apart.

The dark keeps Swain alert. "You're pushing the law of averages every time you fish at night," Swain said. Tankers and tugs also ply these stretches of the river, representing a constant danger to the fishermen. There have been no black shad boats on the Connecticut since a tug towing an oil barge to Hartford rammed the last one 20 years ago, killing the fishermen.

Our drift was over in an hour. Two men hauled in the net, squeezing the shad through the mesh with quick thrusts that popped the fish to the deck where they lay stunned. The shad piled up, gaping yet tenacious; their mission is to get upriver and they don't give in easily.

Swain picked a powerful roe shad from the deck, nearly two feet long, about six pounds. It was deep-bodied with saw-like scales on its belly that can cut you badly if you're not careful. He held it to the light admiring the translucent scales, "black and shiny like a new car," he said, indicating it was at the beginning of its journey. In contrast he showed me a fish so worn and emaciated it seemed to be another species. It was a "racer," a shad that had already spawned and had been struggling seaward on the outer limits of its reserves. In the warmer rivers of the South, shad live to spawn only once, and pelicans and gulls line the banks to gorge themselves on the dying shad floating by. But in the cold Connecticut at least a fourth of the shad will survive a return to the sea.

The others on this reach will fish another drift before the tide trips. But Swain goes home. He is officially disabled with a bad heart and explains to inquisitive government people that he is not fishing when he is on his boat, he is teaching. This night he taught us to the tune of 300 pounds.

Published April 1980

Today, six to eight commercial fishermen continue the nighttime drift-net Connecticut River shad tradition. Several towns along the river boast notable shad festivals. One of the most famous is the Essex, Connecticut, Rotary Shad Bake, held in early June since 1958. The shad are baked on wooden planks, the same way the indigenous populations feasted.

Billy Starr's Long Ride

There are people who possess a gift they don't really know they have, until something unexpected happens and their life takes a turn, and then their gift becomes life itself. For instance, Billy Starr.

In the summer of 1973, he had just graduated from college. He'd grown up in suburban Boston, a boyhood filled with good schools and sports and summers in Maine. Billy Starr was, as he puts it, "footloose, a late bloomer," with no plans except to backpack around the Himalayas. "I saw the world as an infinite alluring expanse," he once wrote.

That August he was playing in a tennis tournament, and when he came home, his father was crying. "I'd never seen him cry," Starr says. Billy's mother, Betty—"she was beautiful," he says, "she once was a model"—had melanoma. "Life got a lot harder then," Starr says. "We suffered seeing her dying." Betty Starr passed away in December 1974. "My father was never himself again," Starr recalls. "Within three months of my mother's death, he was diagnosed with Parkinson's."

So, this is how life sometimes lines up. Billy's mother was gone, and his father needed him now. Billy Starr wouldn't take off just yet for distant places. He worked for the family kitchen-supply business, but he had to do something with his restlessness. "I was a pusher, always pushing," he says. He hiked 400 miles of the Appalachian Trail, starting at Katahdin in Maine. He was with some friends, and they got lost and rain-soaked;

some turned back. He remembers how hungry and exhausted he became, but above all he remembers the exhilaration when he came through, when he finished what he said he would do. He pushed more. He'd wake at 4 a.m. to bicycle to Provincetown, 130 miles distant, in time to catch the afternoon ferry back to Boston. "Provincetown was a destination," he says, "because it was the end of the line."

The long ride kept calling him back. "I started to think," he says, "how could I turn my interest in sports, my sweat, into something meaningful? I felt there was something more here." On an April day in 1980, he was in the Arnold Arboretum watching the sunset. "I had my epiphany," Starr says: He'd bike alone from Williamstown to Provincetown, point to point the longest way to cross the state, some 300 miles by bike. He thought he could persuade people to donate money toward cancer research for each mile, a way to turn his continued sorrow for his mother into action.

This was long before athletic fundraising became popular. He wasn't sure how it'd all work, but he "knew this was out there to do, people wanting to give back." He brought his idea to the Jimmy Fund, and a woman there asked, "What's really your goal?" Starr said: "To raise money for cancer research." "You think you can do this better by yourself?" He realized he needed others.

Starr handed out brochures on the Charles River Bikeway, and one September morning he and 35 other riders pushed off from Springfield, Massachusetts. "Although I did everything wrong in the planning," Starr says, they ended up the next day in Provincetown. "We finished at MacMillan Wharf. The ferry had broken down and we had to take the bus home. But all I heard was 'We have to do this next year.' I decided, *I've got to make this work.*"

That year the riders raised $10,200 for the Jimmy Fund at Dana-Farber Cancer Institute. Starr pushed more. He learned how to do things better. The next year 210 riders signed on, and when the second ride ended, he gave $40,600. The next year he gave $60,000, and the next, $100,000. Starr had found a calling, and with it the improbable idea that this bike ride with the catchy name, Pan-Massachusetts Challenge (PMC), could raise enough money to let doctors or scientists discover *something* to cure cancer if only they had more time and space to keep looking.

Starr had a lot to learn and he had to do it on the fly. The fourth year, it was 94 degrees, and he didn't have enough water stops. The fifth year, a 24-year-old bicyclist hit a shoulder and was thrown. "We were in the age of innocence," Starr says. "There was no helmet rule." The young man died, and Starr's volunteer staff was so shaken they all left. "I knew the PMC had to go on," he says.

His staff worked through the shock and grief and came back. Each year there were more riders, more money for the Jimmy Fund. In 1985, the Massachusetts Maritime Academy in Bourne opened its dorms to riders, who now had a comfortable landing spot before the final push to Provincetown. A few years later, the rains came for the first time. "I had always wondered what would happen if it's raining at 5 a.m. Will people show up?" Starr says. "It was pouring and yet there was everybody. To walk out into the rain and see all these people. . . . I realized the PMC had taken a huge psychological leap in the minds of participants."

Starr kept pushing. He tinkered with new routes, creating more ways for people of all abilities to do a ride. "There was a time when the event was eating me up," he says. He met his wife through the event and listened when she said he had to delegate. He formed a board of directors and hired full-time staff. He says the years have gone by in a blur, and now here we are, 30 years in. What began with a single $10,200 gift has grown to $239 million. Last year's ride raised $35 million for cancer research, half of all the money the Jimmy Fund receives in a year. There's nothing quite like this anywhere in the world. "When they write the history of how cancer was conquered," notes Dana-Farber president Dr. Edward J. Benz, Jr., "the PMC will be in chapter one."

This year on August 1, some 5,500 riders will start out, each one riding for someone they love, or someone they lost, or someone fighting to get well right now. Hundreds of riders themselves have or have had the disease. "We are not just cancer survivors," one says. "We are cancer warriors."

There are now eight routes, with different mileages, starting points, and endings. The longest ride starts at Sturbridge on Saturday and ends 190 miles later on Sunday morning in Provincetown, the riders sweeping past the dunes in a sea of color, their jerseys and helmets flashing by in the morning light and into the town, as the crowd cheers as if they've done something heroic. "You pedal 200 miles for that last 50 yards," Starr says.

What they've done is to keep pushing one pedal down, pulling the other pedal up, going from water stop to water stop, not questioning whether it matters, because they know it does. Because this is what is possible: to fight back. "The weekend builds hope, and hope is very powerful," says one rider, whose team includes his wife, who has survived two bouts of cancer and one bone marrow transplant. They know why they do this year after year: because this is one ride we all are on.

Published May/June 2009

The annual Pan-Mass Challenge continues to be held the first weekend in August. To date it has raised over $1 billion for Dana-Farber Cancer Institute for cancer research and care.

It Takes a Woman with a Strong Back

Even the seagulls know that life in Prospect Harbor has changed. For years, when the herring arrived at the sardine cannery, the gulls would cry and hover, thick as clouds, and you'd look up and barely see the sky. Now, a few still circle when the lobster boats head out and return, but an unwelcome quiet has come to this little village just north of the Schoodic Peninsula.

The reporters and television crews, they're gone, too. Newspapers far and near, and, of course, the blogosphere, all picked up the story: how in Maine, where sardine factories once thrived, only one remained, Stinson Seafood, in Prospect Harbor. And how on Thursday, April 15, the last oval can would come off the belt, and then an industry that had once sustained the Down East coastline would end. So many reporters requested interviews that Bumble Bee Foods, the plant's owner since 2004, sent people in from California to handle the public-relations fallout, which is what happens when 128 people lose their jobs in a community without other jobs to go to.

Peter Colson, Stinson Seafood's plant manager, said that all the attention beat anything he'd ever known. Bumble Bee had told him early in February, and he'd lived with the secret for days before calling his workers together, many of whom had worked for him for years. "It was killing me," he says. "I couldn't sleep, worrying about them."

And so the world came to know Lela Anderson, 78, who became the symbol of the end of an era. She'd packed sardines since she was 17, had been at Stinson 54 years. "Men couldn't do this work long," Colson says. "It takes a woman with a strong back to pack fish." He calls Lela, who reaches five feet if she stands on tiptoe, and weighs 101 pounds, "the strongest lady you'll ever meet."

Her face revealed every day she'd packed fish: determined, stoic. It was as if the work ethic of sardine workers from Rockland and Belfast, Jonesport and Lubec, had come to rest right here in Lela Anderson. So day after day, she'd step back from her lunch break for a few moments and talk into cameras with an accent so soaked in coastal Maine it made its own poetry. And then there was no longer a need for Lela to talk about her life, because once the doors finally shut that Thursday, for the world beyond the peninsula the story was over. . . .

"On Friday morning I kept looking at the clock," Lela says. "I said, 'I've got to get up. I've got to get ready for work.' And then I remembered: 'You fool, you ain't got to get to work. You're done work now.' I bet I wasn't the only one."

We sit in her neat-as-a-pin two-bedroom house, set on a tidy lawn in Corea, three miles east of Stinson. She bought the house with her husband, Herman, a lobsterman, in 1963, and raised a daughter and a son, also a lobsterman. A weekend has come and gone. The afternoon light filters in through the window, at about the time she'd usually be coming through the door and getting supper ready.

"I've seen it all," Lela says. "I remember my first day packing at Snow's in Gouldsboro. That day I lost my first pair of scissors, and the first week I got paid, I lost my check. Oh, I learned a great deal from that."

She came of age when weirs jutted from bays and coves in every town, capturing the herring as they swarmed in by the tens of thousands to feed in the spring and summer—so many that the water glistened like a sheet of silver when the men rowed out at night with flashlights. In daylight, sardine carriers pulled alongside the weirs; the men pulled the nets tight around the haul, then suctioned the fish onto the boat, before heading to a nearby cannery. Some towns had three or four plants strung along the shore, turning out packed sardines by the millions. (Processed Atlantic herring leave the factories as "sardines.")

"When the fish came to the factories," Lela says, "the whistle blew, telling us it was time to go to work." Factory buses came to the villages to pick up the workers and brought them home at the end of the day. When Lela got to work, she'd tape her fingers and thumb and pick up her scissors, sharp as razors, with the blades ground over and over by machinists at the shop, until they couldn't be ground anymore, and then it was time for a new pair.

"I went through four pair a year," she says. "That's how I got this," and she holds her hand out for me to see the thumb joint on her left hand, her cutting hand, pushed up and knobby, as if the bone were trying to escape the flesh.

"I cut left-handed, so I'd pick my fish up with this hand, the same hand my scissors were on," Lela explains, "and then I'd flip him over onto my right hand and I'd cut his head off, and I'd flip him over and cut the tail. Sometimes they'd bring buses of schoolkids and they'd say, 'Wow, come quick!' They'd run down the aisle: 'Come see this lady! She's fast.' Because I was the fastest one with scissors."

She packed sardines when Calvin Stinson, Sr., who lived right there on the peninsula, owned 11 canneries up and down the coast. She was Prospect Harbor's star packer when the fastest workers from all the plants converged on the annual Maine Lobster Festival in Rockland and faced off, with hundreds watching. Lela packed sardines when canned tuna became the new belle of the lunch ball, signaling a shift in American tastes. She was there when the cannery burned in 1968 and was rebuilt as a spanking-new and modern plant, with machines replacing the scissors, so that by the mid-1970s she could just put presliced herring sections into the cans.

"Well, I liked the scissors, but I liked that better," Lela concedes. "I liked it all cut up, 'cause then you didn't cut your hands." But then her pride kicks in: "You had to be a lot more skilled then, a lot more," she says. By the mid-1980s, frozen herring had come into the plant; Lela's hands would turn cold, and whenever she could, she'd hold them by the heat of her conveyor belt. "You'd just have to suffer it," she says.

Change was happening at sea, too: from the use of "fixed-gear" weirs and stop seines to purse seining, which let fishermen go beyond the coves, to midwater trawling from big boats that moved in on the fishing grounds and scooped up the herring by the ton before they could reach the nets of the local fishermen. The schools that once contained millions of herring were declining. The traditional ways that had sustained the fishery since the time of the Native Americans were in decline, and by the early 1970s the herring were in trouble. New federal quotas revived the fishery, but an inexorable worry set in.

The number of canneries dwindled, even as the plants were having trouble finding younger workers. Where once more than 50 canneries had operated, by 1975 only 15 survived. The Stinson family sold its plants in 1990, and 10 years later the new owner sold them to Connors Bros., a firm based in Blacks Harbour, New Brunswick, that had been buying and closing Maine sardine factories since the 1980s. Connors promptly closed Stinson plants in Belfast, Lubec, and finally Bath, leaving only Prospect Harbor, which was then sending 120,000 sardine cans into the world each day.

In 2004 Bumble Bee Foods merged with Connors. For the first time, Lela's work life was in the hands of a far-off corporation. Then in November 2009 a new, lower herring quota for the New England fishery was proposed: The total allowable catch would be cut nearly in half, to 91,000 metric tons. Soon after, Bumble Bee announced that the prospective drop in herring supply was forcing the company to close Stinson. In the small towns, this statement was met with skepticism. People noted that now the firm's Blacks Harbour plant would have no North American competition. Whatever the reasons, it was over.

On April 15 Lela came to Stinson before 6:00 a.m., put on her apron, hat, earplugs, and blue rubber gloves. A few days before, Peter Colson had thrown a company barbecue and given every worker a surprise book of photos documenting what their work had meant. Now, one more time, the machinery hummed and rumbled, the fish slid down the belts, the cans whizzed by and were packed, covered in sauces or oil, and sterilized.

Shortly before noon, the machines slowed and stopped. Everyone gathered around the packing belt. The last 130 cans to be produced in Maine, in the United States, were taken off the belt and put aside for the employees. Colson told Lela that she would pack the last one. She picked three small fillets and arranged them perfectly. "That was a bad day," Lela says, shaking her head just a bit. "A sad day. The head guy from

California came and talked to us about our severance pay. Then we cleaned our lockers out and lined up to get our papers signed. Peter stood up in front of the line, and we went out saying our goodbyes. You couldn't help crying. You couldn't help it. You knew you couldn't be with your friends. Then we walked out."

She was driven home, and she put her final can of sardines in a glass display case in her dining room. Then she walked to the wharf, where her son was tending his traps.

"I had an operation last year," Lela says, "and Peter had me doing quality control—repacking all the cans that weren't done right. 'Whenever you're ready,' he told me, 'your table is waiting for you.' I was going back on the line this summer."

She looks right at me. "It got harder as you got older," she says. "But I could go with the best of them. I'm a packer. I will always be a packer."

Published July/August 2010

When Lela Anderson passed away in her Corea, Maine, home, October 13, 2013, she was 82. The NOAA (National Oceanic and Atmospheric Administration) included Lela in its "The Women in the New England Fisheries" oral history project, designed to "honor the pivotal role of women in shaping the New England fisheries." Lela's Down East-soaked voice and memories live online.

The Light That Went to the Stars

Barely 200 feet from the shallows of Long Sands Beach, Cape Neddick Light perches so handsomely on its bony 2.8-acre nest of Nubble Island that we call it simply "Nubble Light." Maine boasts more than 60 standing lighthouses. Nubble Light, Maine's southernmost light, may well be the one we love most. In 1977, when the *Voyager* spacecraft blasted off for Jupiter and beyond in search of possible alien life, their capsules carried photos to show what we revered here on Earth. Among those photos: the Great Wall of China, the Grand Canyon, Nubble Light. The lighthouse and the keeper's house are on the National Register of Historic Places and are engraved on York's town seal, as if to say: *Nubble belongs to the country, but here is its home.*

The keepers of the light who lived here from 1879 until the last Coast Guardsman left in the summer of 1987 felt that this was their calling. They tended the French-crafted Fresnel lens as if it were a child, polishing its light until it shone like gold. Sometimes winter blew fog that blanketed the knoll for weeks at a time. The keepers knew that the safety of ships depended on their keeping Nubble's red light glowing 15 miles out to sea. At dawn, they'd extinguish the light, watch the sun creep over the water, and start their chores. Nubble Light is at its finest on a blue-sky day when the ocean scent makes simply breathing worth the trip. Stop at tiny Sohier Park on Nubble Road. Ahead you'll see the gleaming white tower reaching 41 feet high, and beside it the trim, red-roofed keeper's house, a few outlying sheds, and a white picket fence, as if the lighthouse stood on a shady neighborhood street. Lighthouses have become icons of our yearning, speaking to us of lives spare and romantic at the same time. We wish we lived there; we know we cannot. So we carry the light inside, no matter where we live.

Published September/October 2015

Nubble Light is never more loved by those who know it best—the people of York and southern Maine—than when dark descends on the Saturday after Thanksgiving and, seemingly by magic, white lights flow across the contours of buildings, fence, tower. Buses carry people from the high school and the beach to Sohier Park. There is Santa, and live reindeer, and thousands of free cookies baked by locals. Nearly every place in the country has a tree lighting. But only here, in the dark, can you imagine these lights like tiny stars in the sky, shining and forming the perfection of a constellation called Nubble Light.

A World Apart

You don't stay strangers when you pack together on a blue-sky morning in the cold cabin of a snow tractor rumbling up the eight-mile-long Mount Washington Auto Road at six miles per hour. In places, the tractor must break through 20-foot-high snow slabs, its enormous treads rolling over the mounds. Riding the snow tractor is not unlike being on a small boat in a storm-tossed sea.

Seven of us—four men, three women—have signed on for a Mount Washington Observatory "EduTrip," an expedition during which guests bunk and eat with weather observers in the most singular mountain environment in the world. We've come from Canada, Pennsylvania, Maine, and New Hampshire, packs stuffed with cold-weather gear. Crampons and ice axes are stacked in a corner of the tractor's cabin.

The few hundred people who reach the wind-pummeled winter summit find a beautiful, perilous place where storms sweep through with little warning and temperatures drop swiftly, as though you've left one country for another in the blink of an eye. Some visitors ignore the peril, treating a winter climb as though it's a jaunt. Too many of them end up with their names on a memorial wall in the Sherman Adams Summit Building, among the 140 who have died in the Presidentials, most of them on Mount Washington.

This EduTrip is called "Winter Mountaineering Essentials," a chance to learn how to move about safely on icy slopes and how to save our lives if we don't. Our leader is Joe Lentini. He is 55 years old, and for much of his life he's been climbing and guiding within sight of Mount Washington. Coming here with Joe Lentini to learn about winter mountaineering is like taking cooking lessons with Julia Child.

On this morning, the higher we climb, the deeper winter closes in. About eight hours earlier, the observers had clocked a wind gust of 104 miles per hour. The day before it had been 113. But now the wind has subsided to a modest 50 or 60 miles per hour. "A good trip is not beautiful weather," Joe reminds us. "That's not normal."

Joe tells a snow-tractor story while our driver, Gus, steers the beast upward. It happened, Joe says, maybe 20 years ago. On that day, a driver was taking two inexperienced visitors to the summit. About six miles along, a whiteout engulfed the road, and the tractor hit something hard. The driver climbed out of the tractor to investigate, being careful to keep a hand on his machine. Suddenly the wind knocked him away. No matter which way he groped, he could not find his way back. His only chance was to fight his way down. Hours passed. All the passengers knew was that their driver had left them, not to be seen again. All they heard was a terrifying wind; all they saw was the blinding white.

You cannot get farther away from it all than to come here. There's no "it" here, except the wind, ice, and snow. Everything wears a coat of rime, as if torn from a frozen planet. Then there's the startling warmth of coming indoors into the observatory, where now you smell hot soup, homemade rolls, and coffee brewing. The observers, interns, staff scientists, and Marty the cat share spare quarters, where obsessive monitoring of weather has been a mission since 1932. They're young, and nearly always a bit tired, since they work 12-hour shifts eight days straight.

They live in this building, but they live for what happens outside. The weather room is packed with computers, instruments, and charts. They're a world unto themselves, every day hoping a great storm will stop by and make every hourly venture outside to check this or that device a battle of will against the wind. For fun they challenge one another to see which of them can walk around the icy observatory tower in a 100-mile-per-hour blast without touching a rail or toppling over. They call it the Century Club. On the tower the wind punches your breath away. It's both dangerous and irresistible to any observer, intern, or staffer who knows the lore and legends of all the men and women who have lived here before them.

We learn the rules right away. “Nobody leaves without checking with me. Nobody goes out alone,” Joe says. If we go outside, we must never lose sight of each other. We sleep with all outdoor gear within reach. If there’s an emergency and we have to scramble outside with the windchill at minus 50 degrees, there’s no time to say, “Oops, no mittens.” Water is scarce; no showers. The air is so dry people get dehydrated, so we have to drink a lot of liquids. Joe urges us to go to the tower to see the sunset and to wake at 5:30 for sunrise. Many days and nights you see nothing but fog, but when it clears, Joe promises, it’s like nothing we can imagine.

Joe readies us to feel the mountain under our feet. This is not a forgiving mountain, so we need to strap crampons on our boots and know how to use an ice axe. He knows how to grab our attention.

“It was April,” he says. “Two men hiked up here on a windy day. It was the iciest I’ve ever seen. It was scary being up here, hard to get your crampons into the surface. These two guys made it to the top and were standing in the parking lot. And they relaxed and put their ice axes down. And a gust of wind hit them. They went over on their backs. One guy went maybe 200 feet and hit a rock and broke his femur. The other guy went more than a mile. And that’s why I went up there, to bring his body down. It could have happened to anyone. So when you walk out here, always have your ice axe in your hand.”

Walking with crampons on hard snow and slick rocks, you become aware of every step: lift foot, put foot down, lift other foot. Aware of every breath. We wear hoods over our hats, goggles over our hoods, faces covered with balaclavas. We’re thickly layered from top to bottom. It’s a strange feeling to be so cocooned in the bitter cold. Joe guides us to a moderate slope above the Lakes of the Clouds. Just beyond, the headwall of Tuckerman Ravine is lovely in the rare sun.

We’re here to learn “self-arrest”: a technique of stopping a fall that can make the difference between living and not. We climb to the crest of the slope, lie on our bellies, heads to the rise, and, well, let go. We slide, wanting speed, then push down with our body weight on the edge of the axe until we stop. Climb back. Lie on our backs, let go, flip ourselves over. Stop.

Climb back. Then head first, a position to give pause, then flip ourselves over, all the while lifting our legs off the ground lest a crampon dig in and perhaps snap an ankle. One of us doesn't stop until he barrels into Joe, standing like a crossing guard where the slope levels off. Once, a woman in her early 20s climbed not far from here with friends; they made themselves into human sleds, until the laughter ended, when in a sudden and growing mist, she shot past the headwall and into a deep crevasse. Her name is on the wall at the Sherman Adams Summit Building.

Joe's pack weighs 24 pounds. He tells us that these 24 pounds will let him survive any conditions on Earth. On the side of the pack he carries a short-handled, steel-bladed shovel. It weighs next to nothing; hardware stores carry them for $10. We trek across the ridge until we come to hard pack. We dig what looks like a grave—just deep enough and long enough to hold one of us. If we're ever caught in a storm, if it's 20 below and blowing 80, this hole can provide just enough warmth away from the wind to give rescuers time to find us. We take turns crawling inside. When I slide under the lip of the cave, it's as claustrophobic as an MRI tube. "It's not the Ritz," Joe says, "but it'll keep you alive."

The night is clear, the stars startlingly so, but in the morning, clouds sweep through and descend, and snow starts. Joe's happy; bad weather has joined his trip. We start walking down the Auto Road. Once I'm blown nearly off it. When I look up, the group seems to have walked through a hidden white door. I know I'm fine. I'm standing on the Auto Road; Joe is just ahead. But still. . . .

In time, we hear the snow tractor rumbling toward us from the top, where it had gone earlier to take supplies. We are cold, wet. Now and then snow blinded. Nobody wants to get in.

Published January/February 2009

The Mount Washington Observatory continues to lead winter weekend EduTrips to the otherworldly summit, and Joe Lentini continues to be part of perilous mountain rescues. His Moth Radio Hour account of his mountaineering life lives online. The documentary 109 Below *recounts the harrowing winter rescue attempt in 1982 that features Joe Lentini and others. It will stay with you.*

Fridays with Bert

There can't be many farmers in New England more well known or loved by neighbors than Bert Southwick, who lives in the same farmhouse his parents found in 1918 on a ridge set back from Zion Hill Road in Northfield, New Hampshire. Except for a stint with the National Guard in the late 1940s, he has spent nearly every night of his 84 years on this ridge.

The house needs work. His parents papered the walls some 60 years ago, but there's no time for cosmetics. He never married, his parents died, his brother left for upstate New York, and not long ago his sister moved across the river to assisted living, leaving Bert to move relentlessly from one chore to the next until daylight is gone. "I have to do what five of us did," he says.

Some of the outbuildings that sprawl across Bert's 250 acres seem to be hanging on for dear life, but each has a purpose: a henhouse, a slaughterhouse, a sugaring shack, buildings to store machinery and the old tractor and plow he uses to clear his neighbors' driveways, a shed for an ancient green milk cart with red wooden wheels that he bought as a teenager for $25, a barn filled with horses and pigs. Sheds filled with so many bits and pieces and scraps of a farm family's life it seems that little that wasn't edible has ever left the land.

Bert ended his formal education at age 14 so that he could help full-time on the farm. "The only place I ever did work," he says, counting off what seems like a thousand ways he and his father made money here: growing vegetables, spreading manure, selling firewood, haying, selling homemade pork sausage, selling horses, pigs, pumpkins.

He's the most famous man in town—two towns actually, since only the Winnipesaukee River separates Northfield from Tilton, and Bert belongs to both. Over the years reporters and TV people from near and far have found his farm, always on Fridays. They come on Fridays because that's when he hitches his horse to the boxy green cart with red wooden wheels and takes his eggs and vegetables to town, winding through the streets of Northfield, across the river, and through downtown Tilton, stopping at houses, apartments, fire stations, post offices, a nursing home, libraries, a beauty salon . . . door after door, carrying cartons of eggs he's collected, sorted, and cleaned from his dutiful hens. They come because he may well be the only horse-and-buggy egg man left in the nation, but also because in a world of change, he's now into his 71st year of bringing eggs to his neighbors.

Since he began in 1937, seven horses have pulled Bert's cart: Ned, Dinah, Dolly, Misty, Miss Gray, Bob, and Mischief. "I like horses that like to sleep and ain't too anxious to get to some other place," Burt says. "The first day I took Dolly alone was the day President Kennedy was shot," he remembers. "Dolly went with her mother, Dinah, and when her mother was over 30 and failing, I took the harness off her and gave it to Dolly. Then when she was 14, she died with no warning in the heat of summer. So I had to educate another. Misty was three colors. Pretty wide awake. First couple years, had to make sure she was tied. After three or four years, she got used to it. Hard to get any better by the time she stopped." Bert's customers remember when Misty died; tears rolled down his cheeks whenever he'd talk about her. Now Mischief, Misty's daughter, is into her 14th year.

For years Bert's egg route covered some 200 stops, scattered over a six- to eight-mile route that would take him all day, what with kids feeding apples to his horse and small talk with customers. In time, a lot of them moved away, or died, but he still delivers at least 100 dozen eggs a week. He figures he's sold close to six million eggs. If you add up the miles he's clip-clopped down these roads, he's crossed America eight times.

In 1995, when a spanking-new elementary school was built on land he and his family had cleared years ago, the children asked that it be named

Southwick School. At the entrance is a fine engraved sign showing Bert's famous cart and horse. "It was the horse and wagon who named the school," he says, "not me."

Bert made his Friday rounds with horse and cart no matter the weather, sitting beside a small heater, "on days snowing so hard couldn't see two telephone poles ahead of you," he says. But just after Christmas 2001, he lost his footing and stumbled while hoisting himself back into the cart. If he had let go of the reins, people say, he would have been okay, but he held on and the cart rolled over him. He broke four ribs, and pneumonia set in, while Northfield and Tilton held their breath.

His friend Harold Kelley picked up the deliveries in his truck, but the first Friday Bert got out of the hospital, he climbed in beside Harold. He keeps the cart under cover during the winter now and lets Harold truck him around until spring. Then when the snow is gone and the fields green up, he tells Mischief it's time.

One late winter morning with snow piled high on the ridge, I join the men on the route. I find Bert in the barn, carrying hay to his horses. "Good morning," I say. "Where'd you find a good one?" he answers. With the barn chores finished, he squeezes through his narrow front door into the warm kitchen. His knees are shot, and if he sits for a while, he rises stiffly before picking up momentum, so he doesn't sit much, except to sort his eggs and pick feathers off them here in the kitchen, which is heated with the same black Glenwood stove his father bought after World War I for $35. That stove and a wood furnace below have warmed him since birth. I ask about backup heat as he readies his eggs. "Backup is me putting in more wood," he replies.

Bert changes into a faded gray coat—"his Friday coat," Harold points out, "only times he wears it"—and the men fill the truck with eggs and set off. At the end of the long rutted drive, Harold turns left onto Zion Hill Road, past the school that bears Bert's name, and then pulls into the heart of Northfield. Bert tells of the changes in Northfield and Tilton brought by I-93 racing past their borders: how he's seen houses that sold for $1,800 now fetching $240,000, his watery blue eyes reflecting amazement at how that came to be, and how for the past two decades he drops off eggs and rarely sees anyone at home, where for so long he'd be met at the door by mothers with a smile and cozy conversation.

Through the morning Bert fills his arms with cartons and places them inside the doors of houses, and from time to time he finds a few dollars tucked inside an empty carton. He carries a pencil in his pocket so that he can jot down figures, but he rarely does. At one house Harold asks, "Isn't she away?" "She said to leave two dozen a week until she gets back," Bert answers. "She eats more eggs when she's not home."

We stop at the local fuel oil company. A man named Walter Hill sees me sitting next to Bert with a notebook. "So they're still after you," he says. "Well, they're down to pretty small entertainment," Bert quips. The local librarian says, almost apologetically, "No eggs this week, Bert." "Didn't you work up an appetite?" he replies. And so the morning passes, up and down stairs, snatches of hellos whenever someone sees him.

We're back at the farmhouse by early afternoon. Hours of chores stretch ahead. Hens are laying the next week's batch. Slouching against the wind, Bert will soon head off to the henhouse with his wire basket. In a few days he'll slaughter one of his pigs; there's a waiting list for the sausage. The winter would be a lot longer, he says, if he didn't have so much to do. With so much snow it's hard to see spring, but Bert does. As soon as the soil warms, he'll plant Swiss chard, potatoes, cranberry beans, corn—enough vegetables to feed anyone along his route who asks.

And one Friday in early May he'll hitch up Mischief, load the cart with eggs and some horse feed and a cheese sandwich for himself, and he'll start down the ridge, swing left on Zion Hill Road, eggs jostling behind him: a man with work to do who has found that he needn't travel more than a few miles to see all he's ever wanted or needed.

Published May/June 2008

Before Bert Southwick passed away in 2015 at age 91, he transferred the property where he spent his life to the Southwick Farm Trust with the intent that the property would be restored and kept as a living, working farm. After extensive renovations to the house and barn, a family has lived there for the past decade with their horses and chickens, keeping a garden Bert would have been proud to see. The trust Bert left also supports the local library, fire department, a 4-H club, and Winnisquam Regional High School.

Edie Clark, Yankee's *beloved columnist of "Mary's Farm," called her life in the 1762 farmhouse "the most rewarding kind of love." She is pictured in her dining room in 2009, where she hosted holiday feasts for friends whose families lived far away.* Photo credit: Ewa Buttolph

Leaving Mary's Farm

"It might have been the beauty of this land and its dramatic sky that brought me here, but the house, its history, its voices, the thought of the many feet that have touched its floors, this is what is so meaningful to me now. I'm only here to make it better, to make it last." – Edie Clark

On the first Saturday of this past autumn, Edie Clark came home. A van from the nursing home and rehabilitation facility where she had been recuperating for weeks brought her back on a sun-splashed, blue-sky day, with cars lining the narrow country road as far as the eye could see. It was just before noon, and Edie, in a wheelchair, rolled carefully down the ramp, and family and friends were smiling at her, holding out their arms. And Edie smiled back, and everyone was happy to see that.

Only five years earlier, Edie had thrown a late-summer gala here to celebrate the 250th birthday of this homestead, which Benjamin Mason built in 1762 to shelter his family and raise his livestock. The party had been a joyous occasion, marred only by a thunderstorm that sent everyone scattering but which gave Edie, as always, fodder for her column: *"In so many ways, we had summoned Ben Mason into our present, into our 21st-century reality. Maybe he was answering back—maybe throwing a lightning bolt down into the trees to give us the fireworks we lacked—maybe doing some handstands up in heaven."*

For the next few hours, the house and its yard filled with a steady tide of well-wishers. A table set up by a tall shade tree held Edie's books, which spanned 35 years of her stories about New England places and people and, most memorable of all, her columns for *Yankee*. In the latter, she wrote about her life in two houses: one a few miles from here, a place readers knew as the Garden at Chesham Depot, and now this breathtakingly lovely homestead, Mary's Farm, named for Mary Walker, who had lived here for many years.

In the dining room, the table filled with platters, which was fitting because nobody ever left Edie's house with an empty belly. She sat in her chair on the lawn, looking out to the broad meadow and the stone walls and the mountain. Visitors gathered around her, sharing small talk and memories, and a few children romped in the fields. Her neighbor Anne came by, and seeing her face you knew she was also losing something precious. When the sun softened and a breeze came through, Edie asked to go inside, to see the kitchen where she had sat for so many hours facing the meadow and the mountain, writing of the moments that make up a country life: *"If you could look out my front window, you would see a broad, humped hay field. Beyond it is a stretch of forest, mostly tall oak trees and some pine. And then rising above both is the mountain, Mount Monadnock, a long stretch of rock much wider than it is high, its rocky peak exposed like the blade of an old knife."*

We all knew that Edie had been falling, that ordinary things had become more difficult for her. Her legs and back pained her, and she'd been hoping for surgery to bring relief. For several months her neighbor Joan had visited often to tidy up, to shop for necessities, to keep Edie going. We thought Edie was battling another flare-up of the Lyme disease that had laid her low many times in the past. We knew she had blood pressure issues, too, that could cause steady legs to wobble. What we did not know was that, in fact, it was stealthy strokes that had caused her to fall. She would call friends, afraid, abashed to be asking for help, and they always responded, getting her back on her feet, into a chair or bed, and they would entreat her to go to the hospital. She always said she'd be okay. But maybe she knew that wasn't so—much as her dogs always seemed to know, she'd once written, when things would not be okay. Maybe she sensed that if she went to the hospital, she would not return.

"I never thought Mary's Farm would become mine, and to be here is like the best, most rewarding kind of love."

Before Edie moved to Mary's Farm, she had written about her gardens and the seasons and neighbors and small-town rituals while living in a house across the street from an old railroad depot in Chesham. She had bought the house with her second husband, Paul Bolton, a master builder, almost as a declaration of faith in their future: He had spent three years fighting cancer and was then in remission. But just a few months after they moved in, the cancer took Paul at age 39. She grieved deeply, finding relief only when she went on the road to search out the little-known people and places whose stories she told.

Edie had arrived at *Yankee* in 1978; I came a year after. We often walked the country roads that run by these offices. It was 1990, a year after Paul's death, when I suggested she write a column about country life. As she later described it, *"I didn't want to pass myself off as an expert gardener, so I hoped my readers would accept me simply as a lover of the miracles of the earth and a teller of stories."* With each column, her followers grew. Many times I heard people say the first page they turned to was Edie's.

When Edie left Chesham for Mary's Farm, her readers followed the bumps along the way: frozen pipes, snowdrifts so deep the plows broke trying to free her road, snapping turtles laying eggs in the garden, the trials and heartbreak of loving and losing a dog. And they also shared in the burst of beauty that Edie found in every season. Who could ever see frost on a window the same way again after reading this passage: *"I would lie there, still snug in bed, and watch the light of the sun bring the night's frost painting alive. I thought of this window as my winter garden, where blooms came faster and more dramatically than any flower ever could."*

Edie's columns, each about 650 words in length, revealed a life in miniature. Readers understood how deeply one can live alone, especially when one paid attention to life. She once wrote, *"I find that writing the next essay is my best day."* I think that was because each time she sat down to write, it affirmed that her farm was *"my sanctuary from a world that sometimes changes too fast for me."*

I know that if Edie could, she would also write about this day, and what she saw and felt when the van returned in the afternoon, the light fading a bit across the meadow. Those who had remained gathered around her, pressing tightly, cameras clicking. And for one final moment, Edie smiled back.

As I write this, Mary's Farm does not yet have a new owner. The family is hoping to find a buyer soon—someone to drink in its views, to tend its buildings and gardens, and ultimately to become part of its long history. As for Edie, her voice is strong and steady, and the other day she said she yearned to write again. There is always uncertainty with such sudden and radical change, but of one thing I am sure: Whenever people pass by this house and this land in years to come, they will say, "Oh yes, Mary's Farm—the place where Edie Clark wrote."

Published January/February 2018

When readers learned that illness had forced Edie to leave her home, the response was as though a beloved family member had been taken from them. The letters and cards came flooding in, most of them carrying the same message: "Your column was always the first thing I looked for." Edie and I spent hours on the patio of the nursing home, me reading the letters aloud to her, Edie listening, sometimes laughing, sometimes with tears, as she felt the deep affection of her readers, while also knowing she might not be able to reach them again. Edie passed away on July 17, 2024, at the age of 75. She would have so enjoyed the memorial reading of her work by writers who came from around New England to honor her legacy as a packed church audience hung on Edie's graceful words.

FIVE

COURAGE AND RESILIENCE

I once began a series in Yankee *called "Portrait of a Hero." During the series, I wrote about three Congressional Medal of Honor recipients: Ed Dahlgren in Aroostook County, Maine; Michael Daly in Fairfield, Connecticut; and Larry Joel, who was living then in Bridgeport, Connecticut. What they shared were memories of war that they rarely, if ever, spoke about. They shared deep sorrow for soldiers they left behind. And they shared the belief that what they did in battle came from a place deep inside that can never be explained—except they did what they had to do to save others.*

When you talk with someone who has shown such bravery, you ask few questions, and let their words fill the room. When they returned from war, Michael Daly and Ed Dahlgren from World War II, and Larry Joel from Vietnam, they followed different paths. Daly became a successful businessman and one of the leading citizens in Fairfield. Dahlgren returned to the potato fields of northern Maine, where he became a potato inspector. And Larry Joel found that heroism exacted a price almost too steep to endure. The story he shared in "The Battle Within" revealed a different kind of courage needed to save himself.

Perhaps because we live so close together in this small region, when we learn about those who have risked their life to help others, or who have endured tragedy and hardship, we feel we know them. We know where they come from. Maybe they are not so different from us. We have not all gone to war, but any one of us could have been near the finish line when the bombs went off on Boylston Street near the finish line at the 2013 Boston Marathon. The men and women who rushed to aid the injured are our neighbors, the ones I thought about in "The Memories We Choose."

We understand the meaning of courage on a battlefield, or during an act of terror, or during a natural disaster. There is also the courage that Jane Smith showed after losing her husband and famous daughter in an airplane accident. In 1982, Samantha Smith became the most famous child in the country when she wrote a letter to Yuri Andropov, the leader of the Soviet Union, expressing her fear of war, her desire for peace. When she was invited to visit Russia, she was greeted with great affection, while her father and mother watched with a mix of pride and amazement.

When I got to know João Victor, the young man from Angola who arrived at age 15 in Lewiston, Maine, knowing several languages but scarcely a word of English, I could not help but think of what it would be like to be so vulnerable, in a place whose climate, food, and culture might as well have been on a distant star. What he and his teacher set out to accomplish became one of those stories I did not want to see end.

When I leave after talking with the people you meet here, and then for days look over my notes and hear their voices again, and relive their stories, it is impossible not to wonder if when storms come my way, I could find in me what they possessed, knowing that storms always come, and so many give no warning at all.

Life After Samantha

On a Friday morning in a television studio on the outskirts of Portland, Maine, Jane Smith sits in a chair on the stage set of "At Issue," a local public affairs show that airs Sundays at 11:30 a.m., and with practiced ease snaps a microphone onto her sweater beside her necklace. "No, I'm not nervous anymore," she says. "More worried, maybe, that I haven't prepared enough. But I could never be relaxed like Samantha."

She is early forties, jogger lean. She knows how to dress for the television camera: light turtleneck, turquoise sweater, black skirt, silver necklace. Her eyes are brown, and her hair, once brown and short, curls long and light. "Friends say I look like they remember me 15 years ago," she says. "Would Samantha like it? Yes," she says, smiling, "she would. She would like it a lot."

She does not smile easily before the camera. She knows this and reminds herself that television is kinder to a smile. Her face, she also knows, has a tendency to droop. "People look at me and see a grief-stricken mother and widow," she says. "But I've always looked sad. Even as a little girl, people said, 'Jane, you look so sad.'" She put her fingers on her cheekbones. "When I relax, everything just sags." She knows she will be introduced the way she is always introduced—with a pause. She knows this just as she knows the comma will be there in all the newspaper stories. "Jane Smith. Pause. Samantha's mother." She knows someday her obituary will begin,

"Jane Smith, mother of schoolgirl Samantha Smith. . . ."

"I was thinking about that," she says. "I was filling out an application for a grant, and I had to list my honors and awards. I realized that the last award for me was in college. Everything I have received since has been for Samantha."

Five summers ago, she was mother to the most famous child in the world, Samantha Smith, the little girl from Maine who sent a letter to Yuri Andropov—*"My name is Samantha Smith. . . . I have been worrying about Russia and the United States getting into a nuclear war. . ."*—and whose subsequent journey to the Soviet Union became a media sensation. Throughout that time Jane Smith stayed in the background. She knew the journey did not belong to her but to Samantha. In the months of fame that followed, when Samantha grew from celebrity to a worldwide symbol for peace, she was there, attached but barely visible, like the string that holds a buoyant kite.

On a rainy August night in 1985 Jane Smith was waiting at the Augusta airport for Bar Harbor flight 1808 out of Boston when word came that it had crashed 4,000 feet short of the Lewiston runway and burst into flames. Eight people were on board, including Jane Smith's husband Arthur, age 45, and Samantha, then 13. Samantha and her father were coming home from Samantha's film-making session in England for her new television series, *Lime Street.* "Samantha had asked me to come with her this time," Jane says. "She thought her father had been traveling with her so much. But I was the breadwinner then, and I had to stay on my job." With a friend she drove to the scene of the crash.

"When I saw it, I knew nobody had survived." It was then she began the long process of putting what she calls "objective distance" between her life and theirs. "I knew I would survive the loss," she says. "I just didn't know how."

Dave Silverbrand, host of "At Issue," talks with Jane Smith for nearly 30 minutes. They retrace Samantha's journey and the journey of Jane Smith out of grief to her current work, bringing a message that "one ordinary person can make a difference," continuing what Samantha represented through the Samantha Smith Center. They talk about Jane's projects: an international newsletter for children, bringing American situation comedies to the Soviet Union, hosting Soviet children in American summer camps.

At the show's end the address and phone number of the center flashes twice on the screen so that viewers can send for information or, hopefully, send donations. The address appears in bold white letters set off against a black background with a wide red stripe highlighting the words "Samantha Smith Center." After the show Jane Smith shakes hands with the show's director, the man who highlighted the address. "That was beautiful," she says. "Thank you for doing that." In the days that follow there will be only one response, a woman calling for information. "You know what well-meaning people tell me?" Jane Smith asks. "They say that if I want money for the center, I had better learn to cry in public."

She lives today in a pretty two-story house set off by woods in the small town of Manchester, just west of Augusta. "People feel surprised I'm still living in the same house. I've thought about leaving it, getting a fresh start, but I like its familiarity. I've put down new carpet, rearranged and redecorated things. I've tried to make it seem like a different house." The clothes of her only child, Samantha, lie in boxes out of sight in a storage room. Except for the new carpet, Samantha's room is bare. Gone are the silver samovar, the folk art, the toe shoes autographed by the prima ballerina of the Kirov Ballet, the stuffed animals, the dolls—mementos of what Jane Smith calls "Samantha's adventure." Now they reside in a long glass case at the statehouse alongside displays of Maine's other famed resources: deer, moose, brook trout, Atlantic salmon.

"I didn't want to be the kind of mother who lived in a museum," she says. "A scriptwriter asked me to leave the room as it was until he could see it, and I did. After that I took pictures of it, so I could remember how it looked." What she kept was a fancy paper bag that Samantha was bringing home from England and that somehow survived the crash. "In the bag were colored pads of paper with slogans on them and a small glitzy bumper sticker," she says. "One of the pads says, 'So much to do, so little time.' The other pad of paper says, 'A peacock who sits on its tail feathers is just another turkey.' The bumper sticker reads, 'Whoever said money can't buy happiness didn't know where to shop.'"

Every morning, she is at her fitness center by 5:30, jogging and lifting weights. The morning after the crash, Jane Smith kept her workout. "I am a practical person," she says. "I knew that when people woke up, they would hear it on the news. I wanted to be able to deal with everything." A few weeks later she boarded a Bar Harbor plane in Augusta—the same sort of plane, a Beechcraft 99, that crashed in Lewiston. "I thought, 'If I don't do this soon, I'll be afraid to fly.' I sat right behind the pilot, and I could see a big gaping hole in the dashboard. I thought maybe I should stand up and tell everybody who I was and suggest we all get off. But I didn't. It was one of the worst flights I've ever had. But we made it. I made it."

It takes her 12 minutes to drive to her office, down Route 17 to Daggett's Market to US-202 then over the Granite Hill Road into Hallowell. The news on the radio this day is of Mikhail Gorbachev's impending arrival in America for a summit with President Reagan. She parks across from Boynton's Market. Her office is in a tall frame building that was once a stable; more recently it housed an ambulance service and meetings of the Grange. "Our initial funders, who raised $100,000 to get us started, wanted me to move to New York. I refused to do that. When we refused to become the large organization that they wanted us to be, we lost some of that support."

There is no sign on the building, nor on the door, but opening the door she sees a poster of a smiling Samantha beneath these words: "Children Should Be Seen and Not Heard." The "Not" is crossed out. "So many people comment how difficult it must be for me to see this poster every day," she says, "or to watch tapes of Samantha's trips. But that little girl was already gone. Parents will tell you a 13-year-old is almost a completely different child."

She climbs the stairs to the second floor. Nailed to the door is a small plaque: "The Samantha Smith Center gratefully appreciates the donation of this office space." It does not say that the donor is Jane Smith. Inside, hanging from a wall, is Samantha's invitation, in Russian, from Soviet Premier Yuri Andropov. Nearby is Samantha on the cover of *Life,* Samantha on the cover of *Soviet Life,* a framed Soviet stamp honoring Samantha after her death. On a shelf is Samantha's book, *Journey to the Soviet Union,* written with her father shortly before she died. The office is quiet. There is a secretary. Two women volunteers stuff envelopes with information about the center, requesting contributions. The stationery reads: "A non-profit corporation dedicated to fostering international understanding." A smiling Samantha, age 11, decorates the border.

She goes into her office, spacious with sofa and easy chair and a map of the world along a wall, to phone the Soviet Embassy in Washington. "I want to send Gorbachev a copy of Samantha's book as a memento of welcome. But they'll be swamped with stuff. I want to make sure it doesn't get lost in the shuffle."

The summer after Samantha died, Jane Smith returned to the Soviet Union. By then she had left her position as an administrator with the Maine Department of Social Services. With her were 20 of Samantha's classmates from Maine. Where Samantha had gone, they went. By then an asteroid, a flower, a mountain, and a cruise ship bore Samantha's name in the Soviet Union. At Artek, the camp where Samantha had spent the happiest days of her trip, Jane Smith walked along Samantha Smith Alley, entered through a gate where a portrait of Samantha greeted visitors. A package from Jane Smith will reach Mikhail Gorbachev.

In Maine the first Monday in June is officially Samantha Smith Day, when schools across the state will plan activities to help children understand other cultures and to remember Samantha. But on this day the future of the center that bears her name is in doubt. Jane Smith has just laid off her paid fund-raiser. A successful and publicized summer exchange that gave ten Soviet teens nearly a week at a Maine camp—the first time the Soviets had sent their kids to an American camp—depleted the center's funds. A projected donation of $50,000 from the sale of "Joanie's Jams," featuring the blueberry jam recipe of Olympian Joan Benoit Samuelson, collapsed when a sliver of glass was found in a jar of the jam sold in a grocery store. *Samagram,* the center's magazine for young people, had published five issues, but had attracted only 700 subscribers. Jane Smith had hoped for 5,000. *The Samantha Smith Story,* a movie that Columbia Pictures hoped to co-produce with the Soviets, was into its fourth script, and its prospects grew bleaker by the day. The center was to have received a portion of the film's profits. With a friend, she has started writing a biography of Samantha. If it sells, the proceeds will go to the center.

She talks about growing up in the early 50s as the daughter of a minister in Virginia. "My father was a hunter, and he gave me a BB gun. I remember thinking that if the Russians came, I would get my gun and hold them off at the house." And of her days at Hollins College where as a senior she met a young English teacher, Arthur Smith. In 1970 the couple moved to a tiny Aroostook County town with a prophetic name, Amity, "friendship among peoples." They lived in an old farmhouse a half mile from neighbors. Jane was town clerk, worked in the woods as a surveyor, and in time had a craft shop, while Arthur taught at Ricker College, in Houlton. When Ricker folded, the family came south to Manchester where Jane found work with the Department of Human Services and Arthur became a part-time professor in Augusta. He also suffered his second heart attack.

"That was rough on Samantha when we first moved," she says. "She'd come home and say, 'Nobody likes me.' You know how it is when you're eight. Her father was in the hospital when the fair came to town. Arthur stayed home with Samantha, but she was really babysitting him. He had just recovered when she wrote her letter, and one thing I worried about was if he could hold up. My friends were concerned that after the crash, Art got lost in the shuffle. He was a movie buff, so they set up a fund to buy videos in his name at the Houlton library."

The conversation turns toward Samantha, as it always will. Jane Smith has told some of the stories so often that they hold for her the comfort bedtime tales give children.

"She surprised all of us. How she suddenly became articulate in front of the camera. To us she was a 10-year-old who seemed to do nothing but giggle and act like a complete idiot with her friends. Then all of a sudden the camera was turned on, and she could make sense. The first time I saw her on television, I had to go to my neighbor's to watch. We didn't have an antenna. She came on, and tears filled my eyes. I couldn't believe this was my kid.

"When the media crush began, we tried to anticipate questions. We tried to be careful in not telling her what to say, but we wanted her to have time to think about what she might be asked. But she didn't like to do that. She'd say, 'That's okay, Mom. I can handle it.' She was the perfect age for all this. She had no idea of the impact of the trip. It was like she was taking an exciting field trip. A couple more years down the road and she would have been too self-conscious.

"But look," she says, holding the morning's *Bangor Daily News*, "here's a review of a Samantha Smith biography. The writer called me once, talked a little bit, and wrote it. The center won't receive any money, and it might hurt our own book. A lot of people have capitalized on Samantha. And there's not much we can do about it."

She wants to make a video to train other groups who wish to promote youth exchanges. "We have the footage," she says, "but we can't afford to edit it. Part of the problem is that I ignored fund-raising for a long time. I thought this was such a wonderful idea that the money would just come in. In the beginning people told me, 'You have to capitalize on this right away.' They'd say, 'I hope you understand, but the appeal of Samantha is only going to last for so long.' I was brought up where you don't go around asking people to give you money. Asking people for money for the foundation seems almost like asking for myself. And I think one of the problems with our fund-raising—and it's hard for me to tell, because people won't say it to me directly—is that some people think the center is just therapy for me. Just a little project until I get over the hump.

"When I began the center, I was on a lot of TV shows. I wanted to talk about our work, about bringing Soviet kids here, and sending our kids over there. But they wanted me to talk about how to deal with grief. So many letters came from people asking me to tell them how I managed to get through. It still happens. An older man carried my groceries out to the car. He said, 'You're Mrs. Smith, aren't you?' I said, 'Yes.' And he started crying. I thought, 'Now what should I do?' It's very sweet yet at the same time a little awkward." She says, "I still cry, especially alone, at night. But it's not something you can do anything about, except go on. There's so much to do right here." She speaks softly, with no hint of self-pity. Rather, she seems to want to cover the subject, knowing the questions are always asked.

Her secretary knocks, hands her a message. "You know," Jane Smith says returning to the conversation, "at least half of our calls are from people wanting us to help them start an exchange. Which in a way is wonderful. But we're all competing for the same funding. Maybe Samantha's influence has done as much as it can. Maybe I should just be happy for the stimulus she's given to others. But with her name we can do so much. She is a folk hero in the Soviet Union. That is a legacy I would hate to give up.

"When we came home from the Soviet Union, we thought the attention would subside. But it didn't. We kept asking ourselves if everything would be a bore to her after this. But she seemed to be handling the attention so well. She had some problems in school. She fell behind in her homework, and some kids teased her about being a communist. Some teachers bent over backward so much not to treat her differently that, I think, they ended up giving her a rough time. When she went to California to be on the Johnny Carson show, she had a tutor out there who showed her how to do some assignment. When she got back, her teacher said she had done it wrong and ripped the paper up in front of the class. The other kids told me this, that Samantha was in tears. Samantha didn't. If she hadn't had so many good things happen to her, it could have destroyed her.

"When she was invited to be on *Lime Street,* that was a very big decision. It seemed too good an opportunity for her to pass up. She had such an affinity for the camera. But we felt uneasy taking a 13-year-old girl to Los Angeles. Friends called it 'Sin City.' It was all a little scary. She loved the Hollywood stuff. She was the right age to be fascinated with the glitz and the make-up—which worried me. We had put a deposit on an apartment near Columbia Studios, but we weren't sure how we would support ourselves. By then she had gotten very interested in clothes from her trips to California. She'd hang out with Robert Wagner's daughter, who had a wardrobe like Samantha had never seen. When she first became famous, she'd never had a dress on. When she met the governor, she didn't even have a pair of dress shoes. I thought she couldn't go in sneakers to meet the governor, so I bought her first pair of dress-ups. When she returned from California, Augusta didn't have what she wanted. So we had to go to Portland. Some people wrote that they felt betrayed that Samantha had gone Hollywood. But it wouldn't have been natural for Samantha to devote her life to Soviet-American relations at age 11."

It is lunchtime and Jane has a walking date to climb the steep hills of Hallowell. There is one more question on this day, about "objective distance" and a piece of stone. The stone is outside the statehouse, in a grove of birch trees, a life-sized bronze statue of Samantha set against a wall of pink granite. A bear cub, symbolic of both the Soviet Union and Maine, rests at her feet. A white dove is poised to fly from her hand. She wears blue jeans and Nike sneakers, and at Jane Smith's insistence to the sculptor, an imitation Izod T-shirt, the kind she always bought at Sears.

For a moment the distance closes. "In summer, with leaves on the trees, I can hardly see it," Jane says. "And it sounds strange to say it, but in winter I'll go by, and I'll feel she has to have more clothes on. She can't be out there with shirtsleeves."

Published May 1988

The Samantha Smith Foundation ended its formal work in 2012, following more than 25 years of continuing to try and knit together young people from the United States and Russia. America's Youngest Ambassador: The Cold War Story of Samantha Smith's Lasting Message of Peace *was published in 2023. Its author, Lena Nelson, says Samantha Smith was her idol growing up in the USSR. She spent years reading and learning everything she could about her life, and she created the SamanthaSmith.info site to honor her memory. When I wrote to Jane Smith asking how she is, she responded, "As my brother, a retired school psychologist, recently told me about his response to questions about his health . . . he says 'It's age appropriate.' So I'm retired, slowing down, and my health is 'age appropriate.'"*

The Unfinished Journey of João Victor

On the evening of May 1, 2019, João Rodrigues Victor emerges onstage and strides to the microphone, ready to recite a poem that will take about three minutes but which he feels could impact his life for years to come. Later he will say that when he was waiting in the darkness of the wings, "my heart was beating so fast, I thought I was going to scream. I was overwhelmed sitting there waiting. I asked myself, *Am I good enough?*"

He is 18 years old, a high school senior in Lewiston, Maine. In January 2016 he arrived in Maine from Angola with his father and two younger siblings seeking asylum. At the time, he spoke Portuguese and Lingala, a Bantu language, but no English. His father, an outspoken opponent of Angola's ruling political party, had been imprisoned and beaten. A friend and neighbor who also opposed the government had been dragged from his house by authorities and was never seen again; his father felt that he would be next. He was able to obtain only four visas, so he fled Angola with his three youngest children, leaving behind his wife and three daughters. But the audience filling the Lisner Auditorium at George Washington University for the Poetry Out Loud national finals, as well as the thousands watching across the country on a live stream from the National Endowment for the Arts—they know none of this.

Here is what they do know: Months earlier, about 275,000 high school students had memorized and recited a poem in their English class, and from that starting line, schools in every state plus the District of Columbia, Puerto Rico, and the U.S. Virgin Islands, had chosen a champion. What followed was a steady winnowing of competitors, from state regionals to state finals. Now, each state winner has come to Washington, D.C. To the outside world they are all but unknown, but here they are celebrated. They have worked to perfect the art of bringing a poet's words to life with their own voice—something one contestant has described as "crawling inside the poem." The day before, 53 champions recited three poems before a panel of judges; only nine were chosen to perform on this night. The winner will receive $20,000, and two runners-up will get $10,000 and $5,000.

Here is something else the audience does not know: A week earlier, when I first met João Rodrigues Victor, he said, "With poetry I can express how I feel. If a day went bad, I recite poems." As a young man who does not know when, if ever, he will reunite with his mother and sisters, who does not know whether he and his family will be denied asylum and sent back to Angola, he sees many bad days. Asylum seekers cannot apply for federal financial aid for college. He works washing dishes at a hospital every day after school and often does double shifts on weekends, but that money is needed for his family here as well as back in Africa. Though he has been accepted at a small college in western Maine, he does not have the $200 needed for registration. The college told him the cost for his first year would be $20,000.

Onstage in D.C., he wears a raspberry suit coat with black lapels, a red bow tie, and a black shirt, gifted from a J.C. Penney near Lewiston. He has already recited his first poem of the night, Vijay Seshadri's "Bright Copper Kettles," which imagines the dead coming to life not as threats but as comforts. His face is intense, his eyes darting left and right. His hands clasp and unclasp. He takes a deep breath. "'A History Without Suffering,' by E.A. Markham," he announces in his lilting accent. He begins: *"In this poem there is no suffering. / It spans hundreds of years and records / no deaths, connecting when it can, / those moments where people are healthy / and happy, content to be alive. . . ."*

The audience leans in, listening to his voice. After he ends, the ovation is loud and long. He seems confident and composed, but when emcee Elizabeth Acevedo, the poet and National Book Award-winning novelist, approaches him as she does with each of the finalists after their second performance, he becomes shy, a bit awkward and self-conscious, responding to her comments with "Yes, miss." She asks about his early memories of books. He smiles, says he comes from Angola, and he did not have books but remembers singing songs. He tells her he discovered poetry only this year. He waves to the cameras and gives a shout-out to Lewiston and to his brother and his sister, who are watching. He thanks the high school teacher who helped him believe he could do this. Acevedo asks him to pronounce his first name, and when he does, it sounds like *Shu-oun.* He knows how strange it seems to American ears, which is why he tells everyone to call him Victor.

Journalists are not supposed to become invested in the lives of the people we write about. But as I watch this, I want Acevedo to ask different questions. I want her to ask how he came to recite intricate poems in a language he had only recently learned and in a way that makes those who hear him feel he is talking just to them. I want her to ask about the first time he met James Siragusa, his teacher, or the last time he saw his mother. If those had been the questions, he would have started his story in a sweltering airplane terminal at 4 a.m. in the Democratic Republic of Congo. And then it would have become clear why he has wrapped his arms around poems as if they were hope itself.

When Victor tells me the story of coming to Maine, it starts like this: "The last time I saw my mom, it was a January night. We had escaped to Congo in a bus. She was sitting with me at the airport. I was looking at her, and she was making sure my tie was okay. She said, 'You must find your way to succeed. You have to take it.'"

The next days are a blur. There's a flight to Morocco, another to New York, then a bus to Boston, a bus to Maine. Along the way, there are brief stays with those who have already made the journey. One of them advises going to Lewiston, where many African immigrants have settled. Once in Lewiston, Victor's father fills out an asylum petition. They need to wait six months before he can work, which means they must rely on charities and community programs. Victor remembers dragging his luggage against pavement and the bitter cold—"I couldn't feel my hands," he says. "I couldn't talk." Mostly, though, he remembers feeling confused and lonely.

Lewiston High School, with nearly 1,500 students, is the largest in Maine. It is also one of the most diverse in New England: Nearly one in four students in the Lewiston school system is enrolled in the English Language Learner program. Victor enters ninth grade, taking beginner English classes, all the while trying to navigate a school and a social landscape unlike any he has known. He finds if he translates all assignments into Portuguese and back into English, he can understand what needs to be done. Slowly, the new language begins to make sense. He grows less shy about asking teachers to repeat their instructions.

In the spring of his junior year, Victor is watching TV when he sees a Maine teenager named Allan Monga reciting Lord Byron's poem "She Walks in Beauty." He learns that Monga, a high school junior in Portland, is also an asylum seeker, from Zambia. Monga is in the news because he had won the state Poetry Out Loud competition but was being denied the chance to go to nationals because of his immigration status. Only when his high school and the city of Portland made a legal challenge to the contest's permanent-resident requirement was he allowed his opportunity. Victor hears the passion in Monga's voice. "When I saw him," Victor recalls, "I said, 'How can I do this? How can a teacher help me?'"

James Siragusa began teaching English at Lewiston High School in 1984, and in 2019 he was set to retire after 35 years. He is soft-spoken, tall and lean, bald, bespectacled. He is one of eight children; his mother, 96, still lives at the family compound by Lake Annabessacook, 20 miles north of Lewiston.

Siragusa has been involved with Poetry Out Loud since it began in 2005, and though he has seen hundreds of his students recite poems, he will always remember the early morning in September 2018 when he was getting his classroom ready for the day, and a young man ran in straight from the school bus.

"He said, 'My name is João Rodrigues Victor, but it's easier to just call me Victor. Are you Mr. Siragusa? Can you help me do Poetry Out Loud?'" Siragusa tells me. "No one had ever done this. No one had ever come in and said, 'Teach me. Show me how.' Victor was so excited, so enthusiastic. I haven't even heard him yet, but I think, *He can do this.*"

They begin by choosing poems together. There are more than 900 poems on the Poetry Out Loud website for students to select. "I'd never spent so much time reading the poems," Siragusa says. "I'd never spent hours. But when I heard Victor read the first time, I knew we had to find poems with pathos and emotional range. He was a natural. You can't teach expression. He just had it. I wanted to find poems that made you *feel.*"

Siragusa tells Victor not to memorize any poem until he knows its meaning. It wasn't just saying words, it was saying words how the poet intended; you had to know it not just by heart but *with* your heart.

Victor is drawn to the Longfellow poem "The Light of Stars," and when we meet shortly before he leaves for nationals, I ask him why. "Longfellow had a good life, and suddenly tragedy happens to him and he loses everything," he says. "His house burns. He loses his wife and he is badly burned. That showed me I have to stay close to my family. When I talk to my mom, I am sad. I say 'I love you,' and I had never said that before." And then, as casually as humming a tune, he recites: *"O fear not in a world like this, / And thou shalt know erelong, / Know how sublime a thing it is / To suffer and be strong."*

Every morning Victor sprints from the bus to Siragusa's room to practice before the first bell. He is almost always late to class. He returns every afternoon for a half hour more. He keeps asking, "What can I do to improve?" He finds YouTube videos of Allan Monga reciting, and he watches them over and over. He washes dishes at a local hospital for four hours every evening, and when track practice ends, he runs the two miles to that job, reciting along the way. After his shift ends at 9:45, he runs the mile to his house. He finishes schoolwork at midnight. He hears his poems in his sleep.

Siragusa solicits coaching advice from poets and people who know theater and voice. When Victor selects "Bright Copper Kettles" to perform in competition, Siragusa makes a video of Victor and sends it to the poem's author, Vijay Seshadri, a professor at Sarah Lawrence College. (Seshadri emails back, "I'm a very lucky poet to have found such a connection to my world.") Mentor and student sometimes meet on Saturdays, Siragusa sitting, Victor standing, as if they are in a room with judges and an audience watching.

And then they are. Victor becomes his high school's champion, then wins the southern Maine regionals in February. At the state finals in March he is seated next to Monga, who is vying for his second state crown and a chance to return to nationals. "I thought, *Oh my God, I'm competing against my hero,*" Victor says. "He is the one who led me to discover poetry. I couldn't believe it. But I wanted to win. And only one of us can go to Washington."

At the end they stand side by side, the two finalists. Before the winner is announced, they embrace, seemingly reluctant to let go; it's a bond between two young men who understand each other. Without Allan Monga, there would be no João Rodrigues Victor onstage. When the emcee announces, "First runner-up, Allan Monga," the stage erupts with Victor's exuberance, and Monga bows deeply to the new poetry king of Maine.

In one month, Siragusa and Victor will fly to Washington, D.C., for nationals. Siragusa has waited his entire career to find a student with Victor's passion. *"I thought, God gave me a gift,"* Siragusa says. *"A parting gift."*

On April 22, 2019, Victor and James Siragusa meet early in the morning to drive to the Maine State House. Victor wears a suit and a bow tie that Siragusa loosens "so it doesn't constrict his voice," he tells me. It is a week before nationals, and Victor has been asked to recite at the first Maine Arts and Culture Day. Governor Janet Mills will be there, as well as Maine's poet laureate, Stuart Kestenbaum. When Charles Stanhope from the Maine Arts Commission introduces Victor, he says, "We are all following his journey."

Victor recites in the Hall of Flags, a room of marble floors and high ceilings, and when he finishes, everyone stands, applauding. Victor seeks out Kestenbaum and asks if he has any advice. "You're already incredible," Kestenbaum says. "You're not up there showing off. You're respecting the poem." A woman from a dance troupe at Bates College approaches Victor and asks where he will attend college. "I don't know," he says. "I can't apply for financial aid."

Siragusa is introduced to Con Fullam, director of the Pihcintu Multicultural Chorus in Portland. Everyone in the chorus comes from other nations, and they have just returned from singing at the United Nations. When Fullam learns about Victor's plight, he is blunt with Siragusa. "He must get legal representation," he says. "Those who are represented are the ones who get listened to. If you don't, you are just dust in the wind."

Afterward, Siragusa wants Victor to see the lakeside compound that's been in his family since the 1930s, so we drive about 12 miles west. Siragusa's mother, Helen, is there making lunch for everyone. Victor can barely contain his excitement at the lake, shards of ice rimming the shallows, ospreys overhead, and the absolute quiet of the land. He asks if he can bring a girlfriend in the summer, especially if he finds one.

Inside, the walls are covered with family photos. "This is a house of pictures," Helen says, and as I watch Victor walking through the rooms, I wonder what he is thinking. For several hours he talks about carrying jugs of water from distant rivers, and meals of bread and sugar water, and how he felt rich when his parents were able to afford tea. He tells of being beaten in school for talking so much, because he always liked the sound of his voice. He talks quickly, as if a timekeeper will cut him off. He says he learned to speak with feeling from listening to pastors in Angola. "If you are passionate, people will feel it," he says, "and people will want to stand with you."

Looking on, Siragusa says quietly, "I am learning things about him I never knew."

In Washington, Victor meets with Maine's Congressional delegation and recites "The Light of Stars" for Senator Angus King—who then recites a poem back. Victor meets other young people from across the country, surprising them when he is able to comment on their performances, which he has watched so often he's memorized their poems. When he sees Janae Claxton, last year's national champion, he asks Siragusa, "How do you say a female hero?" "Heroine," Siragusa replies. And this is how Victor greets her.

After Victor is named one of the finalists on Tuesday, he and Siragusa return to the hotel room. "Do you think I have a chance?" Victor asks.

"There are only nine," Siragusa says. "Everyone has a chance."

The next evening, May 1, before they leave for the auditorium, Victor asks Siragusa to pray for him. "There was an awkward pause," Siragusa remembers, "and Victor giggled. I realized he meant *out loud.* I said, 'Lord, please help Victor to shine his light on his audience tonight. Give him the strength and confidence to express himself from the depths of his soul and to enjoy this moment forever.' "

Then, shortly after 8 p.m., Victor is onstage after his second poem, and Acevedo is asking about his early memories, and soon all nine finalists are standing side by side waiting to hear who will be asked to recite one more poem, which will decide the winner.

Here is where I want to write that, thanks to all his hard work and passion, Victor becomes the Poetry Out Loud champion, is awarded $20,000, and will attend the college that he feels will open yet another new world to him. But sometimes journeys, like stories, take their own path.

"Everywhere I have gone, every competition," Victor recalls, "I hear *João Victor, João Victor.* Now, for the first time, I did not hear my name." He will tell Siragusa, "I let Maine down."

"Usually when a student is so disappointed, they can hide it," Siragusa tells me. "Not Victor. I told him he had done so well. 'What are we going to do now?' he asked me." Late that night, Victor's phone rings. It is Monga, who tells him how proud he is, that Victor has achieved so much, the first from Maine to be a finalist.

Despite his deep disappointment, when Victor returns to Lewiston, he finds he is something of a celebrity. The city names him its first youth poet laureate, and he gives a workshop on recitation at the local library. At Lewiston High School's awards night, Victor once more recites "The Light of Stars," and though he cannot see them, tears flow down the faces of many in the audience. A man hands him an envelope; inside it is $2,500, a start toward his hoped-for college life.

Just before he left for the nationals, I had asked Victor what he would do with his drive to excel once he no longer had to pour his life into reciting poetry. "I won't stop," he says. "One day I will say to my kids, 'If you put in the work, you have a chance to dream.' I am an Angolan man, and look where I am. I won't stop doing this. I will start writing my own poetry."

Victor begins performing his own poems on stages ranging from community churches to the Waterville Opera House. But more than anything, he uses his poems to help him face life. In fall 2019, Victor's mother contracts malaria, and her sister dies in a bus accident in Congo. "That was the hardest time," Victor tells me. "I couldn't do anything. So I went and wrote a poem so I could keep myself calm."

Right before the school year ends, James Siragusa posts a Facebook plea for a lawyer to take on the asylum case for Victor's family even though they have little money. The mayor also gets involved in the search, which ultimately leads to one of Lewiston-Auburn's best-known attorneys, Michael Malloy, agreeing to represent the family pro bono. "When someone calls and says, 'Will you help this amazing person?' you say 'yes,'" he explains. Before the end of the year, he files the official application for an asylum hearing. He tells me the family has a compelling case, but with hundreds of new asylum seekers from Angola and Congo continuing to arrive in Portland throughout the summer and fall, it might take two years, or even longer, for the case to be heard.

Victor enrolls in the local community college, but without the discipline that bonded teacher, student, and poetry, he struggles with business and math courses while washing dishes 40 hours a week. He says he may wait to go back to school and just work to earn money for the family in the meantime. He knows there are colleges where students study drama and poetry and speech, but he doesn't know how to go from here to there.

His mentor keeps in close contact with Victor, doing what he has done since they first met: believing in his rare talent and charisma, refusing to let his flame be extinguished. When Victor tells him he thinks performing arts is where his heart will ultimately take him, Siragusa begins writing to people who work in the field of drama—another way of praying, he figures.

This is a journey they are now on together, one with a still-undetermined end. Except now Victor belongs to two families, one uprooted and one with generational roots, and that just may be enough for him to find his own way. "I'm still learning," Victor says. "I will use my words to get back."

Published March/April 2020

Joáo Victor is now married with two children. He works as a home care worker in Lewiston. He remains close with his teacher, James Siragusa. His mother rejoined her family in 2022. In early July 2024, the entire family was granted asylum.

The Memories We Choose

We can choose to remember the few seconds before 2:50 p.m. at the finish line of the Boston Marathon on April 15, 2013, this way: three young people dead, more than 270 injured, many with the types of terrible wounds seen during wartime. We can choose to remember the worst of humankind: two men who placed two pressure-cooker bombs packed with shrapnel close to the finish line, bombs whose only purpose was to kill and maim runners and those who came to cheer them on at the moment of their joy. We can choose to believe that the brothers Dzhokhar and Tamerlan Tsarnaev forever changed the Boston Marathon—that their scar of hate and pain and blood will be imprinted on a race that since 1897 has celebrated endurance and the spirit of human perseverance. We can choose to believe that during this year's race on April 21, we will still feel their awful presence, that their names will be on our lips.

Or we can choose to forget their names, to not dignify their ever walking among us, an ill wind that came and blew out to sea, never to be seen again. And then we can remember this: that even during the frightening first moments, when nobody knew what had happened or whether there might not yet be another blast and another, so many people, strangers to those who lay hurt and in shock, found resources to run toward the chaos, toward the unknown, to pour out their hearts and offer help where they could. *Can I help? Let me help* became the words that the injured on the ground and the thousands of exhausted and scared runners heard in the first minutes after the explosions—words that continued to define that day and the days that followed.

Yes, history will record April 15, 2013, as a day when terror came to the Boston Marathon. But we each own our personal history, and we have this choice: We can remember the Boston Marathon as a place where lives were lost, but many more were saved; as a place where the best of humankind, demonstrating bravery and selflessness and kindness, will never be forgotten by anyone whose life was touched by a stranger saying, *Can I help? Let me help.*

A woman watching from her hotel overlooking Copley Square posted this impression on *Huffington Post:* "To me, the image that sticks out is the yellow jackets. The yellow jackets carried runners in their arms and acted as human crutches. I saw runners collapse into their arms and they stood still and held them. . . . They ran back and forth from the medical tent, bringing bags of ice and supplies, pushing empty and full wheelchairs, doing whatever it was that needed to be done. They too had families to call. They too were in a dangerous and unsecured crime scene. . . . For me, the enduring image of the Boston Marathon will forever be of the very first responders: the Boston Marathon volunteers, the yellow jackets who stared fear and evil in the eye and vowed that no matter what, they would not run."

Here's a memory to keep: a photograph. In the photo, one that has been seen over and over, Carlos Arredondo, a Costa Rican immigrant in his early 50s who settled in Massachusetts, sprints to an ambulance with the life of Jeff Bauman in the balance. The image of Arredondo's white cowboy hat soon seeped into our lives: the good guy coming to the rescue, his face taut with urgency, Jeff Bauman's face wreathed in pain and shock. Within hours we would learn more: how Arredondo had suffered the loss of two sons, one to war in Iraq, another whose grief at losing a brother led eventually to his taking his own life; how he had emerged from his own despair to become a peace activist and who was at the finish line to cheer on a member of the National Guard running to honor his sons, Alex and Brian.

"He was conscious," Arredondo told a reporter that day about finding Bauman. "I let him know that the ambulance is on the way and he's okay. . . . '*You're okay, stay with me, stay with me.*'"

In the weeks that followed, Arredondo and Bauman became two of the enduring symbols of a moment when the lives of strangers fused together. In late May, as Bauman, who lost both his legs, continued the long process of recovery, Arredondo stood beside him at Fenway Park while thousands cheered for them, and for themselves, perhaps. Cheering because none of us knows when a storm not of our making may engulf us, and when we may need our own Carlos, who says, *It's going to be okay, hang on, hang on.* And here was Jeff Bauman to tell us that he had.

Here is another memory to hold close: In the first hours after the blasts, more than 8,000 people in Boston and surrounding towns took to social media and offered their homes and apartments to any of the 27,000 runners who needed shelter, food, a friend. A typical message read: "Please come to Brookline if you need to feel safe. I'm two miles from Copley, but you are welcome in my home." Another: "I live in Hopkinton but would happily drive anywhere to pick up a runner who needs food, shelter, and comfort."

Ali Hatfield, a runner from Kansas City, Missouri, posted an Instagram photo of the food, drink, and comfort she'd been given at the home of someone she'd never known. "There is love in this world," she wrote. "A sweet woman opened her home to us and gave us food, shelter, and beer! Our hotel is locked down. We can't get over there. So scary. Praying."

And at a time when so many were still struggling to make financial ends meet, $61 million in donations poured into The One Fund to help the injured and the families of those who had died; more millions were raised in separate social-media efforts. It was as though America's heart beat for Boston.

Here is another memory: So many runners and Bostonians made their way to blood-donation stations that soon the American Red Cross tweeted that it had enough: 500 units of blood were on their way to local hospitals, where doctors, nurses, and technicians pushed aside fatigue and found the composure to match their expertise. "There's stress," said Dr. Ron Medzon, an emergency-room physician at Boston Medical Center. "You really want to do the best for every person. I got my patient stabilized and just started running from patient to patient to make sure that everyone else was also getting the attention they needed. And every single patient had at least two or three super-competent, compassionate people working on them. Every single person had a limb-threatening injury, a life-threatening injury. And I think 20 people came in over 40 minutes, which is just incredible."

Nearly 40 injured victims were rushed to Brigham and Women's Hospital in the first hour—and all survived. Dr. Peter Fagenholz, a Massachusetts General Hospital (MGH) trauma surgeon, worked 35 hours straight. He had come on at 7 a.m. and performed six operations before the bombing, then scrubbed in on at least four surgeries, perhaps as many as six or seven, after it, working on the injured throughout the night; he finally left the hospital the following day at 6 p.m. An off-duty trauma surgeon, David King, also at MGH, had completed the marathon and was heading home when the explosions went off. Though physically spent from the race, he went.

There were so many moments of courage and extraordinary kindness amid the noise and sirens that we can also choose to remember the quiet acts, the ones that happen when nobody's looking. Think of Jessica Kensky, a nurse at MGH. She was newly married, and in a flash both she and her husband were wounded badly, each losing a leg. Coworkers—fellow nurses, cafeteria staffers, maintenance people—donated 7,000 of their time-off hours to Kensky—three-and-a-half years' worth. Because of that, Kensky has time to recover, to adapt to a life so suddenly changed, while remaining secure as a full-time employee with health-care benefits.

And here is one final memory, still to come. This year, on April 21, whether the day is warm or chilly, sun-splashed or gray, some 36,000 runners will await the call to begin in Hopkinton, finishing 26 miles distant in Copley Square. There will be a sea of athletes: young, old, men, women, able-bodied, in wheelchairs. A year earlier, many were forced to turn away before the finish. They've put in thousands of miles training to do what they love: to run in this beautiful city on a spring day, with tens of thousands of supporters pressed close on the streets, shouting for them to keep going. And as the miles go by, as they stream through Ashland, Framingham, Natick, and Wellesley, turning into Kenmore Square and down Commonwealth Avenue into the heart of the city, they will hear the shouts that will always be the true legacy of the Boston Marathon, the same as it always has been: *Keep going, keep going.*

Published March/April 2014

The tragic events gave rise to the "Boston Strong" rallying cry, which continues to reverberate today. Jeff Bauman's memoir, Stronger, *became a film of the same name that featured Jake Gyllenhaal as Bauman. Carlos Arrendondo and Bauman remain close friends. As Arrendondo received plaudits from organizations like the Daughters of the American Revolution, attention was also given that he had arrived illegally to the United States as an undocumented immigrant from Costa Rica, before becoming a naturalized citizen in 2006.*

Against the backdrop of Seaside Park in Bridgeport, Connecticut, in 1982, Larry Joel, wears his Medal of Honor for his actions as a medic during a fierce firefight in Vietnam. He was the first medic in the Vietnam War to receive the honor, as well as the first Black soldier to live to accept the medal. Photo by Carole Allen

The Battle Within

"... he searched for wounded, exposing himself to hostile fire; as bullets dug up the dirt, he held plasma bottles high, completely engrossed in his lifesaving mission...."

– Medal of Honor citation for Lawrence Joel, March 9, 1967

The meeting was set for eight o'clock, but now it's past nine. "It's his car," his sister says. "The car's nothing but trouble. He should've left Hartford at five." It's the start of Washington's Birthday weekend, and outside light rain falls on the quiet Bridgeport street, the houses separated by small muddy lawns and a scattering of fences. She hears a car pull into the drive and nods. "He's home."

Larry Joel walks in, a man in his early fifties, tall, slender, with a groomed Afro—"Took me six months to grow it after I retired." His face is soft and round with shy brown eyes behind glasses. He apologizes for the delay; there were errands and lots of traffic. He leads the way to his apartment on the second floor, a bag of groceries in his arms. He takes the steps slowly. "There's arthritis in my shoulder, arthritis in my leg," he says later, "but I don't let people know I have pain. I tell myself I don't hurt, then I don't hurt as much."

He's lived in the apartment above his sister's since he retired from the Army in 1973, commuting the hour to Hartford where he works for the

Veterans Administration as a counselor. "The drive's wearing me down," he says. "Maybe I should move to Hartford." He puts water on the stove for the instant coffee he gulps incessantly. "I haven't had a drink in four years," he says. "This is my replacement."

He puts a pack of Kools on the kitchen table, saying it's the only habit he has left. "I haven't talked about the medal," he says. "Too many bad experiences earning it, and too many bad experiences living with it. I've been wanting to talk about this for a long time. But I haven't been ready."

Larry Joel was a medic in the 173rd Airborne, the first ground troops sent to Vietnam. He arrived in May 1965, the rainy season. "They told us to bring bathing suits, we'd be there only a few weeks. We'd patrol days and never run into the enemy. We had to simulate death so we'd know how to deal with it. One night something was moving in the bushes and some trigger-happy guys let loose. The next morning, we found two hogs, 250 pounds apiece. We put one on a chopper and made a barbecue pit at camp. We smoked up some delicious ribs. That's what the war was like for us, until November 8, 1965.

"I was 37 and a lot of the young soldiers followed me around like I was their father. They'd come to me with their problems. Except for our platoon sergeant, who'd been in Korea, none of us had seen combat. We were told to travel light that day—we had one more area to check out, then we'd be lifted out. I had a premonition that morning. As I was walking, my mind flashed to my daughter and wife and son. They say we crossed water that morning, but I don't remember going through water. I guess there are some things I'll never remember. We stopped at a clearing where hills rose on two sides. We saw fresh camouflage had been broken; we knew something was in there. Nothing was moving. But there were three regiments of North Vietnamese just waiting for us.

"All of a sudden it was like the Fourth of July. I was with four riflemen, and we dived behind this little rock jutting up by the side of the hill. The rain had washed away the soil, and we just piled on top of each other. We could hear bullets ricocheting off the rock. One of the men with me got hit in the kneecap. He was bleeding bad, and I bandaged him up, gave him morphine and a can of albumin serum. I thought for sure he would make it. After about half an hour it got real quiet. I heard, 'Medic.' That's all I could hear—'Medic. Medic.' I looked over behind the rock and saw them lying on the side of the hill, some sitting up with rifles across them. That's how they got killed, as if they were sitting on the side of the hill sightseeing.

"I'd always wondered what combat was like when I heard my buddies tell World War II stories, and I always figured I'd be a survivor—until it happened. They were calling for me and I looked out and I couldn't see anything but jungle, though I knew the enemy was all around. I was afraid, and I just froze. I couldn't move. . . . "

When he pauses, you can hear the steady drip from the shower across the hall from the kitchen. He gets up stiffly to put on more hot water and knocks the tape recorder to the ground. "Is it all right?" he asks. "I'm opening up, but I can't do it myself." He gets his coffee and, taking no chances on disturbing the tape recorder, changes his seat.

"I could hear a kid named Swoboda moaning. I called over to see if he could make it to where we were, but he acted as if he didn't hear me. He'd just turned 18 and it was his first patrol. I could see him lying on the side of the hill and I thought, 'If they ever ask, hey, Doc, where were you?' I wouldn't be able to live with myself. I tried to run to him, but they opened up on me and I got hit in the leg. I ran back to the rock and bandaged it up and gave myself morphine. I tried crawling back to the kid. That's when we called in the artillery. It fell short and hit some of our own people. One of our guys went wild from the pain, and we had to run and catch him and hold him down while I patched him up. I got mad then. I just forgot my fear. I said a little prayer, 'If I get hit, please don't let it be a vital area, because I'll be knocked out of action. Let it be just a little bit, so I can still do something for my people.'

"All morning long we moved the wounded, but the helicopters couldn't get in to evacuate them. Another company came to help us and got pinned down. I ran out of supplies and grabbed some more and began treating their men too. The other medics were a lot younger than me and weren't moving fast enough—I just took over and told them to straighten bandages. Three different times I had a cigarette in my hands and never got to light it. A few hours later I got hit in the leg again. It swelled real bad, but I didn't want more morphine. I got a stick and used it as a crutch. I'd throw it to the ground, treat the soldier, then move on to the next one.

"Once it got real quiet. I said, 'Please let them be going home. They've hurt us enough. Let us pick up our sick and dead and let us go home.' Then they blew their bugles on us—they were charging—the saddest sound I ever heard. The battle lasted all day and into the night. That night I went back to where I thought would be a clearing for evacuation, but there wasn't a clearing, only the wounded and dead lying on ponchos. I found the soldier who'd been hit beside me that morning. He'd become delirious, knocked his I.V. out, and he'd died. It's always bothered me knowing that if I'd stayed with him, he'd have lived. But there was too much going on.

"It rained that night and we sat up under ponchos trying to keep everyone dry. In the morning the choppers came to get us out. That's when I gave myself another shot of morphine. Our battalion had 69 killed, 110 wounded. Nearly half the men of my company were either killed or seriously wounded. My platoon sergeant told me, 'Doc, you did a good job. I'm going to put you in for something, if it ain't nothing but the Silver Star.' At the camp when they got ready to pull my bandage off, I broke down and cried. I couldn't find tears on the battlefield. I wanted to cry, but I couldn't."

Larry's 17-year-old nephew, with whom he shares the apartment, comes up the stairs. He's quiet with strangers around and quickly goes into his room. Larry stands up, stretches, puts water on to boil. He goes into the living room, where a framed jigsaw puzzle of a covered bridge hangs on a wall. He shows off his tropical fish and his old army footlocker painted green, which he uses as a small table.

During the last months of World War II he dropped out of school. Too young for the Navy he joined the Merchant Marine. When he turned 18, he joined the Army and was shipped to Italy. "It was a segregated Army then, and they had so many Black troops they didn't know what to do with us. The only contact we had with white troops was our white company commander." He stayed in the Army until 1949. In 1952, while working in a Baltimore munitions factory, he got "Army sick. I missed my buddies. I wanted to go to Korea as a paratrooper. I went back for the jump boots and the glider patch that said I was one of the elite." He was too late for action, but he decided this would be his career, he'd stay for 20 years.

There's a shout from downstairs. A friend is borrowing his car to take Larry's sister to work. Larry checks the time. It's 11:15. He wipes his eyes and gets his coffee, spooning Sweet 'n Low into a mug printed "Larry." He sits back down at the kitchen table.

"They operated on me that morning. That evening my company commander came over. He said, 'Doc, they're writing you up right now for the Medal of Honor.' I didn't believe it. All I did was my job—I didn't take no hill. General Westmoreland came to my bed and congratulated me. About a week later I read my citation and shook all over. It took a long time before I could read it and not shake. Gangrene set in my wounds. For two weeks they squirted vinegar and water in them. I'd put gauze in my mouth, stick my head under the pillow, and holler as loud as I could. I wasn't gray when I went to Vietnam. I was in the hospital two weeks before I saw my face, and I looked at my beard and it was white.

"I was in the hospital in Japan for three months. I'd keep hearing how far my citation had moved up the chain of command. I returned to Vietnam February 25, 1966, three days after my 38th birthday. I went on patrols for another month, then left for home on April 7. We came through the terminal in San Francisco with our uniforms on and our combat ribbons, and the people just went about their business as if we'd been on a joy trip."

He yawned deeply. "Oh, my jaw's getting tired," he said. "What's your first name again?" I told him.

"Strange war," he said. "Strange war. My wife told me to catch the limousine at the airport. She didn't come to meet me. I came home, and my little daughter was out hanging clothes on the line, and my son was in the house and he greeted me and gave me $3 to pay the limousine. My wife was working at her beauty shop. An hour later she came home, took an hour off to greet me, then went back to work. I'd been gone one year."

There's another shout from downstairs. His car has gone dead downtown. I drive us the mile or so to the lipstick factory where his sister works. "I know what's wrong," Larry says. "It's loose on the connection." There's an old broom handle in the back seat of his car, apparently a well-used repair tool. He presses the battery cable connection with the end of the broom handle while I work the ignition. The engine roars to life, he throws the handle in the back seat and drives home.

At noon on Washington's Birthday he is cleaning his apartment, wearing a black robe. It's his birthday also, his 53rd. He says he's had trouble sleeping, the talking has made him restless. He's had bad dreams, but for the first time he feels like finding the guys in his old outfit. It's about 50 degrees outside with a high clear sky. He dresses in his sharp blue Medal of Honor Society blazer for a photo session at nearby Seaside Park. There are lots of joggers along the walk beside the sea in the early afternoon and some kids playing softball in the mud. When he poses, he holds his back military straight, seemingly shedding five years. We drive to a small Greek restaurant, a "mom and pop" place, in downtown Bridgeport. He orders bluefish and spinach and coffee. Behind the grill the tall swarthy son of the owners is in high spirits—that night he will fly to Greece to be married.

"I always thought that the girl I married would be my wife forever," Larry says. He lights a cigarette. "But I'm getting ahead of myself. . . .

"My ceremony was set for March 9, 1967, and they laid the red carpet down for me. I would be the first medic in Vietnam to get the medal, the first Black soldier to live to get the medal in any combat action. No Black soldier ever walked away with it. I was the first and I felt very proud. The day of my ceremony was a nice warm sunny day—it seemed made just for me. I trooped the lines with President Johnson as the bands played. I was told, 'This is your parade. If you want to stop and say hello to friends, go ahead. Don't worry about keeping in step with the president; the president will keep in step with you.'

"From that day on I became a celebrity to the Army, and I went on tour—Denver, Chicago, Cleveland; schools, hospitals, recruiting appearances. Every time I looked around, I was called to the White House for some function. I was in Chicago and a reporter took me to the family of Milton Olive, a GI who'd thrown himself on a grenade. His parents showed me his room. They showed me his trains—he was just 19. They showed me his cameras—he was training to be a photographer like his father. It looked like they had his room all set up waiting for him to come home. The reporter asked us to take a picture together. I had my medal and they had their son's medal in their hands. He was killed in the same war I was in, and he was my son's age." He stopped then and swallowed. "The word 'posthumous' goes right through me.

"Sometimes I just wanted to be by myself and forget. I drank more and more to suppress it and not talk about it. I never felt I was a hero. At the base I'd walk into a bar and never have to spend a penny. I'd get done one and there'd be another waiting. I couldn't go anyplace without somebody making an announcement and I'd have to take a bow. Once my wife got a speeding ticket and it made the front page—'wife of Lawrence Joel.' I learned to be so careful about what I did, what I said, how I said it.

"My wife would work very late in the beauty shop, my children were nearly grown and off on their own, and I was home alone. We had some terrible fights. She'd say I wouldn't have risked my life if someone hadn't been watching. Sometimes I'd run out of the house and stay drunk for three days. I didn't know what I was going through. I figured I was just feeling sorry for myself. I didn't know that everybody has problems when they first get the medal. You have to learn to live with it. There's some that put it away as soon as they get it and never mention it again. When they die, they find their ribbon as clean as the day they first got it. And everyone who goes into combat gets wounded, whether they know it or not. It leaves a mark forever. I'd changed, but I didn't know it. I was traveling and people called me a hero, but I felt like nothing. It got so bad at home I got a room in the barracks. My son was caught in the middle. Once we were fighting and we looked up and he was gone. We broke up shortly after that.

"Some officers looked down on me if I refused an appearance. Others thought I was avoiding detail and was just chasing glory. I felt tossed between the Devil and the Lord Almighty. I got sick of trying to please, so one day I said I wanted to go back to Vietnam. I spent that Christmas 1969 in Vietnam. That's how bad I wanted to escape.

"I stayed 17 months that time. I was assigned to the brigade commander, and I'd go with him in his helicopter twice a day when he directed operations. I asked to go on patrol, but they wouldn't let me. When I came home, I couldn't adjust to regular soldiering. I got a ticket for drunken driving and I saw the handwriting on the wall. I had my 20 years, so I retired. I had five sisters and a brother in Bridgeport. All I had was my footlocker, $1,500, and some medals. I got a job at the VA and threw myself into it. I put myself in the hospital to stop drinking. I'd tried stopping so long for other people—when I tried stopping for myself, I found

I could do it. I don't think I really came back from Vietnam until the day I finally stopped drinking." He finishes his dinner in silence. Because he's diabetic, he downs another coffee in place of dessert. When he walks out the door, he calls to the young Greek, "Good luck."

A few months passed. He applied to be health administrator of a veterans' nursing home, a job he wanted very badly, and was rejected. He said he was really feeling the strain of his job, often feeling he was on the wrong side, having to tell veterans their claims were not justified under the law. Sometimes the wrath of a veteran denied benefits would be directed at Larry; at such times he said he felt powerless. He just wanted out. In summer word came that Larry was in intensive care in the VA hospital, stricken with an ulcer.

"If the doctor had told me I was dying," he'd say later, "I wouldn't have gotten excited. Least I'd have been out of pain." He brooded. "Seems I'm hustling backward, seems I'm winding down." In the hospital he made plans to file for a government disability pension. He had few needs, and he would get by on that plus his $200 Medal of Honor pension and his Army retirement. He looked forward to writing the story of his life. "It'll be like *Roots*." In November his disability claim was rejected.

We met the day after Christmas. He had moved with his sister across town, next door to another sister, a roomy four-bedroom house, still crowded with nine people. He shared his bedroom with his nephew. With little privacy his patience wore thin, and sometimes he'd yell at his sister's three young grandchildren at the slightest provocation. I drove to his house, but he wasn't there. He phoned. He had a flat tire across town. Could I pick him up? We came home for his insulin injection, then drove to a nearby steak house. He was wan, tired.

He said he knew he needed help to get his life in order. He would start back at the VA in January, part-time, and was debating whether to move to New Haven or Hartford or to stay put. He would work on getting medical evidence that he could no longer tolerate the stress of his work.

I wondered if he realized that soon it would be 15 years since he received his medal. He shook his head in surprise. "I tell myself it's going to be better," he said, smoke trailing from his cigarette above his glass of milk. "I don't let myself stay down. I saved a lot of people's lives once. Now I've got to help myself."

"You were a good medic, weren't you?" I asked.

He brightened. "The best," he said, "the very best."

Published March 1982

After Larry Joel's death from complications of diabetes in February 1984, he was buried at Arlington National Cemetery. His hometown of Winston-Salem, North Carolina, named its new coliseum that opened in 1989 the Lawrence Joel Veterans Memorial Coliseum. The Joel Auditorium at Walter Reed Medical Center bears his name, as do three U.S. Army clinics at Fort Moore and Fort MacPherson in Georgia, and Fort Bragg in North Carolina. In March 2025, Joel's citations were among those taken down from the Arlington National Cemetery website honoring soldiers of color.

On a broiling summer day in Worcester, Massachusetts, Red Sox baseball scout Bill Enos ("A Scout for All Seasons," page 244) celebrates his 59th birthday the same way he spends nearly all his days—watching young players, hoping to find the exceptional talent that hits him like "a bolt of lightning." Photo by Carole Allen

SIX

GOOD SPORTS

Here is how a young writer gets to spend a few days at Ted Williams' fishing camp along the Miramichi River in New Brunswick.

Williams was one of the greatest players in Boston Red Sox history, someone intolerant of the press, and known for his impatience with those who did not share his passion and talent for outdoor sports. I was press, I had never hunted, I was a neophyte fisherman, as likely to tangle a line as attract a fish. But I was friends with his fishing buddy.

I first met Bud Leavitt, the outdoor columnist of The Bangor Daily News, *in the winter of 1978. I was writing about a wildlife biologist in Maine named Roy Hugie. Hugie was researching the black bear population in the state, and Bud Leavitt had opinions. I rode snowmobiles deep into the Baxter State Park winter wilderness with Hugie, as he tracked the radio-collared bears to their dens. During my reporting a black bear bolted from her den and bit the first obstacle she met holding a protective net—me. I think my encounter in his native woods impressed Bud that I belonged.*

Bud had become a newspaperman right out of high school, and we talked as much about reporting and writing as we did about his life as one of the best-known outdoors writers in the country. Because of him I enrolled in an L.L. Bean fly-fishing course. When I finished, I bought a good rod, a nice vest, a tackle box, and a collection of tied flies that would have all been terrific if I had also possessed the talent to match.

I spent time with Bud again in July of 1980. The occasion was what was billed as "Moose Tuesday," the controversial public drawing to determine the 700 men and women who would be the first to hunt moose legally in Maine since 1935. It became a national story. Officials transported 32,297 cards from Augusta to the Bangor Civic Center in a state police van, guarded by two state troopers and two game wardens. The cards were placed alphabetically into a transparent drum used especially for lotteries and the drum was rotated. Boy Scouts in crisp uniforms plucked the cards from the drums. Alas, the cards never shuffled thoroughly. One scout pulled the name Clemens seven out of eight times, an embarrassment made greater when it was learned they were all related. The show, one that Bud Leavitt likened to three hours of watching bingo, produced one of the largest audiences in the history of the public television network.

Because I had lived nearly ten years in Maine before I came to Yankee, *I gravitated to writing stories from there, especially stories from the wilder part of the state, with its way of life that was so different from my own mid-Atlantic upbringing. And whenever I had a chance, I'd pop in to see Bud Leavitt. His world fed my desire to write about those who knew the forest and isolated lakes and rivers.*

That is how I got to go with him to see his friend, the fisherman Ted Williams.

Whenever I am introduced at some gathering where I am a speaker, it's always mentioned that I "fished with Ted Williams." I want to set the record straight. No fishing line of mine touched the water beside Ted Williams, considered the greatest fly fisherman of his time. What I fished for was a story of friendship. When he barked at me on the bank of the Miramichi River: "You can stay as long as you ask interesting questions," I learned a lesson about this work that has stayed with me.

The Celebrity

"Everything that's happened to me since we won the gold medal is something I once could only imagine. And I don't understand a lot of what's happened except the country needed something, and it was us. People were looking for heroes. But we could have lost and none of these people would be around. That's why I've said all along, my whole life is my family. These people will keep me from changing. They will keep me being me."

– Mike Eruzione, 1980 U.S. Olympic hockey team captain

The houses press close together along the narrow street, shouldering each other for space. They were built long ago when boats filled with immigrants docked in East Boston, and the more prosperous, earlier arrivals drifted here, three miles east—to Winthrop, where the Eruziones live in the middle floor of a three-family house. Above and below them live blood relations.

The parents have known each other since their childhoods, growing up first as best friends, then falling in love and marrying. The family ties read like something from the Bible. Eugene ("Jeep") Eruzione's sister, Annette, lives on the third floor, married to Anthony Fucillo, brother of Jeep's wife, Helen. Annette's twin sister, Ann, lives on the first floor with her husband, Jerry Jaworski.

They moved together into the house more than 20 years ago, and they say they will never leave, that they will die there. Among them they have raised 14 children, all first cousins, nearly all named after grandparents or uncles or aunts. The children call it "a house with one door," and growing up, if they didn't like what was cooking at their mother's stove, they would scamper either up or down and find a place at another table, no questions asked.

The wood of the house is a weathered green, and for years the house has been called by neighbors "the Green Monster," partly because of its size, mostly because the laughter and shouts and noise from parties cannot be contained by the walls and spill frequently onto the street. There is a porch on every floor, and in the infrequent times when activity is stilled, you can see them sitting out, third floor, second floor, first, perched like birds on wires, listening to ball games on their radios.

They drive used cars, handing them down one to another, nursing them into six-figure mileage, and on holidays the flag flies outside. A statue of the Virgin Mary, cracked with age, stands by the front steps, and no matter how late they party on Saturdays, they go together to Mass on Sunday.

When I first met the Eruziones, an unexpected feeling of nostalgia came over me, as though I'd come upon a long-forgotten landscape. They are a tie to another time, before families scattered like pods, blown away so easily by our freeways. The children who married strayed no farther than a few blocks, and on holidays the house, as ample as it is, bulges with three generations.

I had wanted to meet them because I wondered what happens to a tightly knit family when one of their own, Michael, scores the winning goal in a hockey game against the Russians, and suddenly and without warning no longer belongs just to them, but in becoming a hero belongs to the country as well.

On one of those slow dark Sundays in late fall when the men have moved indoors like bears to doze before the TV, I found Jeep Eruzione asleep on a sofa, beneath a painting of an ocean sunset. He awoke with a start when I knocked on the side of the open door. He is the kind of man you like instantly, a man with the unruffled manner and good nature of a favorite barber. He removed his glasses and rubbed a sleeve across his face, the habitual gesture of a man who gets by on little sleep. He has almost never held only one job. Three nights a week for the past 25 years, after spending eight hours as a sewage-treatment worker in Winthrop, he has gone to a popular pizza cafe in East Boston called Santarpio's to wait on tables and tend bar. There were times when he held a third job as well, earning what he could so that his six children would not have to do without sports equipment.

"I don't really mind it," he said, "but I do get more tired than I used to. Saturday is a long night behind the bar. But the guys who work there, we've been chumming together since we were kids. So I just keep going.

"The guys at the bar tease me sometimes. They know Mike's a celebrity now. 'Oh, you got lots of money,' they say, 'time to retire.' I says, 'What do you mean? I still work two jobs. I don't ask my Michael for nothing.' Whatever he's doing is on his own. He wants to do for us, you know. He wanted to buy me a new car. I said I don't need a new car. Just get me four new tires and fix the fan belt. I tell him, 'Just do the right thing and put your money where it's supposed to be. Don't be stupid or foolish. Later in life you're going to need it.' I tell him what do I need the money for now. Like today, I got up and went to 9 o'clock Mass, then came home and got in the car and shot down to the track. It's only ten minutes from here. I played only three races. There was a horse called Mike's Luck running. The horse wasn't any good. Everything I need is right here."

I stared at the glossy family portrait hanging above the television. I remarked that Michael resembles Jeep. "Yeah, some of the guys were just telling me that," he said. "When you go into the bar, there's a huge picture of Mike along the wall. I'll look at it, and sometimes I think of when I'd take him down on a Sunday when he was little. He'd go through the seats and benches on his knees, holding a flashlight, looking for nickels and dimes dropped the night before. Sometimes he'd find 80 or 90 cents. Now people come in all the time with their children and call me over. They tell their kids to shake hands with Mike Eruzione's father. And sometimes I'll run out to my car and get them pictures of Mike, and they sit there beaming."

The volume was turned low on the television, but it was obvious the New England Patriots were being upset again. They fumbled on their opponents' two-yard line, and Jeep winced. "Can you beat that?" he said. "That's it. They're done." We talked about the Olympics then, and his face brightened. Excitement edged into his voice, and his fatigue seemed to slip away effortlessly.

"The only game I missed was against Czechoslovakia. A reporter from Chicago was with us, and we're here watching it on TV. And I'm telling people Mike will always score, and sure enough while we're talking, we hear the announcer, 'Score by Eruzione!' We went crazy.

"'See that,' I says. 'Every time you expect something from Michael, he comes through.' The good Lord must have been on his side from the start. It was uncanny. The score was 3-3 in the Russian game, and I'm sitting next to my wife and I said, 'You know, Helen, Michael's not done nothing yet.' I says, 'C'mon, he's due.' I no sooner got through talking than I see the puck slide across to him. And as soon as he got the stick on it, I yelled, 'Shoot, Mike, shoot! Don't waste time!' And he did. He just let it go. I saw that net stretch and I said, 'Oh my God, that's it.' It was beautiful.

"And I started to think—this goal here could be a big thing. If it could stay up with no other team scoring, I knew the impact it was going to have. I held tight to my St. Anthony medal. 'This is for my Michael,' I said. 'Make this thing end 4-3. No more, No less.' 'Cause I knew what would happen. He's the captain. He's got the winning goal. And the people will never forget that.

"The parade they had for him here in Winthrop was scary. I was in a Rolls Royce with Michael and Helen and his girlfriend, Donna. People swarmed on the car. I thought we were going to be crushed. The police had to get him in a police wagon to protect us. I saw him get out of our car and thought, 'Is this for real?'

"Now after we got home, I'm still thinking he'll turn pro and play NHL. The clubs were interested. To tell you the truth, I wanted him to play. The guys in the bar always said he was too small for the NHL. I'd say, 'C'mon. He's got heart and can dig in the corners; he passes and he's smart.' But then I'm hearing Michael talking, why he doesn't want the NHL. He said, 'Dad, you can't beat this—what we just achieved. I'll never score another goal to equal the one against the Russians. This is something I'll never forget.' So he got me thinking. So he signs for 40 grand. He'd get kicked around. Maybe bust up his knees, then have to sweat it out the following year. All that at 25. And I started seeing things coming into the house for him, like a free car, and I said to myself, 'This kid's got it made.'

"And it's unbelievable that what I have to work for a whole year in one regular job, Mike can make giving a few talks. But he's surprised me with his speaking. Even my buddies tell me he's a nice talker. It comes from his heart when he talks to people. Someday, if this thing doesn't get too big for him, I'll see him be a coach, because I really think what he'd like to do the most is come home and settle down and have a bunch of little boys."

He left the room for a moment, and I could hear him rummaging around in a closet. When he returned, he had a box of videocassettes of all the American victories, including the closing ceremonies where Michael stood on the podium, the gold medal draped on his chest, and sang the national anthem, his eyes glistening. Then Michael flung his arms aloft, fists clenched in a triumphant salute toward his family sitting ten rows up at center ice.

"Helen and I have seen these a thousand times if we've seen them once," he said. "But sometimes Michael comes home late, and when everybody's quiet and in bed, he puts it on. I think everything went by so fast, it's a chance for him to enjoy it."

He put on the Russian game, just before Michael scores his famous goal. "Here it comes," Jeep said. And suddenly Mike is being pummeled by his joyous teammates. Then conversation stopped, and Jeep's back arched closer to the screen during the last tense minutes. At the end Jeep watched the American players fall on each other with unrestrained emotion. The announcer's voice filled the room, "Do you believe in miracles?" "Yes!" Jeep said, caught somewhere between the past and his living room, "Now I'm the happiest guy in the world."

"Every Saturday my mother and my aunts meet upstairs and have breakfast. Then my father's other two sisters come over from East Boston, and they play cards all day. They've been doing this since they were nine years old. They play for pennies and nickels and at the end of the day maybe someone's won 60 cents." – Mike Eruzione

I met Helen Eruzione on a rainy November night. She was where she once spent most of her days, in the kitchen, doing what she is famous for, baking lasagna. The kitchen smelled sweetly of flowers hanging by the windows, and from the pantry came the sharp odor of peppers, which she grows and roasts for her husband. She is a stout, friendly woman, and her fresh blue dress was marked by the blood color of tomatoes on her sleeve. When her children had grown up, she went to work at the local high school, ready to help girls with any problems, physical or personal—doing what she can't help but do—be a mother.

"Mike gets mad now when he comes home late, and I'm sitting up for him," she said, "but I've always waited up for my children. When he was playing, I'd light a candle to St. Mary that he'd come out of it all right. At games I'd do my rosaries. Now all my concentration goes on my other son, Vinnie. He's so small, but he plays as hard for Holy Cross as Michael did for B.U. When they check him against the boards, I look at his face to see if he's wincing. I was at a game once and Michael was on the ground and they were hitting him on the ground, and the guy in front of me was yelling, 'Kick him!' and I was taking a fit. It was an away game, and my daughter told me to hush, before they started beating on us."

It was a strict household run by Jeep and Helen, one not always enjoyed by the children. It was especially difficult at times for the four daughters. Their boyfriends would arrive and find a row of uncles and aunts waiting to inspect the young males. The children had curfews and dared not disobey them.

"Even now Vinnie is 19 and has a curfew. I don't care what his friends do. He has to be in the house by 12:30. I tell him, you want a beer with your friends, come home and drink it. Michael wanted to buy Vinnie a car, but I said no. I want him to earn it.

"Both my boys hated to lose. But I'd tell them, if you lose, leave it on the field. When they lost, they'd go into their room to be alone, and they wouldn't come out until they could be pleasant."

But along with the strictness, it was a house known for its gaiety. "We never had family parties, we had house parties," she said. The parties were legendary. At special times Jeep would bring out his guitar, and all the cousins and all the uncles and aunts would sit on the floor and the songs would go on, raucous ones and sweet soft ones, and none of the children would go to sleep, ever, until they were done.

"That's the hardest part. We miss Michael now," she said. "He's important to our parties. It's not the same without his tenor. Now," she said smiling, "he comes home, and I get his two big suitcases. And I wash and fix his clothes, and when I'm done, he's packing again, and he's gone."

"Right now I like the travel. I enjoy meeting people. I enjoy telling people about what we did at Lake Placid. And when I don't want to do it anymore, I'll come home. My escape is my house. If I don't want to see anyone, I won't. They have to go through my family to get to me." – Mike Eruzione

My appointment to see Mike Eruzione was for five and now it was past six, and I was hopelessly lost. I phoned the house. One of his sisters answered. "Oh, Michael's sleeping," she said. I said I was supposed to meet him. "Wait a minute," she said. Within seconds Michael was on the phone. He had told me previously that he would have to leave by seven. He was going to a party. I asked if perhaps we shouldn't wait for another time. "No problem," he said and proceeded to give me quick directions to the house.

He had come home again, this time for an interlude of three days in a solid month of travel to Minnesota, Colorado, California, working as a technical adviser to a forthcoming movie based on the Olympic victory to be called *Miracle on Ice*. The next day filming would begin in New York, and a party was planned that evening at Santarpio's. When I came in, he was drinking a Budweiser, watching television. His sisters were home, and his sisters' children, and his cousin Bobby from the third floor, and his mother. Jeep was working at the cafe. Sitting beside him was Andrew Stevens, the actor who would portray him in the movie.

He had been Mike's shadow for several weeks, absorbing his speech and brassy manner, and now his family. "I was an only child," Andrew told me. "My parents were divorced. I never had any of this," he said indicating the general clamor in the house. "I wish I had."

Mike brought me a beer and led me past the kitchen, past the bedroom that he shares with Vinnie, past the bedrooms of his sisters, and took me to the outside porch, where we looked down at a large yard.

"That's Cousins' Stadium," he said. "We didn't have any money, but we had this." He pointed out home plate and the pitcher's mound for the stickball games, a horseshoe pit where games sometimes continued all night, a volleyball court, and a basketball net. "This family," he understated, "is very competitive. This is where I learned to play hockey. My cousin Tony would give me a dime and put me in the goal, and all his friends would shoot at me. After a while I'd go upstairs and cry. Then he'd give me another dime. And they'd shoot at me some more.

"My uncle Tony had the philosophy the yard was for fun. There used to be a nice apple tree in the yard, but we cut it down. And halfway up the trees you don't see any branches because we chopped them off. My aunts would be upstairs screaming. 'What are you doing?' And we'd say, 'The ball keeps hitting the branches. We don't know if it's a home run or not.'" Mike shivered from the night air and walked inside and sat at the kitchen table, his sisters and Andrew joining him, his mother stirring gravy on the stove.

"Everyone expected me to change because suddenly I was making money. I've probably made more since the Olympics than my dad's made in 10 years. But I don't come from money. It doesn't concern me. If I make it, fine. If not, fine. I want to spend my money on my friends, and two other people—myself and my family. Because if we'd lost, I wouldn't have had a damn thing. I'd be down at the gym tonight playing basketball, because the adult school is open. Probably coaching hockey somewhere. But we did win, and when you win in America, you're rewarded. And maybe all the work my mother and father did, and all the work my uncles and aunts did is coming out now in me, and we can say finally, 'Hey, enough is enough. It's time for the Eruziones to do something good.'"

Soon he left to get dressed for the party, leaving me with a tape of a speech he had given at a hockey banquet. "If anything, this family has gotten closer," his sister Nancy said. "We saw something threatening the closeness, everybody wanting a piece of him. After Lake Placid the phone never stopped ringing. 'Where's Mike? Get him.' Nobody wants us to be pulled away, so we pull together a little more."

I had a notebook and I passed it to Mike's oldest sister, Connie. I asked her to write the names and phone numbers of the members of this sprawling household. I turned on the tape.

"My dad hasn't lost his perspective," Mike told his audience. "An insurance company sent him a check for $50. My dad gets the check, and he cashes it. He gives my mother $25, and he takes the other $25 and goes to the track and he loses it. My mother's all upset. 'You're supposed to take me out to dinner.' 'No, no, there was a good horse. A chance to win.' And maybe that's how we were—taking a chance to win. Nobody thought we had a chance, but we changed things around. . . . "

I realized how much they had changed when later that night, I looked at my notebook. There were names and phone numbers across a page, neat and cleanly written, but beside Michael's name there was a smudge. His Winthrop address had been crossed out. Instead, his sister had written: "Mike—USA."

Published February 1981

Jeep Eruzione was prescient about the enduring legacy of his son scoring the winning goal in one of the most memorable sporting events in U.S. history. Mike Eruzione has lived the last 45 years in the light of that moment. He has given motivational speeches around the world, has coached college hockey, and served as an ambassador for Boston University, his alma mater. In 2020, on the 40th anniversary of the game, his memoir, The Making of a Miracle, *brought the game back to life. Though goal number four took him places he never imagined, he remained in Winthrop with his wife and three children. His father lived to age 92, seeing the family grow to include 15 grandchildren and 12 great-grandchildren.*

A Scout for All Seasons

We played baseball on summer evenings in a ballpark without lights. Parents and girlfriends and lonesome men sat on weathered bleachers down the third-base line, and children and dogs chased foul balls in the weeds behind the backstop. Then Jon and Bobby grew up, joined the league, and suddenly baseball took on an unexpected edge: Scouts came to town.

They wore dark trousers and sunglasses and talked quietly to each other between innings. They smoked cigars, spat tobacco juice into the grass, and used stubby pencils to write in notebooks they held on their laps. Watching them sitting as still and remote as desert vultures, we thought they possessed magnificent knowledge; and in our eagerness and optimism, we fancied ourselves prospects, knowing baseball contracts sat folded in their pockets.

Of all the dreams of youth, that of being a big-league ballplayer was the hardest to give up. The summer that the scouts came was when most of us dropped that dream hard, once and for all: For they had watched us, then walked on by without asking our names.

That was a long time ago, and while little in professional baseball links that generation to today, the backbone of the game remains the kids with talent and the scouts who must find them.

Scouting, too, has changed, but its folklore endures: independent, shrewd, eagle-eyed watchers, comfortable with loneliness, but never at a loss for words; who get lost in their hometown but can find a ballpark anywhere. Probably no scout evokes the image of this baseball maverick more than Bill Enos from Cohasset, Massachusetts, who beats the bushes for the Boston Red Sox in the north country of New England.

It is 95 degrees and rising at 10 a.m. on a late summer's day when I meet Bill Enos. The day is his 59th birthday, which he will celebrate at a Babe Ruth Tournament in Worcester, Massachusetts. He sits in the shade of a hotdog stand, his face wreathed in cigar smoke, reading the local sports pages. His lawn chair, his third of the season, sags where his excess weight has settled, a girth Enos likens to "a Montana mule."

The field is deserted now except for the groundskeeper watering the infield. Other scouts joke that Enos arrives to put the flag up, but he doesn't mind. The Red Sox, whom he joined in 1973, are the fourth team he has scouted for in nearly three decades, and his routine has never varied. Though he wears floppy hats and his shirt tail sometimes hangs outside his trousers, he is a man of precision.

He gets here early so he can walk the field. Small, possibly crucial details run through his mind: Is the pitcher's mound high enough? Is it even? The rhythm of a good pitcher can be knocked haywire pushing off from an uneven mound. Is the distance from home to second the same as in Fenway Park? It may be useful to know if a young catcher's peg here would arrive on a hop at Fenway. Is the infield smooth, or are there pebbles to distract the infielders? Will the wind affect fly balls? What's the background like for hitters? But mostly, he arrives early today because there is no place he'd rather be than at a ballpark. "It's been that way ever since I could think."

Enos is dressed for comfort in checked pants and a yellow sports shirt, three plump cigars protruding from the shirt pocket. He wears a prominent ring with "Enos" engraved on the side—the American League Championship ring won by the Red Sox in 1975. I ask how the Red Sox did the night before.

"Everybody expects me to know that," he says, "but last night I was at a Legion game on the Cape watching a 15-year-old pitcher. He's 6'3", 175 pounds, with a real good easy motion. His fastball moves, and already he's throwing 83 miles per hour, one of the best kids I've seen all summer.

I could follow him for three more years and want him for the Red Sox real bad, but with the draft, there's no way to predict."

Gone are the days when scouts competed fiercely for players in a no-man's-land with few restrictions except the limits of a scout's cunning and his team's money. In their place, since 1965, are three days in June in offices around the major leagues, where baseball conducts its annual draft of eligible amateur players. The draft has brought order to the doling out of baseball talent, as the team with the worst record the previous season selects first, the second-worst selects next, and so on. Now the scout's keen judgments weigh less than the place of his team in the standings.

"The draft can break your heart," Enos says. "I loved to compete for players. I'd find out everything about a kid and his family, even what they owed on their mortgage. I might buy the father a half pint or bring the mother a gift, but I made sure they looked forward to seeing me. One mother loved Whoopie Pies. I'd always show up with a box of those big fat cookies."

On this day, he is laying the groundwork for the 1980 draft. The games will be but two of some 450 games he will scout in a season that begins in Arizona in March, scouting major league teams for possible trades, until late October when New England colleges finish their fall season. Now in late summer, when Babe Ruth, American Legion, and semi-pro summer leagues hold tournaments, he's able to squeeze a day dry with baseball. When games begin at 10 a.m., he can scout five games in three states in one day. "I drive fast," he says.

He has no hobbies or interests that do not involve baseball. He has never taken a vacation with his wife, Grace, and his daughters, Anne and Karyl, because he could not imagine two weeks, let alone two days, without going to a game. In ten years, at age 70, he will face mandatory retirement from the Red Sox. He shrugs and says he'll just keep going to games, maybe becoming a "bird dog," a part-time scout, for his replacement.

Now he spends restless winter days poring through high school and college baseball schedules, matching them with his foot-high stack of player evaluations. With careful planning and luck, he hopes to see the best players a dozen times before making final judgments. "If I put eight players on my draft list," he says, "they *better* be the best in my territory. With the draft, you can't afford to make mistakes."

Early in the spring, he stuffs his schedules, his lawn chairs, and his hats in the trunk of his Cadillac, whose license plate proclaims "SOX." In the next seven months, they will travel about 25,000 miles. The schedules are his weapons against the capricious New England spring. Nothing frustrates him more than a day of rain when he's anxious to see a player, and he'll thumb hastily through his schedules looking for other games, while phoning contacts around the region, seeking a more cheerful weather report.

Being the local scout for a popular regional team puts him on the hot seat. People unfamiliar with the draft ask how he could have missed native New England major leaguers like Mike Flanagan (Baltimore), Jim Beattie (Seattle), or Rich Gale (Kansas City). "I saw those guys more than I saw Grace," he explains, but nevertheless he is expected to somehow keep New England players at home for the Red Sox. Baseball fans phone him day and night with tips he cannot afford to ignore, no matter how far-fetched.

"I woke up at 6:30 yesterday to hear over the phone, 'I've seen a kid who throws 95 m.p.h.!' 'Hold on,' I said. 'The fastest I've ever gotten is 91.' He says, 'Bill, the kid throws smoke!' So I work him out. I could have caught him in my handkerchief." He shakes his head. "Sometimes people will run you ragged, but I want to be the one checking."

He has seen so much baseball in his scouting career, it's dizzying to compute: over 36,000 hours, more than four years' worth of watching baseball. "I've never gotten up and said, 'I don't want to go to a game,'" he says with disarming sincerity. "My first years of scouting, I rolled out of bed and thought I'd find another DiMaggio. But I lost that. I don't expect to find Babe Ruth, but, hey, I might find somebody pretty good." He puffs his cigar and smiles. "And don't the good ones hit you like a bolt of lightning? You sit up straight and say to yourself, '*That's* what I came for. He can play.'"

A bus pulls up to the gate. Players emerge wearing white uniforms with bold blue letters. Their baseball shoes are slung casually over their shoulders, and they are laughing. "They look so young now, even the coaches," Enos murmurs.

Enos rises. He walks to his car and removes a leather case. Inside is a $1,000 radar gun. If he sees a pitcher today who shows promise, he may want to know if he can throw as fast at the end of a game as at the beginning. We walk out of the shade of the tall trees by the hotdog stand and into the broiling sun. He carries a chair, notebook, radar gun, and stopwatch behind the backstop. He will view the games through the diamond-shaped slats, but he doesn't care. He never watches the game and is at a loss to say who is winning or what the inning is. He is like a mechanic beneath the hood of a car, with the whole reduced to a series of parts.

With Bill Enos, the parts fit neatly on ruled cards 8½ inches long, 6 inches wide. There is space on the card to list the players for both teams with columns marked Arm, Run, Hit, Power, Field, Prospect. There is a separate listing for pitchers with columns for Fastball, Curveball, Change, Slider, Control, Field, Prospect.

During a game he will pencil in, next to their names, numbers that reflect his evaluation of their abilities, ranging from 2 (poor) to 8 (superior). On the cards, though, these kids today will be up against tougher competition than they know—the Boston Red Sox. The numbers do not reflect how they stack up against their peers but against people named Rice, Lynn, Yastrzemski. A 5 rating means major league ability *right now*. Not many young players score 5s. When they do, "That's when the bolt of lightning hits you," he says.

He moves his chair close to the screen and props his feet up so that from a distance, with his hat shading his eyes, he appears to be dozing. But he is especially attentive to the pregame ritual of infield practice. The coach hits a sharp ground ball to the shortstop, who must run far to his right, pivot sharply, and throw off balance. His throw skips wildly past the first baseman.

"There," Enos exclaims. "I may never get to see him have to make that play, the hardest for a shortstop, in the game." He is watching as well the fungoes sailing out to the outfielders. What he is looking for is devastatingly direct: raw speed and throwing power. "If the kid has God-given speed and strength, maybe we can teach him to hit. If a kid can do something, he'll show you. And if he can't, he'll show you that too. If you watch them play long enough, they eliminate themselves."

Each summer, over three million boys play baseball in America, and more than 1,000 each June are drafted. Of those drafted, perhaps half will filter through the minor leagues, greatly reduced to only 2,000 players since its heyday after the war when four times that number played; only a fraction of those will reach the major leagues.

"It's not a job for the soft-hearted," he says, "because you see so much desire in some kids. I may see some kids a dozen times, and *they see me,* and I know they're wondering: 'Why doesn't he sign me?' But if I ever lower my sights, I'm dead. I'll make a hundred stops like today to find one kid who can play. But maybe nobody knows how the kids feel like I do. I've spent a lifetime in their shoes."

In 1936, during the Great Depression, *The Sporting News* offered 10 boys selling the most subscriptions a free trip to a tryout camp in Arkansas. The 15-year-old Enos "wanted that tryout so much I could taste it," and with the tenacity that would later mark his scouting career, he finished second in the country. He was a lithe and graceful high school first baseman who caught the eye of a St. Louis Cardinals scout. Enos signed for $80 a month and spent a dizzying month traveling with the Cardinals, the legendary Gashouse Gang, managed by Hall-of-Famer Frankie Frisch. Their star, Dizzy Dean, called him "Kid." Then Enos was sent to the minor leagues for seasoning.

One year, he hit .315, and Paul Waner, another Hall-of-Famer, called him "the best fielding first baseman I've ever seen," but through 11 years and 22 teams, he stayed a minor league journeyman, his career broken only by a four-year hitch in the Navy during World War II. The buses were rickety and sometimes caught on fire as they groaned through the southern nights. The fields were stony, the people mostly friendly, and one of his sharpest memories is of young mothers sitting together behind the backstop in a Mississippi town, nursing their babies.

After the war, he became a player-manager for Class D teams in Baxley, Georgia; Pittsburgh, Kansas; Mayfield, Kentucky; Ada, Oklahoma. He saw the kids moving up, veterans coming down. He had a player so obsessed with his inability to hit southpaws that he snatched back a donation to a blind man in the street when he saw the man was left-handed. He learned how "can't miss" prospects would sometimes wilt from homesickness and fatigue. He didn't know it then, but he was learning how to scout.

At the end of the 1952 season, the St. Louis Browns, a sorry franchise soon to move to Baltimore and become the Orioles, asked Enos to scout a prospect in Belleville, Illinois. Enos was 32 years old, the youngest scout in baseball. He became the top "troubleshooter" for the Orioles, constantly on the road. He married Grace Jones, a nurse, in November 1954, left on a scouting assignment in January, and did not return for ten months. "Every time I'd get close to home, say, York, Pennsylvania, the club would say, 'Long as you're in the area, why not poke around Valdosta, Georgia?'"

He joined the Kansas City Athletics as their New England–New York scout in 1957 and soon had more South Shore players under contract than the other 15 teams combined. "One kid I signed is a surgeon in Connecticut. Another is in jail. But I'm not signing doctors, and I'm not signing jailbirds. I'm signing ballplayers, and after that, well, the ball takes funny bounces sometimes."

Enos today does not trot out a list of major leaguers he's signed. When pressed, he offers Skip Lockwood, Bill Travers, Tito Francona, and Ellie Rodriguez. It's a slender list, in part because he spent years as a "super scout," one who cross-checks the judgments of other scouts. He is prouder today to talk about the 10 players he's signed who were invited to spring training by the Red Sox. "Not bad for six years," he says.

I wonder aloud what he would have done if he had not gone into baseball. His eyes open wide, and he stammers. It's as though he has entered a terrifying place. "What *would* I have done? I took a test in the Navy, and they said I'd make a good electrician. Hah. I can't even screw in a lightbulb."

Enos has moved next to a rusted machine used to smooth the infield. He lays his notebook, radar gun, and glasses on top. "My office for the next few days." He has a guest in his office, then another. Dick Foley, a New England scout for the Central Scouting Bureau, is here, as well as Al Harper from the Montreal Expos. They share a warm but reserved greeting, like friends competing for the same woman.

The Central Scouting Bureau sounds vaguely sinister, and to some scouts steeped in the old way of scouting, it is. Operating from California with a roster of 60 scouts, it offered computerized, updated reports to any team for $100,000, a fraction of what it costs a team to maintain its own scouts in the field. Seventeen teams joined, and more than 200 scouts lost their jobs, including Al Harper, who was with the Mets at the time. It was a curious new world for the remaining 450 scouts. Scouting judgments, formerly as guarded as diaries, were suddenly being passed around like chain letters.

Most scouts go back a long way together, their lives knit by shared experiences in a singular profession. But in their souls, they are hunters, and it's not for nothing that they proudly call themselves "territorial scouts." When the game begins, Foley retreats down the left-field line, Harper sits on a grassy knoll behind third base, while Enos holds down his office.

By the third inning of the first game, Enos is sure he won't see anybody of interest. His quick notations "NP"—no prospect—save him his elaborate rating system. He was hoping to see a pitcher here, because a coach always uses his best pitcher in the first game of a tournament, but the ones on the mound are only fair. "I don't look at the speed of a pitcher's fastball as much as his movement. Does it hop? If the ball hops, it means he has a lively arm, and I pay attention to the other details—his fielding, his pick-off move, his motion."

I ask who the best pitcher was he ever scouted. I expected he would take a few moments to reply as he sifted through his memory, but instantly he blurted, "Skip Lockwood!" He signed Lockwood in 1964 to a $100,000 bonus with the Kansas City Athletics. He was a star pitcher and slugging third baseman from Norwood, Massachusetts, the nation's most sought-after schoolboy.

Enos savors the memory. "He had an arm so alive the ball cracked into the catcher's mitt. And he had great desire. He turned down a hundred scholarship offers to play for Kansas City. He was 20-1 in high school. I signed him the day after he lost his only game 1-0."

I express surprise that he could recall such details after a lifetime of seeing so many good players. "I may not be able to tell you what I ate for breakfast today, but I know Skip Lockwood ran to first base in 3.9 seconds in 1964. Hey, you don't forget the good ones."

Though the game we are watching is uneventful, void of promise for a scout, Enos will not leave, even to get refreshments. "I think of how parents would feel seeing a scout walk out on their boy. I never leave a game." The home plate umpire talks with Enos between innings. The night before he umpired in nearby Boylston and was impressed by the pitcher, a recent high school graduate.

"What's wrong with you?" he asks Enos. "That kid has really learned to pitch this year." Enos knows the pitcher. He's seen him pitch several times. But he pumps the umpire with questions. "Big kid?" "Real big," the umpire says. "He hurt his arm last year, maybe that put you off him. But you should get up and see him." Enos settles back and makes a mental note to check the pitcher.

In the second game, he takes immediate interest in the catcher, a tall, husky football player. Enos measures him with a well-practiced eye and announces: "6'2", 188 pounds." I check the roster. He is off by two pounds. The catcher shows a strong arm during infield practice, but he's terribly slow. "He looks like he wants to go to sleep out there. I bet you an ice cream soda you could beat him running to first base." The roster indicates he is a senior, and doubting further development, Enos' interest wanes. In the second inning, however, his coach walks over. He thinks Enos should know that the item on the roster is in error. The catcher is a junior.

"That makes all the difference in the world," Enos says. "Everything I do is based on potential. I look at the kid and figure he may grow another inch, maybe two. He could go 210 next year. After I watch him hit, I'll know more."

The catcher pops the ball up. "Doesn't matter. I don't care where the ball goes. I look at the swing. His bat is quicker than his feet. Good quick hands. No matter how a batter stands, or where he holds his bat, he still has got to meet the ball out front." The kid later will rate a stamped post-card addressed to Enos. It is a formality—it will tell him if the catcher is interested enough to send it in.

The second game refuses to end. The innings roll by—9, 10, 11, 12—the teams locked in a 4-4 duel. If the players consider themselves "NPs," it doesn't show. "Let's move our seats," Enos says. "Maybe we'll bring some-one luck." He picks up his chair and walks to the grassy bank by third base. Twilight, and in the 14th inning, the game is won by the catcher's team. Enos reminds me we have a doubleheader here the next day. We've already agreed to meet in Lawrence the night after that for an American Legion doubleheader.

"You're a treasure hunter, Bill," I say. "You won't stop until you find the gold."

"You're right," he says. "But if I find the treasure chest, then what? I'd just have to go out and find more." And he lights a cigar, blows a luxuriant cloud of smoke into the sky, and bids good-bye.

That night he detours by way of Quincy. He knows there is a ballpark there with lights, and "My car can't avoid lights. It's like a moth." He has checked his schedule and sees a game with a second baseman he remembered from two years ago. He is disappointed. The kid has not improved; in fact, Enos thinks perhaps he was better before.

He stops afterward to eat. Arriving at a sleeping household, he tiptoes into his office that is tucked into a pantry beside the kitchen. In his office are a desk, a lamp, and boxes of file cards representing games and players. It is all the space he needs, he says, because he takes his real office with him, a lifetime of baseball savvy that, he points out, "fits underneath my hat."

He flicks on his lamp and finds the card he wants. There is the pitcher's name who had so recently impressed the umpire. As he expected, the card reads: "Slow arm." He'd given his fastball only a "3." He is a big kid, all right, but in the judgment of Bill Enos, not a prospect. Satisfied, he replaces the card and flicks off the light. It is time for bed, and hey, only eight hours to wait for the next game!

Published June 1980

When Bill Enos passed away in 2014 at age 94, news stories featured tributes and memories from the baseball world. Ken Ryan, who Enos signed out of Seekonk High School, in Massachusetts, enjoyed an eight-year major league career. He remembered, "Bill would come to my games with a lawn chair and he would place it down with his back to me. I was always excited when he came to watch me, but every start I had, he wouldn't turn around to watch me until about my third or fourth inning. At that point, he would watch me for about two innings. No radar gun, just his eyes. After about two innings, he would turn his back again and continue chatting with parents and those at the game. This happened at almost every game he came to. It puzzled me. When he signed me in June of 1986, I asked him why he always had his back turned at the start of my games. 'Because you never warmed up correctly,' he replied. 'You would throw about 20 pitches to a catcher and you thought you were loose. It took you about three innings every start until I saw the real you.'"

The Education of Doug Flutie

The father of Doug Flutie drives slowly through Natick, a town of 31,000 west of Boston. It is a summer night; the air conditioner hums softly. Now and then the radar detector beeps a warning, but Dick Flutie pays it little heed. His wife, Joan, sits in the back. They are showing me landmarks in the life of their son, Doug Flutie—the most famous football player in New England history—so he drives as if these streets were pages from an album he could turn.

"That's where Doug and Laurie were married," Dick says in front of St. Patrick's Church. *LIFE* magazine was there. "Natick's royal couple," I say. "Yes," Dick says, "they were." Four years have passed since the wedding, a new granddaughter has been born, but he still has trouble accepting that Doug has a life away from them, even though the life is lived but two miles away. "That's been the hardest," he says. "Not the football. Just Doug not being around as much."

We ride in a 1985 Ford LTD Crown Victoria. It is maroon, the school color of Boston College, Doug's alma mater. In the winter of that year, at the height of his fame, Doug made a television commercial for Ford; as payment he could select a car. He told his father to take his pick. "I was in a grocery store with Doug," Dick says, "and I felt tears in my eyes. I pulled him over in an aisle, and I told him that for me not to have to worry about car payments . . . well, nobody had ever given me anything like that. Ever."

Bolted to the front bumper is a Boston College novelty plate, presumably in place forever. Lying on the back window is a New England Patriots banner that—should Doug be traded—can easily be removed.

Five years ago Doug Flutie threw a ball that traveled 65 yards through the rain in the twilight of the Orange Bowl, defying a wind that shook the palms outside the stadium and a clock that read zero. Some 30 million people watched on national television. The longest pass in football history, one writer said, because it traveled into myth. When he threw the ball, the score was 45-41 in favor of the University of Miami, the defending national champions. When the ball came down, Gerard Phelan, Doug's roommate, was waiting two yards deep in the end zone. Later, in the bedlam of the Boston College locker room, a player said, "That wasn't Gerard Phelan who caught the ball. God caught that ball." "No," replied a teammate, "God threw it."

America wanted a hero. Here was Doug Flutie: handsome, modest, a Rhodes Scholar candidate who played with the bravado of a fighter pilot. He said his parents were his best friends. He played touch football with his old neighborhood pals. And his story read as if scripted in Hollywood. Standing a shade under 5'10" and only 165 pounds, he was seen as too small for big-time college football. Though time and again he had rescued his Natick High team from certain defeat, the Boston College coach had rejected him. Then the coach resigned. A new coach, Jack Bicknell, arrived from Maine. Dick Flutie phoned him. "Take another look at Doug," he urged. "Look at the films." There was one scholarship left to offer, and his son received it. When Bicknell came to the house, Dick told him, "You don't know what you have just signed. You just don't know."

Doug became what the *New York Times* called "a cultural icon." Stores sold out of football shirts bearing number 22. A week after the "miracle in Miami," he won the Heisman Trophy, awarded to college football's best player, and soon after helped Boston College win the Cotton Bowl. A television producer toured New York with him and said in wonder, "It was like being with Sinatra."

For years Dick Flutie had been Doug's coach, his cheerleader, his historian; he roamed the playing fields snapping photos of his three boys, athletes all, and sold them to the local papers for $5 a shot. A computer engineer, he arranged work schedules so he could attend practices. Once

Doug's high school baseball coach told Dick not to come to practices anymore. The two men have not spoken since. At Boston College he obtained a photographer's sideline pass. At times during games, he could almost reach out and touch his son.

Dick grew up lonely in Baltimore without brothers, with an alcoholic stepmother and a father who seldom made time for play. He never forgot his ineptness when he tried out for Little League against the boys whose fathers had helped them along. When his father refused to let him play football, he cried himself to sleep and joined the golf team. As soon as he graduated from high school, he married Joan Rhodes, his girlfriend across the alley.

The children came, one after the other—Denise, then Bill, then Doug, then Darren. Dick worked days, went to college at night, formed a dance band, moved the family to Florida, gave his kids music lessons, and dreamed of the day he would have a family band. They had no other family in Florida as, later, they would have no other family in Massachusetts. "All we ever had was each other," said Joan. "We depended on each other."

Baseball became football became basketball. The boys measured themselves against each other. Bill was the biggest, the fastest. Darren was the toughest. Doug was the most exciting. "Bill made all the plays," remembered Joan, "but Doug was so much fun to watch."

Joan joined in, coaching softball, girls' basketball, running the concession stand at the games. "I learned about sports the same way I learned mothering. It's there to do, and you just do it."

Dick taught his sons a game called spoons. "You have a card table. You put one spoon in the middle. A person says, 'Ready . . . go!' The first person who can grab the spoon and bring it back wins."

"The furniture gets broken," Joan said.

"It's a good way to improve hand speed," Dick said.

"I don't know. It sure broke a lot of furniture," Joan repeated.

On this night we pass the barbershop, the library, the town square. On a winter's day in 1985 Doug rode down these streets in an open Thunderbird convertible, Dick and Joan in a convertible up ahead, waving to 50,000 people who ignored the cold to celebrate Doug Flutie Day. "The greatest parade this town's ever seen," said the police chief. As they rode, loudspeakers on the sidewalk blared again the football announcer's frenzied shouts from November 23, 1984. *"He did it! He did it! Flutie did it! He got Phelan in the end zone! Touchdown! Touchdown! Touchdown Boston College! No time on the clock! It is over! It is over!"*

Soon in Natick there was a road called Flutie Pass. The youth football championship game was called the Flutie Bowl. People came to Dick and said, "You must be so proud of Doug." "I'm proud of all my children," he replied. "Doug is proud to be a member of our family. The good times come and go," he said, "but the family is forever."

In February 1985 Doug signed to play for the New Jersey Generals of the United States Football League (USFL). He became wealthy. Said Doug: "It almost seems like I have had too many good things happen to me." A rival quarterback simply said, "Sooner or later, the miracles will pass him by."

Dick drives a few minutes out of town and stops in front of an expanded Cape, their former house in a neighborhood of modest, attractive homes where Wilogreen and Murdock Roads converge. "You're sitting on Doug Flutie's playground," he says. "That was our dining room," Joan says. "Out that bay window we'd sit there and watch them play."

They found the house in the spring of 1976 when they moved from Florida. Dick thought the schools would be better in New England. And, Joan explained, "the father of the high school quarterback in Florida gave lots of money to the school. Dick didn't think money should decide who played." A Boston friend suggested Framingham. On their drive north—four kids and a dog packed into the backseat—they turned off the Mass Pike and stopped at a McDonald's in Natick. Dick asked some patrons which town had the best sports teams. "Natick," they replied. He hustled the family to the local newspaper. A realtor saw him scanning the real estate pages and took them to Wilogreen Road, their suitcases still in the trunk; only hours after arriving in town, they bought the house. The Natick Babe Ruth league told Dick the teams had already been selected. Dick told them if he could have Bill and Doug, he'd form his own team from the boys who'd been rejected. That team nearly won the championship.

The family struggled financially, getting by week to week. Dick moonlighted as a wedding photographer. Joan worked part-time in a deli. "Sometimes car payments didn't go out," Dick said, "so we could send the boys to football camp. But football camp gave them the edge." Some people said that the Flutie kids were spoiled, that all they did was play. The phone was disconnected once, and Doug took his only high school job, frying clams at Nick's Drive-In. When he earned the money to turn on the phone, he quit.

Dick shifts in his seat. The lights are on in their old house. "We could go in," Dick says. "They told us to come by anytime." "That's Doug's bedroom up there," Joan says. "He had the biggest room." "When Doug played," Dick remembers, "we'd hear about the game until he fell asleep at night. We'd hear about every play. Everything that was right. Everything that was wrong. If I was busy, he'd tug until I paid attention."

At the end of Doug's junior year in high school, Dick accepted a promotion to return to Florida. The house went up for sale. His coaches in Natick still remember how distraught Doug was at the prospect of moving again. Doug flew down to meet with the coaches at the new school. He worked out with the baseball team. Dick talked to Doug, alone, afterward. "It's your choice," he said. Doug chose Natick. Soon Dick came home.

"We must have made all the right decisions," says Joan. She is quiet for a moment, then adds, "Up until the New Jersey Generals."

"There's not many kids that young who have their futures guaranteed," says Dick.

"You mean financially? Well, great," Joan says. "That's not what he wants."

"He's still a quarterback," says Dick.

"Chicago didn't want him," Joan says. "The Patriots don't want him. There's got to be someplace that wants him."

They sit outside the house for a few more minutes then drive just up the road. They want to show me where Doug played with his friends, the pasture where balls hit over the stone walls were home runs. New houses have been built since they were up here last; a chain stretches across the path where the kids once ran. A sign reads "No Trespassing." They stop there just a moment, then Dick heads for home, a handsome house, number 22 on the street, with a wide lawn that slopes to a lake; it, too, is a gift from Doug.

On a morning in June, Doug sits at the dining table in his parents' house, a plate of doughnuts and a glass of orange juice before him. On the wall above the table, looking down, is a huge portrait of Dick. On the walls, flowing from room to room, is a river of photographs of Doug and his brothers, framed newspaper clippings, framed magazine stories. When Doug first became famous, a reporter asked Dick how long his son had been a star. "He's always been a star," Dick replied.

The previous night Flutie's agent had wanted him to attend the celebrity opening of the Hard Rock Cafe in Boston, but instead he came here to eat pizza and watch the Leonard-Hearns fight. He looks tired. He wears navy blue sweatpants. His light blue T-shirt reads "Bermuda." A summer of golf has tanned him dark as a lifeguard. Sometimes his mother looks at him with his hair flowing down the back of his neck and laments what she sees as the influence of his rock star friend Jon Bon Jovi. Sometimes when she complains, he shoots back that if she hadn't been smoking when she carried him, perhaps he would have been 6'3" like his brother Bill.

She has warned me that Doug dislikes interviews. "He can't sit still," she said. This is true. But also the past years have made him leery of the press. With the New Jersey Generals he sometimes took a pounding from the New York papers. "Doug was upset," recalled Chris Palmer, a former Generals coach, now at Boston University. "I said, 'Doug, you can't read the papers. This isn't Boston College, everyone on the same scholarship. Your salary makes you CEO. And people expect you to play like one, every game.'" After his free-wheeling college heroics he felt stifled by the Generals' conservative offense, but he never sounded off to the press. Sometimes, though, when he came back to Natick, he'd start fussing with Joan that his eggs weren't right or the toast was burnt.

He phones now to check on whether he got the longest drive at a golf tournament the day before. The prize is a dozen free golf balls. He returns from the phone with the news that he got the longest drive, 286 yards.

"I thought you got 312," Joan says.

"That was downhill," Doug says.

"Who cares," she says, "312."

He picks up a football lying under a chair. It is soft, the dogs have been chewing on it. He shifts it from hand to hand, squeezing the seams. To his fans he appears slight, a wraith among giants, but his forearms and hands seem to belong to a much larger man. Nearly every day he runs several miles, plays basketball, lifts weights, and the muscles have matured his face and body. A few years ago it was reported that the Patriots had refused to draft the local hero because coach Raymond Berry thought he lacked the strength for the NFL.

"Lifting weights has nothing to do with playing quarterback," he says. "In high school I never touched a weight. I weighed 165 pounds and I could throw a football 65 yards. I can bench press 250 pounds now, and I'm twice as strong, and I throw the ball the same distance. But I want to beat out the other quarterbacks in all the strength tests. Then I'll stop lifting."

His friends and former coaches say that the frustrations of the past five years have taken their toll on the unflagging optimism that once sparked his play. "See, he knows he can't have a bad day," Jack Bicknell said. "A bad day means he's proved all the people right who say, 'See, he can't play.' I saw him a couple of times in the pros and I knew it wasn't him. Because he sort of went into a shell. In fact, I wrote him. I said, 'Doug, what the heck are you doing? Play the way you've always played.'"

Already he has made three professional stops: the Generals, the Chicago Bears, and now the Patriots. He heard his first boos with the Generals, endured ridicule with the Bears, was benched for the first time with the Patriots. His genius for turning routine plays into unpredictable adventures costs him dearly with the pros, who place a premium on game plans and consistency. In Chicago the Bears' most visible player, quarterback Jim McMahon, called him "America's dwarf." When Flutie started and lost a playoff game against the Washington Redskins, the city of Chicago blamed him for the defeat.

"Doug grew up a lot in Chicago," Joan said. "He always felt people were good, period. We both grew up in Chicago. It never entered my mind that people would be so nasty. That was Jim McMahon territory. Doug would come home at night in Chicago, and people had written things or thrown eggs on his garage door, and his neighbors would go and clean it up."

I said I'd ask Doug about that.

"No, please don't," Joan said.

He came from the Bears to the Patriots, the team he had always hoped to play for, in the last days of the player strike in 1987, crossing a picket line he said he would never cross except for the opportunity to come home. "When Doug came home," said Joan, "everything seemed right. Everybody was right where they were supposed to be."

Last year Doug, a substitute, came into the fourth quarter of a game that seemed lost. Joan ran out into the street. "Doug's in," she cried. "Come over, come over!" The neighborhood poured into her home and saw him electrify the crowd and score the winning touchdown. It seemed that day as though the indefinable Flutie charisma had been grafted onto a dormant Patriots team. He would start the next nine games, winning six, including a four-touchdown-pass game that earned him sweet revenge against the Bears. Of his days with the Generals, he once said, "Whenever I felt I was in control, I did well. Whenever I felt like I was being dictated to, I didn't." Soon it became obvious that with the Patriots, Doug had little control of the team's offense. Finally, he was benched at season's end in favor of Tony Eason. A Maine writer summed up the feelings of many Patriot fans: "Flutie has been used, abused, and tossed away. Doug Flutie deserved better."

In the season's last game against Denver, when a victory was needed to make the play-offs, Flutie was sent in only for the final, meaningless play. The Patriots were losing 21-10. He threw the longest pass of his life. The ball sailed 67 yards through the Denver sky. When it came down in the end zone, Denver intercepted. The miracles had passed him by.

Flutie picks up a doughnut. "I could go through a whole season without throwing an interception," he says. "I firmly believe that. But I've always wanted to be aggressive. Go after it. Right now I'm caught in between. Everyone's paranoid that you're going to make a mistake. And it's life or death. My attitude has always been, 'We're going to outscore you. We'll make some mistakes. So what? If they pick one off and score, no big deal. We'll score three more.'" He took a bite.

I thought of what Joan had told me earlier. "Of all my kids, Doug needs the pat on the back," said Joan. "He needs it desperately. And he's not getting it right now. To me, they're mistreating Doug," she said. "I don't care about the reasons. If you're mistreating him, you're on my list. Period." She was quiet. Then she said, "But I'm not Tony Eason's mother." Jack Bicknell simply said, "Doug Flutie's dying now."

Doug pushes back from the table. He flicks the football from hand to hand. "Terry Bradshaw struggled through his first few years. Struggled a lot. I remember him saying he went up to Chuck Noll [his coach] and said, 'Stand behind me, pat me on the back, tell me I'm doing a good job. I'll go out and kill for you.'" Flutie pauses. "That's all he needed."

Outside a squirrel leaps onto the porch. The dogs pound across the room, barking and scratching at the door. Doug throws the ball against the door, scattering the dogs.

While we talk, Joan has been watching a movie on television. The movie is *Winning*, starring Paul Newman. "He won the race," says Joan, "and he kept driving, and a reporter asked him why he didn't stop, and he said, 'I didn't feel like stopping.'"

Doug is at the front door, ready to leave. He walks back, glances at the screen. "Great line," he says. "Great line."

"Remember, don't smother the ball with your hand. Hold it on the fingertips. Leave a little space." The high school kids, all hopeful quarterbacks at the Boston College football camp on the last day of June, kneel in a semicircle around Doug Flutie. He wears gym shorts and a T-shirt. "The easiest way to throw a football is with your legs," Doug says. "Keep your feet under you and step in the direction of the throw. Of course," he adds, "sometimes you're being chased." He smiles. "And you gotta do what you gotta do."

Michael Mucci, nearly 15, stands about 5'11" with time to grow. He is a sophomore from Revere. The number on his high school jersey is 22. In the late 60s his father had played for Boston College; Michael dreams of one day wearing the maroon and gold. When the quarterbacks form groups for passing drills, Michael is without a partner. "I've got him," Doug calls. They kneel, facing each other. The throws from that position must be firm, right at the chest. Doug's are darts. Michael's are not. Doug walks over. Soon his lessons—put your finger here, your shoulder there—help Michael's passes spiral in a way they had not before. That night Michael's excitement will all but burn the phone wires to Revere. Guess who had coached him one on one?

There is a moment when Doug, his work over, stands alone in the center of the field, flipping the ball in the air, catching it, flipping it up again. The next day he will leave for Long Island and another camp for high school kids, then it will be time for the Patriots. He walks to the sidelines, and before disappearing down the tunnel beneath the stands, looks back at the field at Mucci and all the kids whose games stretch ahead of them forever. A short time before, we'd been talking about football and fun and how seldom you hear the word *fun* spoken by NFL professionals.

"Last year," he said, "I went into camp a week early with the rookies and free agents. And we scrimmaged the Washington Redskins. By the end of that week, they believed in me so much. See, all of a sudden I had a group of young guys who rallied behind me. It was just different in the huddle. I'd go out on the field anytime with them. I mean, it would be great."

Once, Doug Flutie made everyone remember the dancing days of childhood when miracles happened every day on every playground. I told Jack Bicknell this, and that Doug once seemed the counterpoint to the technocrats and computers, a free spirit who won by improvising, challenging everyone who said, "No, you can't."

"They're winning now," Bicknell said. "The computers are winning."

Maybe. Maybe when you read this, Doug will have been traded or suffered an injury. Or perhaps he will merely be the man in waiting. "Any story on Doug has got to be open-ended," Dick Flutie said. "The saga continues." Better than anyone, he knows what a computer cannot calculate, that once there was a 13-year-old boy who, on the eve of moving from Florida to Massachusetts, took care of a nagging piece of unfinished business. "I was second trumpet in the school band," said Doug. "I challenged the first trumpet for his chair. We were leaving the next day. It didn't mean anything. But I beat him."

Published November 1989

Like Dick Flutie predicted, the Doug Flutie saga not only continued but created its own legendary chapter. Before Flutie retired from football in 2006, he silenced doubters by playing for 21 seasons—eight of those in the Canadian Football League where he won the Grey Cup, Canada's Super Bowl—three times. He returned to the NFL in 1998 with the Buffalo Bills and was named to the Pro Bowl as well as earning Comeback Player of the Year. In retirement Flutie became a fixture as a television sports commentator. On November 15, 2015, his father, Dick, suffered a fatal heart attack. An hour later, Joan Flutie had a sudden heart attack and died. "They say you can die of a broken heart, and I believe it," Doug posted.

In the fall of 1981, on the banks of the Miramichi River, where Red Sox legend Ted Williams (right) kept a fishing camp, he and his friend, outdoor writer Bud Leavitt, exchange the friendly barbs that began in a Red Sox dugout in 1939. Photo credit: Carole Allen

Fishing Buddies

These were fly-fishing-only waters. Beyond the small river towns with the houses and general stores pressed close to the road, signs appeared "Salmon Flies Tied" and "Fishing Guides." Sometimes we could see the fly lines of the fishermen drop gently in the water that sparkled beneath the waning sun, and at such times Bud Leavitt would glance from the road, looking for the strike of a salmon.

It was on one of the final weekends of September 1981, near the close of the fishing season. Bud Leavitt drove down a dirt road a few miles outside of Blackville, New Brunswick (population 987), and stopped between two cabins, a small one for guests, and the main lodge set on a knoll 100 feet above the Miramichi River, the summer home of Ted Williams for 20 years. This was where Ted Williams had honed his skills as perhaps the finest Atlantic salmon fly-fisherman in the world; where Bud Leavitt came to renew a friendship that spanned four decades and, if he was lucky, to catch fish.

Bud Leavitt at age 64 is an institution of the Maine woods. His daily column,"Outdoors," is in its 35th year for the *Bangor Daily News,* and his "Woods 'n Waters" public television series has twice been voted the best outdoors show in America. "Anybody who goes fishing in Maine and doesn't have Mr. Leavitt as his leader has gone wrong somewhere, probably in boyhood," wrote the late Red Smith. Bud writes before dawn. After that his phone rings: "Are the mackerel biting?" "The smelts running?" "Will bass take better on rubber worms, or artificial bait, or natural worms?" Sometimes he answers calls from people who know their only hope of getting through to the reclusive Ted Williams is through Bud Leavitt.

On the surface their friendship seems improbable. Both are strong-willed, stubborn, proud, profane, loud men with biting wit. One is a sportswriter; the other has a legendary distaste for the pryings of the press. But the outdoors became their shared playing field.

Early in his Boston Red Sox career, which established him as perhaps the greatest hitter of our times, Ted Williams turned to the woods, especially the woods of Maine, as his sanctuary. He remained merciless in his drive for perfection, whether on a ball field or on the water—both salt and fresh—and in Bud Leavitt he found a tenacity and a love for the outdoors to complement his own.

It was past six o'clock when Bud Leavitt arrived. There was a bite in the air and the leaves of the white birches that ringed the cabins had begun to change. Down below he could see a few fishermen plying the evening waters of the Miramichi. Ted Williams was sitting at the end of a dining table perched by the windows overlooking the river. He glanced up from his dinner of spaghetti, salad, and pie served by his long-time housekeeper, Edna Curtis, whose husband, Roy, has guided Ted for 25 years.

"You said five o'clock. You've messed up our evening's fishing already," Williams flung to Bud in greeting.

"I can go home," Leavitt replied.

"Do you know how lucky you are to be here?" Williams said.

Hand-tied salmon flies poked out from the patch of lamb's wool on Williams' fishing vest, worn over a tan chamois shirt ripped down the sleeve. His face was etched with a deep tan and his eyes were red from the sun.

"I'll tell you, Bud, it's the poorest fishing I've ever seen on the river. I'm coming to feel anglers are silly to try and save this fish," Williams said. "I throw back hens and grilse [salmon between three to five pounds returning after only a year at sea] and they're netting 400,000 metric tons in the high seas. The fish can't survive the pressure. I've caught only 43 fish—caught, not kept. Usually I'd be around 100 by now. We're seeing a species die here."

They talked that night sitting on the porch until it grew too cold and they moved inside. Few sentences slipped by without jabs about the other's weight or lack of talent in the outdoors or taste in equipment, arguing over the proper number of pockets in a fishing vest, whether raincoats should have pockets at all.

Before dawn the next morning Ted Williams was at his tackle bench in the basement of his cabin, working amid small mounds of animal hair, bird feathers, and tinsel, tying salmon flies. Fly-tying began for him in 1946, the year the Red Sox won the pennant. He'd sit at his tackle bench in his hotel room, tense from a game, and he'd tie until finally he'd be able to sleep. The night they clinched the pennant, Williams was in his room tying flies, while his teammates partied and popped champagne corks.

His creations now are all tied on single hooks. He doesn't believe salmon, scarce as they are, should be fished with double hooks, as was once his custom. This morning, he worked up a beauty, a Number 8 Cosseboom, that he couldn't wait to test. There was a guy with a gimpy leg across the way to whom he had promised his next salmon.

At seven o'clock Roy and Edna Curtis arrived. Roy is a stocky, ruddy-cheeked man who likes to say he has never fished in front of Ted Williams in his life. "I want Ted to get first crack at a fish," he says.

Ted came out on the porch and peered through the mist to the river. Sea smoke, white and ghostly, hovered over the dark river. "Water near came up over five inches. I can see that rock—I think it came up six inches." He curled a hand to his lips and blew his version of the Marine Hymn down to the river. "I'm alerting the river," Williams said.

Roy packed the pickup. Edna handed him the thermos of black tea and a sack of homemade doughnuts and sandwiches slathered thickly with mayonnaise, as though fearful one of the fishermen she saw to the river would lose an ounce of flesh while in her care.

Ted waved his eight-and-a-half-foot rod in front of Bud. "That's the best equipment you ever had your hands on," he said. "The question is, is it too much equipment for you? Too sophisticated for you?" Bud, who had been kept awake most of the night with mice scurrying through his cabin, mumbled, then Roy and Bud and Ted climbed into the pickup and left for Gray Rapids.

The first words Ted Williams ever spoke to Bud Leavitt were, "Hey,

Bush, come down here." It was 1939 and Williams was a brash rookie of 21. Leavitt was in the Red Sox dugout interviewing Billy Goodman for his sports column in the *Bangor Evening Commercial.*

Leavitt was an imposing-looking man of 22, a former Maine high school hammer-throwing champion. He glanced over at the tall, wiry Williams. "I'm not through talking to this man," he said. At the end of the dugout Williams stood waiting, gripping a bat, taking half swings before the game.

He said, "I'm Ted Williams."

"I know that," replied Leavitt.

"I hear you're from Maine," Williams said. "Tell me about it."

After Leavitt told him what he could in a few minutes, Williams said, "I'll call you," and a month or so later they were bass fishing on a small pond in Washington County. Leavitt's world fascinated Williams—the wardens, the woodsmen, the cooks and waitresses in the small-town diners—and whenever he could, he returned. Leavitt kept his distance when distance was needed, and whenever Williams said, "Off the record, Bush," it remained so.

In 1941 pressure mounted as Williams made his historic run at batting .400, finishing at .406. Leavitt would come to Boston, and they'd dine in Chinatown and never mention batting. As each season ended now, Williams, in need of peace and quiet, would come to Maine. Bud and his two daughters would meet him at the airport, and he'd sit behind the wheel of Bud's 1939 Packard Touring Sedan convertible driving through downtown Bangor while people hollered, "Hey, Ted." He'd sprawl on the king-size divan in the Leavitt living room, downing Barbara Leavitt's lemon pie with a quart of milk, before heading out the next day to Fish River Lake, or the Red River country in Aroostook, or the Machias, where fishing and woodcock hunting waited.

One memorable year Leavitt was given the executive coach of the Bangor and Aroostook Railroad to bring Williams back to Maine at season's end. It was a sight Leavitt has never gotten over—the great engine pulling one car with two men and their steward northward in luxury through the night from Boston to Presque Isle.

They reached the Miramichi together in September 1958. It was the day after Ted won his last American League batting title at age 40, beating out Pete Runnels on the last day of the season. He flew that night from Washington, D.C., to Boston, and then to Bangor. After resting for a few hours, they left at three in the morning on the final day of Atlantic salmon fishing. Driving through dense fog, they narrowly missed colliding with two cows that reared suddenly from the mist near Fredericton. Nearly 12 hours later they arrived. Roy Curtis was their guide.

"The wind was blowing awful bad," he recalled. "That morning, I crossed the river in the canoe and the sun was coming up over the mountain. I could see every rock and every fish in the pool, and there was a rock in the middle with 10 fish laying around it. I said to Ted, 'You wade out and cast and I'll tell you when the fly's coming over the rock.' The whitecaps were high, but he got it out there. I said, 'Now you're over the rock.' He stood there and stood there! He had staying power. And didn't he get one!" The fish, a 20-pound hookbill, gave Ted one of the greatest fights of his life, convincing him to one day build a cabin on the river. That night he told Bud, "I could go on forever."

Ted was 42 when he played his last game in Boston on a cold day in late September 1960. Bud sat with him in the dugout before the game. In the eighth inning Williams sent a towering home run into right centerfield, ducked out of the stadium, and went to his hotel where Bud was waiting with some of Ted's friends from Maine. From then on, he called himself "Ted Williams, fisherman." He never really retired.

It was 30 minutes down a rutted, bone-jarring road to Gray Rapids, where Ted owned one of his four fishing pools along the river, pools worth thousands of dollars. In the towns along the Miramichi, it was a source of tension that wealthy outsiders could own native waters. Sometimes cabins were burned and private pools poached with nets, but Ted had been left alone.

A parking area was cut from the woods, and already several trucks were there, their owners plying the public stretch of water below Ted's private pool. An outsider can pay $1,000 a week to rent a cabin and a guide on the Miramichi, while natives fish the river for the $20 license fee. It was a steep descent to the river, the path slippery from the rain a few days earlier. Ted caught his breath, coughed deeply, and called to the men he saw almost every day fishing Gray Rapids. Some were well-to-do;

others were unemployed mill workers from nearby towns. But in their waders, suspenders, and hats studded with flies, there seemed to be no difference.

"I've got something for you," Ted said to one of the fishermen who had come to the riverbank. He took out his fly box and held it open. "I want you to be happy—take any one." Ted glanced at Bud. "This won't be an easy decision for him," Ted said. The fisherman then offered Ted his reel. Ted shook his head, visibly touched.

"Give it to Roy," persisted the fisherman.

"No," Ted said, "he's already spoiled."

Ted started upriver to fish his pool. He glanced back at Bud enjoying a cigarette on the bank. "I've got a chance to catch fish behind my friend," he said loudly. "Maybe catch one he's missed." Then he was walking carefully on the loose rocks, disappearing around a bend through the alders, his rod flexing like a wand in his hand.

I walked with Ted to his private pool. "Do me a favor," he said. "Ask interesting questions." He waded out about 50 feet and dipped a thermometer into the river. "The water's pretty cool," he said. "Fifty-seven. I bet the fish are laying in Boyd's Pool on Black Brook."

He stripped line from his reel, tugging it downward on his forecast and backcast, shooting the line in a high tight loop before releasing it to the water. He worked his way slowly downriver, his goal a bunch of rocks barely visible above the water. "They like to lay in there," he said. "There's holes seven feet deep where they sit and rest."

He looked downriver where the fishermen were spaced at 100-foot intervals. "I can tell a guy by the style of his cast," he said. "The trick is the consistency of the cast, keeping the angle the same. And you have to know your limits—don't cast more than you can handle."

He measured his line by bringing it in and stretching it across his chest, his arms flung open to a six-foot span. He figured 90 feet into the east wind. "Not a lot of fishermen can handle that," he said. "Sometimes I fish all day knowing the water temperature is no good and not many fish are coming. But you never know, you never know. The other day I wanted to see what Roy was doing, but as I turned, I said to myself, 'Be ready for a strike' and boom there it was."

He stayed close to the bank, feeling for the black rocks beneath him disguised in the flowing water. The bank to his left was a mound of high grass with a few dead tamaracks in a grove of young birch. Across the river was a knoll with houses painted white and a blue tent on a lawn where a campfire smoldered, a scattering of trailers, and two canoes beached on the shore. Four mergansers flew past and above them streaked an Air Force jet: for a moment the fly line, the ducks, and the jet shared the sky above the water. He looked up.

"Four hundred fifty knots," he gauged. "See that fly swinging now. That's a hot spot. There's plenty of action in the water, lots of oxygen for the fish. Now the next hundred feet will really be hot. I'm in a good place here, mercy, mercy."

As he cast, his mouth hung open just a bit and his body leaned toward the water on his follow-through. "Yi, yi, yi. I'm in a good place! I remember all the spots, and that's a lot of memories. I remember where I cast, where I got a boil. Every time I approach that rock, I remember that little roll I got, so slow and pretty. Fourteen pounds. This fish gets under your skin so bad, so bad."

Across the way a young native fisherman called out from his canoe. "Happy birthday, Ted. I heard it on the radio. Pretty soon, Ted, the salmon are going to put the shift on you."

Williams laughed. "Pretty good. Forty years ago," he shouted back, "I was whistling along at .413 right about now."

Suddenly his voice lowered. "I don't know but I could have had a fish boil under me there. I'm probably wrong, but I'm going to give it another cast. Now that's just close observation and I may be altogether wrong. I thought I might have had a little disturbance underneath. I'll give it one more cast, one more chance." He cast to the same spot and spat into the river. The water boiled. "Goddam, there's one! What do you think of Ted Williams now?" he shouted. "What do you think of Mr. Williams?" as the salmon leaped and cut the water with a flash of silver. "It's a good fish, 12, 13 pounds," he said.

Roy appeared with the net, drawn by the shouts a hundred yards away. Ted let the salmon into the net carefully so it would not thrash and injure itself. It was a hen filled with eggs. Roy lifted her by the tail. "Fresh from the sea," he said. "Sea lice still on her."

For a moment Williams seemed undecided, thinking perhaps of his friend across the river to whom he had promised a salmon. "I hate to keep it," he said. "I hate to keep it."

Roy looked over, then put her in the water, stroking her belly. A minute or two later the fish put her nose to the current and moved upriver. A local fisherman who had scurried over said, "Lucky she got caught by you. I don't think I could have let her go."

Hours later, Williams called from the river. Was it 12:30? He was hungry. It was 2:15. He was surprised and came slogging through the water. "The thing to do now," he said, "is agitate Mr. Leavitt."

He was delighted to find Bud downriver, his hook tangled in some grass. "First time I've seen his rod bend," he laughed. "C'mon, Porky, get in here." Bud waded onto the bank and asked me to dislodge a hook caught in the back of his vest. Williams raised his eyebrows, made some unflattering noises.

"Didn't you ever hook yourself?" asked Bud.

Williams considered. "Maybe once," he said. "In '57 or '58."

A fisherman was approaching, holding a grilse, the only evidence of any action since Ted had released his fish. He had white hair and wore a hearing aid. "Look at Williams," he said, "all solid meat, not an ounce of fat."

"He's after a fly," said Bud.

"The man's just being honest," replied Williams.

The fisherman displayed his fly case, filled with a summer's worth of donations by Williams. Bud angled over for a look. "Don't show him," hissed Williams.

"Hat flies," spat Bud. "Never been in the water."

"There's a lot of jealousy here, a lot of jealousy," Williams said. He poked through his own collection. "There's a winner," he said and handed it over.

Time moves slowly on the bank of a salmon river when few fish are showing. The conversation percolated through layers of memories. Sometimes it drifted to baseball and paused there awhile like a slowly passing cloud. Someone asked about Yastrzemski. Williams was silent for a moment then smiled. "First off," he said, "Yaz fishes with worms. . . ." But at the slightest movement in the water the talk swayed back to fishing.

Bud was talking smallmouth bass fishing, about a river where "there's no way you're going to hit the water early and not catch 10 to 15 fish."

Williams hooted. "You told me the same thing about the St. Croix, and we didn't catch 15 fish the whole week."

"Well," Bud said, "we caught a bunch of pickerel."

"Little pickerel," Williams said, spreading his hands a few inches apart. "If it's so good up there," he added, "I'll make a movie with you. I'll put your show on the map. I'll give it a good rating."

"I had a floater with a plug," Bud continued. "I just threw it in and it exploded."

"How big was it?" asked Williams.

"Four and a half pounds, a helluvafish," Bud said.

"And you think that's a good place for bass, huh?" Williams asked, his interest aroused. "And you just go along the shoreline?"

"Yeah, you just poke along," Bud said.

"That's fun. That's fun." Williams said.

Soon Bud began fiddling with his reel. "When it comes to mechanical ability," he said, "I can't screw a lightbulb in, but I know there's something wrong with this reel."

Williams reached over and began tinkering. Bud looked on, keeping his peace. Williams was obviously having trouble putting it together again. "It's a little tricky getting this spool on," he said. "Got to get it just right."

"Yeah, well the moral is if it's working, don't open it—use it as it is."

"Is that right?"

"Yeah. You think you're Thomas Edison?"

"Did I ever tell you you're terrific?" said Williams. "You're terrific." In the distance he saw a fish break the surface. He handed Bud his reel, all in one piece. "I'm going back in there." He stood up and took a fly from his fly case. He squinted. "Not many fish see this one."

Then he smiled. "Oh, we'll be tired tonight. Love it when we're tired." But there was no more action on the river that afternoon. Emerging from the river, he walked stiffly until circulation returned to his legs.

After dinner Bud came out on the porch. "I want you to hear this," he said, inserting a cassette into the tape recorder. He said it was a re-creation of the 1941 All-Star game, recorded by a California sportscaster. Ted came banging outside. "Let's get excited!" he said, peering toward the river.

Roy tugged his waders on. Ted was moving ahead, down the rough-hewn steps leading to the river.

Bud flicked on the recorder. The voice was grainy above the steady roar of a simulated crowd. "Two out, bottom of the ninth. The American League trails 5-4. Ted Williams the batter, tying run at third base, winning run at first in Joe DiMaggio. Williams is one for three with a walk. Takes a pitch, just misses for a ball. Williams is batting .405 on the season. Two balls one strike. There's a long fly, home run off the parapet in the top deck! The American League wins 7-5."

"He laughed going around the bases," Bud said. "People said they'd never seen him so happy." He shook his head. "Three years ago, he walked on the field at Winter Haven with his balloon uniform that Johnny Orlando had outfitted—and it had to fit perfectly even then—and the writers crowded around. Who else, just by putting on the uniform, can do that?"

We strained our eyes to see Ted as he worked his pool. From inside we could hear Edna straightening up the pots, waiting for Roy to take her home. Outside it was quiet, and Bud had turned up the collar on his jacket. Down below we could see the twitch of motion, Ted's line hitting the river. As the dusk deepened, even that was lost, and all we could do was sit and wait for Ted to come back.

Published April 1982

After "Fishing Buddies" appeared, J.J. Nissen, one of Maine's largest commercial bakeries, saw an opportunity to have these two famous friends debate whether white or whole wheat bread was better. Their TV spots became one of the classic Maine commercials of their day. Anyone could see on the riverbank that each barb, the sharper the better, was how two burly men expressed an affection that they could say no other way.

SEVEN

MEMORIES

Two miles north of my house sits a metal and concrete storage unit, among hundreds of other similar units in one of those storage neighborhoods that take root on otherwise open terrain. Inside is what seems to be a chaotic collection of musty cardboard boxes and plastic crates. This messy world is where memories grab hold: of lives lived, of people loved, of work that brought pride and pleasure and once filled days and weeks.

When my two sons moved away and sold their mother's house after she died, their art projects from childhood, collections of shells and knick-knacks, video games, and mementoes from proms and sports—all found homes inside crates I squeezed into nooks and crannies.

When I ask what they want me to do with it all, they say let it go, all of it. But here is where I find a child's blue ski helmet. I do not see an old blue ski helmet that can never be worn again. I see the little boy flying down a slope with his brother, and the flash of blue is how I spotted him when I looked up the mountain.

Inside another box is a framed photo of my dad in his Army uniform from World War II. He is only a few years older than my sons, who never knew him. And here sits a dusty brown leather satchel. Inside are large manila envelopes that have not been opened for decades. They hold letters my father wrote to my mother during the war. When I leave this earth, nobody will ever want to see them.

I find a set of audiotapes held together with a rubber band with my handwritten scrawl: "S. King." They keep his voice from nearly 50 years ago. Another set reads "Alan Shepard." And here is where I keep the notebook I used for my first Yankee *story, a profile of Ma Dudley, the wife of a Maine potato farmer who would feed the workers every day and who opened a small restaurant in her homestead after her husband died.*

I know the wisdom that says you will not miss any of this stuff. It has been dormant here for years. You will have $125 each month that now simply goes to a closed door. I know this makes sense. But what lies inside once meant something to people I cared about; and notebooks and interviews were the tools of my life's work but of little meaning to anyone else. I know that. It is a dilemma shared by many of us.

One day I went to the locker determined to lighten the load of the past. It was time. And this is where I found a yellowed letter paper crumpled beneath a few notebooks. It was handwritten by a girl named Jamie. She would have been eight or nine years old. She was on a youth baseball team I coached in the early 1990s in Keene, New Hampshire. Only a few girls played then, and she had been unsure she fit in. I read: "You have showed me so many things that I never knew I could do. If it weren't for you, I would still be that wimpy scaredy-cat I was when we started. But now I'm someone who can go up to the plate and hit, swing hard, and not strike out and be upset. Thank you so much for getting me to be the ballplayer that I've dreamed of being."

She had decorated the top and bottom and both sides of the paper with colored stars. Tell me, how do I toss it into a bin, even if I have not seen it for 30 years? Because now I have, again, and it fills me with the same pleasure as when I read it long ago. I fold it carefully and place it in a new box that I label "Keep."

The Worst 30 Minutes of My Entire Life

They told me later that conditions for racing had seldom been worse. It was bitter cold, nearly zero, that March weekend in Rangeley, Maine. A blustery wind gained force steadily, swirling the snow so that dog teams seemed to disappear through a veil of white—a "white-out" they called it. The spruce cuttings that marked the trail on the lake (five and a half miles for five dogs, nine miles for seven or more dogs) became all but useless as a guide, and the experienced drivers relied on the instincts of their lead dogs to see them through, though I learned later that even veteran drivers struggled. More than 50 dog teams raced that Saturday, one being driven by me, the greenest of greenhorns. After I left the starting line of my first sled-dog race, Ivan Beliveau, a leading sled-dog trainer and racer, owner of my team, turned to his wife, Kathy (the publicist for New England sled-dog racing who had helped concoct the scheme of letting me get the "feel" of the sport), and said, "We've made a mistake." But all of that I learned later. . . .

I arrived in Rangeley just before midnight that Friday. It had been a desolate ride—for the last 75 miles I had passed by perhaps two dozen houses. There had been time—too much time—to ponder what Ivan had told me earlier. Weeks of rain and mild weather had wiped out the heart of the racing season and had interrupted the training a racing dog needed to stay sharp. "These dogs are going to be nitsy, sore, sour, and miserable," Ivan had said. "There's no telling what they'll do. They'll be so keyed up that there could be a lot of interaction with other dogs—and that's where the trouble begins. The biggest thing," he added, "is not to be afraid. The dogs will sense if you're afraid and they'll take control of you—just bolt. If you're fair with them, they'll respect you, but if you do something that makes no sense, they'll look for a situation to get rid of you."

The streets of the town were lined with trucks, with dogs sleeping two to a hut built onto the cabs. I checked into the inn, then walked down the street. The snow on the street crunched beneath my boots. I could hear dogs shifting in their boxes as I went past, and sometimes I caught a glimmer of eyes peering out. I went back to the inn.

I awoke early from a fitful sleep to the sounds of barking as dogs were turned out up and down the street, and now and then a howling began in a pocket of town and spread. Then just as quickly as it began, it faded and died. At about 9:30 a.m. Saturday, Kathy told me Ivan had agreed to let me run. It seemed a good day for the race. There were five inches of hard snow on the lake, and it was cloudy, cold, and tolerably windy, good weather for dogs bred for the cold. The trail seemed well marked with spruce cuttings. "Remember," she cautioned. "If you get off the trail, you're on your own. There are 18 miles of lake, and we'll just be waving good-bye to you."

I began tingling with the curious mixture of fear and excitement that I hoped would be taken as a sudden case of the chills. I had two hours to wait before my race, and I spent much of it walking between the racing area and my room, trying on combinations of clothes before deciding on long johns, wool pants, a turtleneck, a sweater, and a wool coat. Still I shivered as I watched Kathy and Ivan prepare my team. Sobi, the leader, was let out first and tied on a short chain to the truck; this set a dozen other dogs yelping with anticipation. Sobi had been debarked six years before, when neighbors complained about the steady clamor from the Beliveaus' place that reached a crescendo every evening at feeding time, and as she strained against her leash, a curious, rasping woof rose from her throat.

Ivan cautioned me. "My dogs know I'm the leader of the pack. I'm stronger and they know it because I've proven it. If I say 'straight ahead,' they know it's straight ahead. But you're a newcomer, and you have to prove you're the boss. Sobi's the toughest. She's the dominant leader. Sobi would just as soon thumb her nose at you—say 'see ya later.' When you give the commands [*gee, right; haw, left*], it's not how loud you say it, it's how firm."

So Sobi, the lone female, would be my leader. Behind Sobi would run her son, Thunder, and alongside him would be Buzz, a buff-colored dog. They were both just two years old, in their first full year of racing. "They're learning from Sobi not to make mistakes," Ivan said. "They're in training for my team and I can't afford to have a young dog on my team make a mistake." Pulling up the rear would be Streaker, once a member of the North American championship team and purchased by Ivan for breeding; and Lobo, Ivan's $800 "mystery dog."

"Impeccable genes," Ivan said, shaking his head, "but I can't unlock him. When I tried to make a leader of him, he just turned around and wouldn't run." Over the din of the barking and yelping the loud speaker boomed: "Twenty minutes until five-dog teams."

Ivan reached into his pocket, took out a package of small matches, makeshift suppositories, and inserted them quickly into his dogs. "A dog that stops to poop," he explained, "well, that 20 seconds can lose the race. I've lost a lot of money for 20 seconds."

There are other rituals. Kathy greased the paws to prevent snow balls, and most curious of all, Ivan began howling to the dogs, his cry piercing the air, and the team caught his cry with theirs—except for Sobi's whispered effort—and they trembled with pleasure. "It's how Ivan gets them to shake the kinks out," Kathy explained.

The dog teams were started at two-minute intervals, racing against the clock rather than each other, and Ivan hurried over to the timekeeper to check my position. "Ten minutes," he shouted on his return. He clapped his mittens together. "It's wild, woolly, and cold," he said. "You're going to get windburn, sure. It'll give you a feeling for how tough it is."

I knew he felt a certain satisfaction that his sport would not be a picnic for me. "Don't worry," he shouted, "you're sandwiched between people who know what they're doing. Our friend Jo Ann is ahead of you. If you get in trouble, she'll help."

"Should I tell Jo Ann that Mel's a beginner?" Kathy asked. "No reason to," Ivan replied.

When the dogs were hitched to the sled, they thrummed with tension. With the exception of Sobi, a Siberian husky, the remainder of the team was a cross between greyhounds, shepherds, and Siberians, in racing circles known as Quebec hounds. They are bred for excitability, for furious energy, and it showed as they howled and lunged. Sobi at the lead was straight as an arrow, and it took all our strength to hold the sled still until Ivan and I had grabbed the lines. By the time we had walked the dogs to the starting area, I was panting and perspiring from the strain.

Kathy shouted instructions. "If you fall off, never let go of the sled, even if they have to drag you. The dogs can really hurt themselves if they get tangled and panic. When you come upon another team, you yell, 'Trail,' and they have to let you by. Then you say to Sobi, 'Straight ahead,' and she should go by. You have to pump your foot, just push off the ground, because they'll lag a little. If a team comes upon you and says, 'Trail,' slow down, but don't stop. The potential for getting in trouble is there when you stop. And don't put Sobi's nose up another's rear end. You've got to give room."

There were four minutes left. "What happens if their dogs attack mine?" I asked. "They shouldn't," Kathy said. "If," I hissed, with a disquieting sense of rising panic, "I've got to know the ifs."

"Then you've got to plant the snow hook and separate them—but you shouldn't have that problem. Jo Ann is a pro and so are the others in front. Just talk Sobi on by. You say, 'Straight ahead,' and you say it rough, like you mean it."

Ivan yanked us to the starting line. I watched the team before me speed ahead, the snow beginning to blow harder across the lake, and soon her dogs all but dissolved in the mist. "Kathy," I blurted, "if they went with you first, wouldn't they know the trail better?" She peered into my face, seeing perhaps for the first time its rigid, vacant look, surprised at how quickly it had been drained of confidence. "You're not seizing up on us, are you?" Ivan yelled from the point. "You'll be all right," Kathy said. "You can't let them know you're nervous. They can smell it, you know. Just pump hard. Like you're riding a scooter. Just pump hard."

The dogs strained forward, like arrows drawn taut on a bow, and the starter counted down "four, three, two, one . . . " and we sprang forward.

I was conscious of two shouts before all noise faded before the wind. One was the send-off from the starter, a burly man hooded in his snowmobile suit who yelled, "Don't let go of the sled!" And the other was Ivan's hopeful cry to Kathy, "Did you tell Jo Ann to watch out for them?" And his quick burst of distress, "You didn't? You didn't?"

Two hundred yards along the trail I saw to my horror that the driver of the team that was supposed to take care of me was herself in trouble, her team turned crossways to the trail, as we headed straight for its unprotected flank. The only call I remembered was "Straight on," and I shut my eyes. When I opened them, Sobi had veered away at the last instant. But relief was short-lived on that wild lake. We quickly gained on the team in front, one that had also become confused and that also lay crossways to the trail. This time we hit, becoming entangled in the lines. The other driver, a seasoned veteran, leaped into the fray, untangling my dogs, heaving Sobi toward the trail.

"Straight on," I hollered, as I murmured embarrassed apologies to the other driver. We turned around an island that formed a hub for the course, Sobi hard on the spruce track until suddenly she followed the scent of an errant team and ran toward an open expanse that for all I knew stopped in Quebec. A young man stood his ground, doing his job—which was to frantically wave dog teams back onto the trail. I pressed the brake hard, and Sobi stopped. "I don't know what to do," I shouted. His eyes grew wide beneath his enormous parka. "I don't know either," he said. "Can't you get the dog to follow you?" I asked him to hold the sled. He approached slowly, as though half expecting me to run off, leaving him to drive the dogs home. Ivan had told me to throw Sobi back on the trail when she got off, but I wanted to keep my distance.

"C'mon girl, here girl," I implored, my arms motioning to the trail. I clucked as though I were calling my own dog. I whistled. Sobi stared at me briefly then looked off into the distance. Dog teams passed by 30 yards away, heading home. In desperation I grabbed Sobi's neckline and yanked her toward the trail, pulling the team 30 yards until I was so winded I feared I would be ill. I rode the sled runners then, not even pretending to pump. When we turned the far point toward home, the teeth of the wind, now gale force, struck full-bore. It seemed to drain the will from me. Jo Ann's team, which had had difficulty staying to the trail, came so close that I kept kicking her leader. Again Sobi veered off the trail, though there was nothing left of a trail except runner marks. "What do I do?" I shouted. "Yell 'haw,' " she answered. I yelled it over and over to no avail. "Get off and haul her over," Jo Ann shouted. I yanked Sobi around, but confused, she headed back the way we had come, straight into Jo Ann's team.

The two teams, tired, irritable, and confused, began to growl. "Oh," Jo Ann muttered, "now we're in a fix." She yanked her team in front of Sobi, and for the last mile we crawled home following Jo Ann's team. I didn't care. I just wanted what until then had been some of the worst 30 minutes of my life to be done with. A half mile from the finish I saw Ivan, his arms folded, his face tight, staring at me with what I imagined to be disgust. "At least make it a good finish," he said. "Pump it in."

Kathy was waiting. "I've been praying for the dogs to come back." She saw my hands stiff from clutching the sled. "You're not supposed to have a death grip on it," she said.

Later, after they had watered the dogs, my humiliation changed to relief. Time and again someone came over, clapped me on the shoulder. "You finished, that's the main thing," they said. I perked up. My time was 35 minutes and seven seconds. I felt better knowing one team was out nearly an hour. Later, in the dark, in the cold, I found Ivan and Kathy tending their dogs. Ivan's tattered gloves were off, one dog had wet in the stall; two others, Sobi and Cleo, both leaders, had started fighting and Ivan had separated them. He knew their muscles would be sore and was dropping aspirins in their feeding dishes before scooping their homemade dog food—chicken breast bones ground up with chicken fat. It smelled like dried blood.

I thought of something he had told me the night before. He was racing once in Vermont over a course laid out across a field. Barbed wire had been hidden by the snow and nobody knew it. Another racer had gone over the wire, hooked it with his brake, and lifted it up enough to catch Ivan as he passed close behind. He wouldn't let go of the sled, and as the dogs lunged, the wire ripped through his jacket, cutting his stomach open. Nevertheless, he had finished the race.

"Ivan," I asked, "why do you do this?" "We were just talking about that," he said. "You know somebody said a few years ago we were just chasing a fantasy. Mine is to have a sponsor someday, to be able to retire into sled-dog racing. Who knows," he shrugged, "maybe someday people will get bored with golf; maybe this will take off one day."

He told me of friends who had lost their houses and their families to pursue sled-dog racing in Alaska; of a nonstop 1,200-mile drive, 20 miles per hour for 40 hours, bringing the dogs from a race in Wisconsin; of 200-mile drives to find enough snow for 30-minute training runs; of the meager winnings and the tremendous expenses. He explained it simply. "A lot of people in our sport are obsessed," he said.

Saturday night we sat in the bar of the inn, and every so often a driver would go outside to check the dogs, and when the door opened, you could hear the dogs yelping as they dropped to the ground from their boxes. Ivan came in on one occasion from dropping his dogs (letting them out of their boxes). "It's really wild out; it'll be awfully bad tomorrow. And they'll be sore—and they may decide this isn't any fun. So the real test may come tomorrow." I yawned and stood up. "Well, folks," I said cheerfully, "I can go to bed knowing as bad as it was today, at least tomorrow will be worse." "Don't lose your nerve," Ivan said. "They allow a change of drivers only for heart attacks." "Well, at least there are alternatives," I said, then went to bed, where I drifted to sleep to the sound of crying from a baby next door.

Sunday came clear and cold; by 6:30 Ivan had dropped the dogs and was waxing the runners of the sleds. "I want you to cut five minutes off," he said. We started slowly, the dogs and I, heading into the wind, and I braced for the worst. But Sobi knew the trail now, and with every stride I realized we would be all right. We rounded the island and Sobi kept her nose low to the trail. My spirits soared. It didn't even matter that inexplicably I forgot Sobi's name. My mind searched madly through a collection of names until I settled on Lobi. "I'm helping Lobi," I shouted. "Here we go, move it! He wants five minutes—we'll give him ten off! I'm working Lobi," surely one of the stranger cries heard on the lake that day.

I pumped the sled hard, the ground sliding by beneath my foot, and when I approached the finish, I saw Ivan smiling and I didn't care that at least I had survived. I wanted to know my time. I had come in at 28 minutes, 11 seconds, nearly seven minutes faster, good for 15th place! Ivan clapped me on the back. "For a cheechako [greenhorn], you did all right," he said. "I wasn't sure you could pull it off. If you'd had a whip to crack, you could've taken two more minutes off. I'll make a sled driver out of you yet. But you have no sense whatsoever of a big dog team. I mean 16 dogs, 64 legs, over 1,000 pounds of dogs. Very few drive them successfully. You have to dominate all 16."

We said good-bye after lunch. Ivan had finished with the day's second-best time. He was satisfied. The drive home seemed an eternity when darkness came on and weariness replaced my euphoria. The roads were narrow, hugging the woods, and there were few lights or passing traffic. I remembered reading in a sled-dog book what a young Danish soldier had written upon learning to drive a dog team in Greenland: "Nobody who has been admitted to that mystery is ever the same again."

I knew the mystery was far from my reach—if anything the dogs had controlled me. But for many days afterward I was haunted by the demonic yelping of the dogs as they braced to race; of the moment when we would pass another team and the heads of the dogs would snap to the side, and sometimes there would be a low growl and a fleeting nip and then we would be past. And there was a dream of another race, when I would have 16 dogs, their string reaching so far in front I could barely see my leader as we raced furiously, noiselessly, across the snow.

Published January 1982

While I never raced sled dogs again, on my second date with Annie, who later became my wife, I read her this story. She laughed so hard, she nearly fell off the sofa. I thought that was a good sign.

Summer Times

Sometimes when I write my editor's note, the unexpected happens. While reading the pages of our summer issue last week, I thought about how summer memories seem to hold on tighter than those of any other season. So I started writing down mine, certain that many reading this will remember their own.

Twilight. We chase fireflies; we ride bikes up and down the street. Then suddenly comes the jingle of the ice cream truck as it turns toward us. No day could offer a better end than this. . . . *Fourth of July.* My sister and I scoop up our baby brother and dash in and out of the lawn sprinkler. Our springer spaniel is torn between the tantalizing scent of my father's grill and our calls to join in. . . . *After mowing.* The smell of cut grass washes the air; the heat of the day is just beginning. I go to the neighborhood ball field for a pickup game with friends. No grown-ups, just bats and balls and time.

And here is what might happen when you start writing summer memories: Out of nowhere, one pushes aside all the others.

On the night of July 20, 1969, I watched Neil Armstrong step onto the moon with "one small step for man." I remember the moment for its magnitude, of course, but also because I was at Bill Freeland's home. And it was the last time I would see the teacher who, perhaps more than anyone, led me to the writing life I have known.

I first saw Bill Freeland when I was 11; he was probably in his late 20s. It was 1957, and he was standing outside the little Quaker elementary school I attended. He was not only a new teacher but also the first male one I'd encountered. Although he was imposing, with a thick mustache, what struck me most was the fact that he was wearing sandals. I asked why. Frostbite in Korea, he said.

I blurted, "Did you shoot anyone?" And I have never forgotten this: He looked at me, then softly and deliberately he said, "You never ask that question."

He taught art, reading, and PE. He built sets for school plays. He'd turn off the classroom lights and read Edgar Allan Poe to us. As we memorized Tennyson and Longfellow, he made us care about the sounds of words. He was larger than life to all of us. Two years after I moved on to junior high school, he left to teach at an art college, and in time his own art and sculpture would gain a following around the world.

The summer of 1969, I came home on leave from the Peace Corps to get married. The one person I wanted my future wife to meet was Bill Freeland, so I phoned. It had been 11 years since I'd been his student, but he invited us over to watch the moon landing. And when we left, he gave us a painting.

Soon after, I, too, was teaching children, and I, too, turned off the lights and read aloud to them. I wrote him then to tell him that. Afterward, I lost touch—as it is too easy to do—and then in 2009 I read he had died at age 80 in Ireland, where he kept a studio.

I lost his painting some years ago, after one too many moves. But even as I type this, I am back in that dark classroom, the one where Bill Freeland is reading aloud and giving us chills we don't even understand. And I do not know it then, but I am taking my first small steps on the path that led me here.

Published July/August 2024

After this essay appeared in Yankee *I heard from admirers of Bill Freeland's work, including friends from Ireland where he had made his home. His son Erik, a video producer, offered one of his father's paintings to replace the one I lost long ago.*

The Boy Who Walked on the Moon

I was in my early 20s when I taught my first fourth-grade class in a small Maine town. My only experience was that once I had been 10 years old. I was hired because the district wanted a male teacher for a group that had frustrated their educators in earlier grades. I had just returned from the Peace Corps, and the thinking seemed to be that if I could survive the rigors of an equatorial mountain town, I could tame 27 country kids with attitudes.

I taught 80 children during my three years, and today they are pushing 60; no doubt a number have grandchildren, perhaps even some entering fourth grade. Occasionally I get the urge to see my former students again, because I knew them when they were young, and I wonder what happened after. And maybe I want to know if they remember, too. Back then, wanting to help them succeed often kept me awake at night.

One winter day there was a knock on the classroom door. A woman stood there, and beside her was a boy. She said he was from another town and he had come here to live with a foster family. He was short, sandy-haired, unsmiling. He said his name was Faron. The other kids looked on in silence, aware there might now be a shift in the class dynamic.

I asked him to write his name on the blackboard. He didn't move. I thought he was shy and said I'd walk with him to the board. He motioned to me. I leaned down, and he whispered, "I don't know how."

This was back when instruction was done in groups separated by ability, especially in reading. Faron and I became a group of two, and each day we sat together reading "books" I wrote for him. They were no more than 10 handwritten pages, stapled together, and they came with bold titles in black Magic Marker. Faron flew with Neil Armstrong and Buzz Aldrin on Apollo 11, and as Armstrong stepped onto the lunar surface, so, too, did Faron. He fought through cold and ice-choked waterways to plant a flag at the North Pole with Admiral Robert E. Peary. He stood with Edmund Hillary on top of Everest. He set sail from Plymouth, England, aboard the *Mayflower.* He was a scout with Lewis and Clark. He was the lone survivor at Little Big Horn. He found his way to this little Maine town where he was brave enough to tell me what he did not know.

I don't know whether he learned to read that year or whether, as I suspected, he memorized the stories from all the times we read them, and the words flowed. Soon he was reading the tales of his exploits aloud to a larger group, and a few months later the school year ended, and Faron disappeared from my life.

Not long ago, I typed his name into Google. What I found was his grave marker and, beneath it, the year 2002. He had not yet reached 40. He had died on a street in Portland. Maybe he kept those stories for a while. Maybe not. Teachers rarely know if they change lives, but sometimes—if they are lucky—they can change a few months here and there, when even a little boy with so much stacked against him can be a hero, when he reads aloud about the night he walked on the moon.

Published January/February 2023

When I speak to writing students, I tell them that I learned more about the craft of holding the attention of readers while teaching nine- and ten-year-olds than from any class or book on writing. I heard from teachers who had known their own Farons, and who also wondered and hoped they had made a difference.

The Seasons of Ice

People who live along inland waters in northern New England know there are only two seasons: ice-in and ice-out. All else is but prelude and aftermath.

I learned about ice the year I lived beside a lake near the foothills of the White Mountains. It was a small lake, a mile across and five miles around. I watched the lake ripen and freeze, then, months later, rot and thaw. The ice became a constant companion, always changing, never dull. There are people who confuse a frozen lake with stillness and silence. They should live beside one. The ice seethes with activity. With sharp temperature fluctuations, it contracts and expands.

As the ice is pushed and pulled, it groans, pops, shudders, and at times makes a curious soft sigh—winter songs at once startling and comforting, each retort a signal of change. In winters of heavy snows, the sounds are muffled, as the snow insulates the ice from drastic temperature changes; but there are times when the first hard crust of ice, pure as crystal, stays long into a snowless winter. These are the winters of black ice, days of breathtaking skating over transparent ice, the deep, dark waters gleaming below.

I stood on the shore of my lake one night in late November when the stars burned and the cold whipped down from Canada. I made a fire on the beach and stayed warm while the night worked its way on the waters of the lake. At dawn a surface of ice, thin as mica and clear as a mirror, floated at the cove. It did not freeze hard and true then, but a few weeks later after a few light snows, the nights snapped cold and sharp again. With little wind to ripple the waters, this time the balance was tipped to the ice.

Along that shore there lived only my wife and me, and our neighbors Tom and Sue. Tom's grandfather had first come to the lake in 1938, and since then generations of his family had spilled along the shore, six houses lined up, filled with uncles and cousins. They came in summer from suburban towns in Massachusetts; Tom was the first to live there in winter, arriving from Florida burnt out from a corporate job and discouraged.

We were all unemployed, in transition from jobs that failed, living as cheaply as possible off small savings. It was a vulnerable time in many ways, but we were happy enough, and without saying it, we were all aware, I think, that the days and nights on the lake were but moments caught between our own days of expansion and contraction.

I will always remember the night of the black-ice skate. This was on New Year's Eve, after an unseasonably warm day. The ice remained hard, and that night only a few pale stars poked through the clouds. We made a small fire in the middle of the lake and placed bottles of tequila against the ice to cool. We skated from the center, each on a different axis, and from across the lake you could hear someone shout, then another shout, and in time we skated to the center, gulped the harsh drink, then skated away again. It was dark enough on the lake to fear weak ice, or just the dark, but the momentum of the night kept us going. A strong wind picked up, and we unzipped our coats, opening them out to our sides, as though they were wings. We needed frictionless ice and a north wind to sail that night, and we got it.

In time a snowstorm came howling from the northeast, burying the ice beneath a foot of snow. The morning skates around the lake were now gone, replaced by long walks across the lake to the post office. The snow on top of the hard ice attracted the ice fishermen, whose closely stacked shacks sprang up on the lake by late January. Early on cold mornings I'd see the men trudge across the lake wrapped in thick coats, until they disappeared into their brown weathered shacks, not emerging for hours on end.

By late March we knew the ice was changing fast. Sometimes while walking to the post office, we'd pinch through the ice, and it would give slightly, as though suddenly grown rubbery. Along the shore, we'd see the same needlelike crystals we saw at the first signs of freeze in November, as though we were unwinding a tape of the winter. The ice could no longer be trusted. As the lake thawed, the water reached its coldest point of the year, but the balance had shifted and the spring deathwatch for ice-out began.

The ice broke free from the riverbanks first, and large cracks appeared. The shoreline eroded faster each day. It was no time to be loose on the ice, though giant cakes of it remained, seemingly thick enough to support a horse, but now rotten and weak, its tension destroyed.

One warm afternoon the thermometer read 70 degrees beneath a bright sun. Tom and I chipped ice ten feet from shore to make ice cream. Small pools of open water formed like potholes between the ice floes, and for over an hour Tom eyed them. When the ice cream had thickened, he stripped quickly, leapfrogged among the ice floes, and jumped into the water. Two weeks still remained until the lake was free, but watching Tom lift himself from the water, his elbows extended on the ice, emerging in shivering ecstasy—this signaled ice-out for me.

In town, though, ice-out was not official until you could put a boat into the lake at the dock behind the post office and could travel to the head of the lake, no matter how many twists and turns were needed to dodge ice floes. People wagered small sums, usually 10 dollars, on when that would happen. They'd keep watch on the south wind that would jam the ice together. Tom and I would take his canoe and go on long rides between the chunks and islands that formed natural canals.

I would have liked it if the ice had gone out with a final shudder beneath a star-filled night. But there were only a few days of warm drizzle and the fog that held the warmth close to the lake. On the last day of April, a wind blew from the north, breaking the last floes apart. They rode across the lake with white caps whipping at their heels, and within a few hours, people from town came down the road to watch the first open, blue water of the year, not minding the slightly acrid odor of lake-bottom water now rising to the top.

Soon the lake shore filled with smelt fishermen, released from winter bondage of their own, who had driven for miles to fish this lake, one of the best smelting spots in the state. Tom had heard from his parents, his uncles, and cousins. When the weather warmed they would fill the shoreline, and their motorboats would hum across the lake. The lanterns of the smelters played out over the lake, and even as Tom and I dipped our own nets silently into the still-icy waters along the shore, we could hear the faraway shouts of revelry.

Published January 1980

My writing life began that winter in an unheated cabin by the lake in Waterford, Maine. I had no running water, the owner having drained the pipes before he left in late fall. Winter mornings I chopped a hole in the frozen lake and carried buckets of clear, cold water into the cabin, where we heated it in a big pot on the always-stoked woodstove. I lived on one end of the lake, and after writing all morning, I walked across the lake to visit with Alice Rounds, the postmistress and owner of L.R. Rounds General Store, the social hub of the village. The store was separated from the post office by short swinging doors. Her cry, "I'll be right there," bounced back and forth between the two rooms. I had never sent stories out to magazines before, and Alice wished each one a fruitful journey when I delivered it into her hands. In a Maine village, where locals took time to warm up to new faces, she skipped all the preliminaries and became a friend.

Rinty's Song

Rinty is coming this month and there are things to do: oil the sewing machine, clear space for thread and needles and cloth, sharpen scissors. Her name is Orinthia. But to us she has always been Rinty. At 79 she is beset with aches and pains so that the journey from her home in Jamaica to mine in New Hampshire will be an ordeal. But come she must, she says. She has something important to do here now.

Long ago she was a seamstress, one so gifted that neighbors battled jealously for her services. She arrived early each morning, working alone on an ageless black Singer in an upstairs bedroom in my grandmother's sprawling house. When my mother came home from school, she'd run upstairs, jostling brothers and sisters to be the first to try on Rinty's creations. In 1945 my mother's marriage to an American soldier uprooted her to a small, treelined town where the snows came early and stayed late. Whenever she could, she returned to Jamaica with my sister and me.

We prowled the corridor outside Rinty's sewing room, held there by the bundles and remnants of brightly colored cloth, by the notion of something taking shape. We were in awe of the thin dark woman, glasses perched on her nose and a scarf wrapped around her hair, who filled the room with the whirring, dizzying needle. Gently she'd put her hand over the wheel and the Singer would hush, as if she had stopped its heart. She hummed for hours, breaking into gospel songs in a high, sweet voice, and then she would laugh, and its sound would carry through that big house and find us.

She saw ghosts. People and premonitions arrived in dreams. She knew when trouble was afoot and when good fortune would strike. She never married. A dream foretold she'd travel and find love.

In September 1957 Rinty came to vacation at our house. She fell in love with my three-year-old brother, David. He was very sick but had extraordinary humor and cheerful spirits. She stayed for weeks, then months. The months became years. They shared a room and a life. David slept to the music of her Singer, waking to new pajamas, or a robe, or a pair of shorts.

For years David was unable to attend school. Every day he and Rinty taxied to town and wandered through shops buying the "little cheapnesses" that Rinty sent home to Jamaica. Sales were sacred, and anything that ran on batteries especially valued. They raised ducks and chickens together, watched "American Bandstand," filling the days with little adventures until nighttime when David slept and Rinty sewed.

Only my sister and I grew up to leave home; David could not. Two years ago he died, in September, when Rinty was away. She sleeps in David's room when she visits my widowed mother. In her dreams David whispers in her ear and they are laughing. She sews all day long. My mother cannot wear all the dresses that Rinty's Singer must make.

Soon my first child is due. For more than 50 years every child born into this family has been clothed by Rinty. So Rinty is coming and everything must be ready. It is Rinty's gift, making things complete. It is what she does best, taking fragments and making them whole.

Published September 1985

When Orinthia (Rinty) Fender passed away in Jamaica in 2011, she was 105, and in her last years The Gleanor, *Kingston's daily newspaper, visited and was amazed at the clarity of her memory. When my two sons were young, they visited Rinty at her cottage in Jamaica, and a circle closed.*

The Keeper

In my family I am the keeper. When loved ones die, I am compelled to bring them home, or at least their belongings. The odds and ends that cluttered their lives now clutter mine. I tell everyone to stay alive as long as possible, death enough already, and my house is too small.

Pushed against a wall by the stairway in my house is a white leather chair. Its size, color, and style are at odds with the rest of the place. In daylight I say it must go. At twilight I know it must stay. Every evening for 40 years my father sat in that chair, his feet on a hassock, turning the pages of his newspaper, taking his ease.

I do not play golf. But I keep my father's clubs in the attic, covered against dust, just in case. Beside them are boxes of textbooks from his college days and cartons of papers and documents. Sometimes at night I carry a light to the attic and pore over the papers like a scholar, looking, I suppose, for the man I never knew—Albert Allen—before my birth. I find the report of his army physical, dated February 27, 1942. He was 34. I hear echoes of my father's pride that helped kill him nearly 40 years later: "Applicant states he has not consulted a physician in past five years."

We took the same size, so I had to make room in my closet for nine shirts and two sportscoats, which in six years I have yet to wear. I wanted my younger brother, David, to take the clothes, but three years later he, too, was gone, and there were more things to keep than I could bear.

I loaded David's things into an 18-foot U-Haul and drove 1,500 miles north to New Hampshire. Sleeping in motels along I-95, I half-hoped that someone would break in and drive that cargo away; yet three times I'd wake in the night to peer out the window, afraid it was gone.

I should not have waited to give his records away. We had eight years between us, and a generation in musical taste. These albums, several hundred of them, I do not play; but for three years I have cared for them, making certain they would not warp. I have needed a friend to take them away, the way a friend will take your dog to the vet for a final visit. David's bookshelf, still filled with his books, crowds the dining room; it would be easier to give them away if he hadn't written his name in so many of them in that loopy scrawl I used to joke about.

Friends who are not keepers don't understand why these things hang around, what with so many auctions and flea markets and Goodwills. I make no defense, for I don't really understand myself why I have kept drawers full of T-shirts with rock stars emblazoned on the chest. A friend, a keeper too, said he gave away his mother's furniture but kept everything that told a story, a knitted wool hat, a scarf, a miniature porcelain swan boat.

My son was born last September. In his room is a beige rug with patterns of flowers hooked by my father the year he retired; on the rug is my brother's rocking chair. Late at night we sit in that chair, rocking; while he quiets, the past quiets too. I named my son for his uncle David and his grandfather Albert. He keeps them for me now in his eyes, in his smile, in his squawks of anger. When I have to move the memories, I'll just pick him up; today at least he weighs just ten pounds.

Published December 1985

Today my son lives in Hawaii with his wife, Allison. In May 2025 they welcomed their first child, a boy they named Jasper.

So Beautiful, So Short

My son Dan was born in late September 1985, on the day that Hurricane Gloria howled through southern New England, drenching us on its way north, leaving two million people without power. The windows of the small New Hampshire hospital were boarded up, and no light peeked through from outside during my wife's 20 hours of labor. (A nurse wondered if maybe the baby knew a hurricane was afoot.) I crushed ice and drizzled honey over it to keep us going, and then in the early afternoon, Dan's first cries signaled the storm inside the room had ended.

A week or two later, I carried him in the tiny pack I wore on my chest and walked through the tree-lined neighborhoods where we lived. The leaves were so scarlet and yellow, it was as if you could breathe the color. I scooped a handful of maple leaves and held them close to his eyes. *This is fall, I said. You will never see it like this anywhere else. You will never forget it.*

Dan lives now in Hawaii, and his younger brother, Josh, lives in Colorado. During their childhood they spent summers at a nature camp called Roots & Wings. Like many parents, I wanted them to spread their wings and reach for whatever and wherever their hearts took them. I just never expected it to be so distant.

We had more than 20 autumns together, and now nearly as many apart. I think about fall with my boys when the leaves begin to change color seemingly overnight, and then after a couple of weeks, a few fall, then more, and then a cascade, drifting down in their twirling dance, draping the yard. We would rake together in the cool air, the mounds of leaves becoming a playground, their dog, Scout, leaping in with them. Now when I rake, I drag dozens of acorns along with the leaves. For the chipmunks that dart across the grass, this is takeout service. Many mornings I enter the woodshed to find their hoard tucked between pieces of wood, hidden in corners, filling their pantry against the coming cold.

I think about fall with my boys when the black walnuts drop with a thud in the backyard. The walnuts are green and look like limes; their scent is akin to citrus, and when I scoop them by the dozens to take to the composting heap at the recycling center, my hands are fragrant with walnut. The small stone wall that separates the backyard from the church parking lot next door is littered with broken shells, the aftermath of red squirrel picnics, as if the animals had been shelling peanuts at a ballgame.

Because Dan's birthday is in late September, every year I send him a gift of home in a box. I buy a quart of maple syrup and a hunk of cheddar and bars of local chocolate, and I lay them on a layer of newly fallen leaves as if they were wrapping paper. My sons' generation does not hold on to nostalgia and sentiment the way mine does.

I know autumn is a paradox. We love it even more because it is so fleeting. We hold it close, and then it is gone, the trees bare and brown. "A time of good-byes," my wife, Annie, once said.

As I write this, I remember a walk after a storm when I carried my son against my chest and showed him flaming red leaves and said, *You will never see it like this anywhere else. You will never forget it. It goes so fast, and one day becomes 38 years.*

Remember, I remind myself, look at the leaves while they hold on.

Published September/October 2023

It Matters Only Here

We begin when snow clings stubbornly to the outfield grass. The ball stings the players' hands through the mitts; when they hit, the vibration jolts them like a shock. They swing again. The town is small, the talent is not. After supper, the fields fill with children and coaches racing darkness, learning how to play this hard game, trying to gain an edge.

We play in a park fringed with trees and picnic spots, and we watch the children year after year, their bats lengthening with their bodies, their fastballs gaining speed. At age 10 they play for the first time under the lights in the chill of the night, when the spotlights gleam and the grown-ups sit on the cold aluminum stands, sipping coffee, wondering silently at how fast our children are growing up. We play 18 games, and at the end, on a Sunday in June, we play to crown the champions.

This photo was taken on one of those June days. The Rookie League Yankees are playing the Reds, whom they will soon defeat 13-12. The game had started with both teams, all eight- and nine-year-olds, standing on the foul lines, facing the center-field flagpole, their hats across their chests, giggling self-consciously as "The Star-Spangled Banner" blared over the loudspeakers. Their parents and grandparents, neighbors and friends, crowded around the backstop, debating balls and strikes. In the stillness between the pitches, you can almost hear the memories from games they had played here once before.

When the game ended, the Yankees flung themselves into each other's arms, the Reds walked off with tears streaming down. The next town over, nobody knew the score—it mattered only here, at this time, on this field, a world compressed into a single run scored on a ball that just eluded the fielder's grasp. And soon after, with the field raked smooth, the next game began, the nines and tens, and when they are done, yet another, the oldest, most skilled, in the finale. By then it was dusk, and it seemed as if everyone in town had come, a farewell to the season, to the children passing through among us.

Published March 1994

The intensity of a Keene, New Hampshire, youth baseball game is mirrored by hundreds of thousands of children across the country, whose games matter only on a small field of play, but whose memories may last a lifetime.
Photo credit: Carole Allen

Once We Were All Children

It's a strange feeling to realize that a story my father told about living through the 1918 flu epidemic is now becoming my story, and the story of all of us, a century later. Then 11 years old, he was living with his parents, two brothers, and a sister in a cramped second-floor apartment above the used-clothing store his Russian-immigrant father owned in Philadelphia. The flu hit the city hardest in the fall, and soon all schools were shut. Before the epidemic abated, more than 12,000 had died, one of the heaviest tolls in the country.

I haven't thought about my father's life in that epidemic for decades. But now I am. I don't know what his family did to survive—there is no one left to ask. Maybe just knowing that they did survive is enough and that the little used-clothing store and that crowded apartment were both still there when I was growing up.

Thinking of my dad then makes me think of children today. I wonder what they will remember, what stories they will tell. Many have computers and video games; they have cell phones. They are confined but not cut off. Still, this is a time they will never forget. I can only imagine the collective sound they will make when once again they can romp on playgrounds and ball fields and run out to recess. We may need to hold our hands over our ears as their joy cascades across our towns.

What started me thinking about children was a message that Amy

Traverso, our senior food editor, sent out to our *Yankee* staff. With all nine of us now working at home, we're using Microsoft Teams to stay connected, send files, collaborate on projects, and, from time to time, get playful. Amy said she was launching a series of challenges under the heading of "Yankee Fun Times," something to keep the bond we shared daily in the office. Think of it as small talk in a world with so much talk about big things.

This week we had to find a favorite childhood photo. I sighed: how to wedge in one more project, no matter how seemingly frivolous. But then there was Amy, giddily playing in ocean waves; Heather, our photo editor, on a Shetland pony named Pepper; our deputy editor, Ian, on a swing, his face full of mischief. There were also photos of future editors in tutus. I had been wrong. Looking at who we once were and knowing who we became, I saw the thread through time. A story on its inevitable loop.

Now we have editorial meetings by way of video conference—which to me is mysterious technological alchemy. Our digital editor Aimee Tucker's two-year-old daughter, Vivien, joins our meetings sitting on her mother's lap, looking wide-eyed at what must seem a strange group of talking heads onscreen—as if we are simply living in some secret chamber in her house, only to pop out once a week. She doesn't disrupt what we do. She patiently shares her mother's attention with us. I do not know what Vivien will remember from these weeks and possibly months. Maybe none of it. Or she may have a glimmer that her mother was always there, even as voices and faces popped up unexpectedly before vanishing in a flash.

One day I want to tell her, "Vivien, your mother woke so early, even before you, and she stayed awake late, long after you, so she could do what she knows connects thousands of people to New England." I will want her to see the photo of her mother when she was a little girl, when she dressed up and danced, because that is what children should always do, even when their parents worry about an uncertain future. "Vivien," I will say when she is older, "there was danger, yet you were protected. You made your mother laugh. You made a whole group of editors smile. That is how life continues."

Published in the April 22, 2020, edition of "Letter from Dublin," a regular column I wrote for Yankee's website during the pandemic.

Leaving Home

The first time I knew the feeling of leaving home, I was a month shy of 11, though what I felt then was home leaving me. My mother, sister, and little brother went to spend the summer on the island of Jamaica, where my mother had grown up and where her parents still lived. I stayed home to play Little League. A strange sense of loneliness soon settled in, as I waited all day in the unfamiliar quiet for my dad to come home to take me to practice or a game, and afterward we'd go to a diner or simply open a carton of ice cream. I never forgot what I learned that summer: Home did not just mean a roof and walls and familiar rooms, but the people you lived with inside.

Since then, I have left numerous homes: off to college, leaving college, leaving the Peace Corps, leaving Maine. Then I came to *Yankee* in October 1979—and never left. I have been part of more than 400 issues of this magazine. I have lived tens of thousands of hours inside this sprawling red building, have worked alongside so many people here, have known and published so many writers. There has been little distance for me between home with family and my second home here with another family—one where day after day we talk ideas, plan issues, look at layouts, meet in hallways and offices, look after each other.

My coworkers have been part of my life for so long that I have been here when their children were born and seen them grow up and have their own children. I have lost colleagues I will never forget, and I have welcomed new ones I will never forget.

For the past few years, when people asked me when I was going to retire, I replied by saying they don't understand the feeling of holding a new issue in their hands, or of finding a story that arrives unassigned, like a stranger knocking on the door asking to come in, and then beginning to read it and knowing *Yankee*'s readers will want to read it, too. They don't understand what it's like to get a phone call from a friend to say she's seen a Facebook post about a Maine lobsterman named Joel Woods, who takes photos of a life that few of us ever know. And then to sit in Woods' cottage on the Maine coast and see his work, and then publish it, and then enter it in the annual City and Regional Magazine Association contest to be judged against photos by professionals across the country. And to feel so proud when his photos take first place.

And then there is that hard-to-define connection with readers, so strong at times I can almost hear their voices when they write. I have kept hundreds of their cards and letters and several thousands of their emails, which speak to a bond that runs deeper than just editor and subscriber. They want me to know how much *Yankee* means to them. They tell of losses in their lives and how *Yankee* kept them grounded, how we have kept New England alive for them no matter where they live. They talk about their family as if we here at *Yankee* all belonged, too.

They write things like this: *Dear Mel, I think I can be so familiar as to call you by your first name though we have never met in person; we have known each other for decades though only through* Yankee.

Or this one, a nod to my long-standing editor's photo: *Check your closet, Mel. Caught between all those red shirts must be one navy-blue or forest-green shirt you could don for* Yankee *issues. Please?*

But there is always an end time. There is always a sense that if not now, when?

In early January, our conference room filled with everyone who works here in Dublin as well as former colleagues who had left or retired. We all enjoyed some good food, and then I told them what they had meant to me, and they told me what I had meant to them. And I am 78, but I felt like a boy as I tried, not always successfully, to choke back tears when a colleague was doing the same.

If you were in the room with us, I would have wanted you to know this: Many days I walk with several editors to a dirt path that runs past a pretty cemetery and ends at a spot where we gaze out upon lake and mountain. And each time I say, "Can you believe how lucky we are to see this where we work?"

I'd want you to know how we pulled together during the pandemic and saw one another only on a screen, and we still put together issues that made us all proud.

I'd want you to know about the time Rudy, my Jack Russell, escaped from my car in the Yankee parking lot and I was certain I'd lost him forever. But within an hour my staff had made "Lost Dog" posters, and everyone fanned out to distribute them and to look for Rudy. And late that night, as I lay in the back of my car at Yankee, hoping somehow Rudy would find his way back, my colleague Joe arrived at the parking lot. Driving once more along the darkened roads, he'd found Rudy walking along the highway and called him into the truck. Now, he held Rudy out to me.

I'd want you to know about working alongside Jud Hale, the former editor in chief whose uncle Robb Sagendorph started *Yankee* in 1935, and hearing him walking to his office calling hello to everyone he passed. And how Sarah, an editor with *The Old Farmer's Almanac,* whose offices are just down the hall, always bakes me a chocolate zucchini bread for my birthday because she knows it's my favorite.

I'd want you to have seen me this past New Year's Day, alone in my office, stepping over the plastic crates I'd brought to fill with what I had saved all these years—which seems to be nearly every manuscript, notebook, calendar, magazine, and newspaper clipping, plus enough odds and ends to fill my newly rented storage unit a few miles away. When I took down all the cards from readers and photos from my bulletin board, I remembered the boy from a long-ago summer who had the sensation of home changing right then and there, and I was glad I was alone on New Year's in my office.

So this is the last issue of *Yankee* with my name at the top of the masthead. I leave knowing that the people I have worked with for so long, who care about this region so deeply, will continue to do the work they do so well. I will always hold them close. I will still come by and join the walk on the dirt path to where lake and mountain appear. And I am certain that if I ever lose my way, they will find me and bring me home.

Published March/April 2025

The cards and messages I received from readers from across the country touched me deeply. Yankee *has endured for 90 years because of its readers, but those of us who make the magazine know so few in person. With the messages came personal stories of what my own writing and* Yankee *itself meant to them—and I wrote back to everyone and then many wrote back to me, and it felt as if I had been given the gift of many friends.*

Acknowledgments

Where to begin to thank those who helped make this collection possible? Maybe with Kenneth Gambone, my high school English teacher who gave me the book *Do You Belong in Journalism?* and convinced me that I did. Also with William Ward and Andre Fontaine at Syracuse's Newhouse School in the mid-1960s, who guided me to report and write better than I knew how to at the time. I owe a debt to Eddie Fitzpatrick, feature editor of the *Maine Sunday Telegram*, who beginning in 1975 sent me across the state of Maine to write a feature every two weeks, and then with a portfolio of stories, I traveled to Dublin, New Hampshire. There I met John Pierce, *Yankee*'s managing editor, and Jud Hale, editor, and soon they wanted stories from across New England, and one day they asked me to join the staff. On October 1, 1979, my tenure began. Not a single story here could have happened without these teachers and mentors along the way.

During all these years afterward, I have worked with so many exceptional colleagues who deserve a thank-you that if I begin listing them all the book would expand to be one of those door stoppers. But many of these stories were first read by two fine writers, Edie Clark and Tim Clark. Art director J Porter designed many of the earlier stories in *Yankee* with a brilliance that made readers stop and want to read. When J left, art directors Leonard Loria, Lori Pedrick, and Katharine Van Itallie put their own visual stamp on my words. When nearly 10 years ago Jenn Johnson became *Yankee*'s managing editor, she always improved what I had written, and she never backed down if I put up a fuss, and the stories were all the better for it. Jamie Trowbridge, president of Yankee Publishing, Inc., and grandson of *Yankee*'s founder, graciously gave permission for me to collect these stories.

This all began with "The Joy of Writing About Others," a talk I gave at a summer writing retreat to students in the MFA Bay Path program. I spoke about some of the people who appear here and what it meant to hear their stories. When I finished, listeners encouraged me to gather the stories in one place. Among them was Erin Gottwald. For her publishing course she focused on bringing this book to life. She offered useful opinions; she also tirelessly scanned printouts from the early years and converted them to Word files. I will always be grateful for her enthusiasm and dogged work, which helped bring this to the finish line.

I enlisted several other readers along the way. Thanks to Ann Klotz, head of Laurel School in Ohio; Lara Beckius in Connecticut; and a special thank-you to Alice Erickson in Wisconsin, who never stopped requesting more stories to read so she could offer her take.

Steve Lewers and I became friends while organizing a memorial reading of Edie Clark's essays, after the *Yankee* columnist's death in the summer of 2024. I cannot imagine a writer being more supported by a publisher than I have been with Steve and *Earth Sky & Water*. Ellen Klempner-Béguin designed these pages and the cover, and working with her has been both a pleasure and instructive. Lida Stinchfield and I closed a *Yankee* copy-editing circle—she once worked on some of these stories when we were both at the magazine. I was fortunate to report many of the early stories with my late former wife, Carole Allen, a talented photographer.

Finally, my wife, Annie Graves, a gifted writer who has written so many stories in *Yankee*, has been with this book from the beginning. It never would have entered the world without her.

And I thank my sons, Dan and Josh, who while raised in New England then spread their wings to distant places. I have written these stories from my heart, and from the day I met them, I felt it widen.

About *Yankee*

A few years ago, Yankee Publishing, Inc., hired a nationally known consultant to find out what *Yankee*'s readers thought of the magazine that came into their home six times a year. After months of data collecting, he came to our Dublin, New Hampshire, office and we gathered in the downstairs conference room to learn what he had found. With the lights dimmed, he showed his PowerPoint of questions asked and replies given on the screen.

What we saw, and what he said, was that he had never found a readership that expressed such deep loyalty, such a profound connection to a publication. He told us that the amount of time a reader spent with *Yankee* was considerably longer than he found elsewhere. They did not just turn pages. They *read*. As an editor at *Yankee* for many years, I was gratified to hear his words—but I already knew what he would find. The letters and the emails that came from readers to my inbox, month after month, told me about an attachment that went beyond that of a consumer to a product.

I wonder how many editors receive calls that ask for suggestions about where they should go for their wedding? Or where they should vacation? Or where to find the best fall foliage, and when exactly to visit? People reach out for help in finding a story that they are *sure*, well "pretty sure," ran sometime 10 or 15 years ago, perhaps later, about a craftsperson who made a certain something that they have never found anywhere else. In the past few years, callers ask simply where should they move to in New England?

This connection has been the thread that ties the *Yankee* of today with what its founder, Robb Sagendorph, envisioned in his first issue, September 1935. It was a homely issue with a cover that featured a basket with an infant left at the door, one whose life continues 90 years later.

"Thus *Yankee* is born today," Sagendorph wrote—"for *Yankee* readers, by *Yankee* writers…his destiny is the expression and perhaps, indirectly, the preservation of that great culture in which every Yank was born. . . . Give him your care, your interest, your heart, and you'll be repaid over and over. . . ."

When I arrived in 1979 at the Dublin, New Hampshire, office where Sagendorph set up a humble shop with a handful of people, the magazine was so ingrained in the life and culture of the region that it was hard at times to know whether New England was shaping *Yankee* or whether the magazine was somehow defining how people saw these six compact states—probably a bit of both. What I do know is that after all this time, at its core remains the quest to get the feel and mood and character of New England between the covers. To understand that even as the years pass, as editors come and go, as populations and life evolves, readers crave the sense of place they see in *Yankee.*

That place is revealed through the people they meet, the food they read about, the famous places and those yet undiscovered, the certainty that *Yankee* gives them insights, a key, as it were, to a kingdom they long for, whether they live close or distant. In the calls I have received over the years, the notes that have come to me, what I see are people looking for the elusive feeling of something well rooted and well tended.

Thomas McIntyre, former senator from New Hampshire in the 1960s and '70s, once wrote about "the craving—to recapture personal identity. . . the feeling that somehow we have lost our way, that to find it again we must retrace our steps."

In writing this book, I have revisited countless issues of *Yankee* and retraced my own steps. This magazine, this writer, have been so lucky to have the most loyal readers anywhere along with both of us.

PHOTO BY JARROD MCCABE

About the Author

Mel Allen taught fourth grade in Maine for three years and believes that his education as a writer began when he had to hold the attention of 27 children through months of Maine winters. From his first two stories in *Yankee*'s December 1977 issue to the January day in 2025 when he closed his office door for the last time, he spent nearly half a century finding people and places whose stories he wanted to know, and assigning countless others to the finest writers in New England. He became *Yankee*'s fifth editor in the summer of 2006, after previous roles as senior editor and executive editor. He has taught magazine writing and creative nonfiction for the past 25 years, divided between the University of Massachusetts-Amherst and MFA Bay Path. His previous book is *A Coach's Letter to His Son.* He lives and writes in New Hampshire and can be reached at melallen716@gmail.com and melallennewengland.com.

About the cover: *Sea Smoke,* photographed by Peter Ralston, depicts "a wicked cold morning at Curtis Island in the mouth of Camden Harbor." Peter is Maine's preeminent photographer of the Maine coast and islands. *Down East* magazine called "Pentecost," his photo of sheep crossing the bay to Allen Island in a dory, the single most iconic photo of Maine. His second book, *Going Deep*, will be published in spring 2026. His work lives at his Rockport gallery and here: ralstongallery.com.